Rhys Tranter

Beckett's Late Stage

Trauma, Language, and Subjectivity

Samuel Beckett in Company

Edited by Paul Stewart

ISSN 2365-3809

1 *Llewellyn Brown*
Beckett, Lacan and the Voice
With a foreword by Jean-Michel Rabaté
ISBN 978-3-8382-0869-5 (Paperback edition)
ISBN 978-3-8382-0889-3 (Hardcover edition)

2 *Robert Reginio, David Houston Jones, and Katherine Weiss (eds.)*
Samuel Beckett and Contemporary Art
ISBN 978-3-8382-1079-7

3 *Charlotta P. Einarsson*
A Theatre of Affect
The Corporeal Turn in Samuel Beckett's Drama
ISBN 978-3-8382-1118-3

4 *Rhys Tranter*
Beckett's Late Stage
Trauma, Language, and Subjectivity
ISBN 978-3-8382-1135-0

Rhys Tranter

BECKETT'S LATE STAGE

Trauma, Language, and Subjectivity

ibidem-Verlag
Stuttgart

Bibliographic information published by the Deutsche Nationalbibliothek
Die Deutsche Nationalbibliothek lists this publication in the Deutsche Nationalbibliografie; detailed bibliographic data are available in the Internet at http://dnb.d-nb.de.

Bibliografische Information der Deutschen Nationalbibliothek
Die Deutsche Nationalbibliothek verzeichnet diese Publikation in der Deutschen Nationalbibliografie; detaillierte bibliografische Daten sind im Internet über http://dnb.d-nb.de abrufbar.

ISSN: 2365-3809

ISBN-13: 978-3-8382-1135-0

Printed in the United States of America

For my grandfather,
William Haydn Jones ("Pappy"),
for encouraging me to apply to university.

Acknowledgements

First and foremost, I would like to thank Neil Badmington for his advice, encouragement and friendship throughout the project. His feedback and fine espressos were the fuel that ensured a steady progression. · I owe a debt of thanks to the following for their support during various stages of the project: Iain Bailey, Elizabeth Barry, Jonathan Boulter, Peter Boxall, Mary Bryden, Mark S. Byron, Julie Campbell, Arka Chattopadhyay, Rick Cluchey, Paul Crosthwaite, Raymond Federman, Matthew Feldman, Peter Fifield, Stanley Gontarski, Dan Gunn, Julia Jordan, David Houston Jones, Seán Kennedy, James Knowlson, James Martell, Ulrika Maude, Laurent Milesi, Irene Morra, Becky Munford, Mark Nixon, Anthony Paraskeva, Bryan Radley, Jean-Michel Rabaté, Laura Salisbury, David Tucker, Dirk Van Hulle, Shane Weller, and Adam Winstanley. · I would also like to thank Series Editor Paul Stewart for his diligence and support during crucial stages, and to Valerie Lange of Ibidem Press for her help and guidance throughout the publication process · I am grateful to the Arts and Humanities Research Council, for their financial support during the principal research of this study · I would like to acknowledge the patient and helpful staff of Cardiff University's Arts and Social Studies Library. · A big thank you to the supportive community of postgraduate researchers based at the School of English, Communication and Philosophy. · Thank you to John Minihan for kindly providing a photograph for the front cover · A big thank you to my family, Hazel, Brian, and Robert Tranter, and to my in-laws Leslie and Don Whitney, for their generosity, understanding, and support at various points throughout the project· And finally, my largest debt of gratitude goes to Jennifer Dawn Whitney, a tireless listener and scrupulous crrritic who has been a constant source of guidance and inspiration. Needless to say, all errors are my own.

Some sections of the material in this book have appeared in earlier versions in the following publications: '"without solution of continuity": Beckett's *That Time* and Trauma Memoir', *Samuel Beckett*

Today / Aujourd 'hui, Vol.27 (2015), 115-128; and 'Late Stage: Trauma, Time and Subjectivity in Samuel Beckett's *Footfalls*' in *Samuel Beckett & The Encounter of Philosophy and Literature*, ed. Arka Chattopadhyay and James Martell (London: Roman Books, 2013) (ISBN: 9380905513), 118-135.

Rhys Tranter
Cardiff, South Wales
August 2017

Table of Contents

Abbreviations

AST 'As the Story Was Told' in *Texts for Nothing and Other Shorter Prose, 1950-1976*, ed. Mark Nixon (London: Faber and Faber, 2010)

AF *All That Fall* in *All That Fall and Other Plays for Radio and Screen* (London: Faber and Faber, 2009)

Cas *Cascando* in *All That Fall and Other Plays for Radio and Screen* (London: Faber and Faber, 2009)

CR 'The Capital of the Ruins' in *As No Other Dare Fail: For Samuel Beckett on his 80th Birthday by his friends and admirers* (London: John Calder, 1986),

E *Embers* in *All That Fall and Other Plays for Radio and Screen* (London: Faber and Faber, 2009)

F *Footfalls* in *Krapp's Last Tape and Other Short Plays*, ed. S. E. Gontarski (London: Faber and Faber, 2009)

FN *The Expelled, The Calmative, The End with First Love*, ed. Christopher Ricks (London: Faber and Faber, 2009)

FAW *From an Abandoned Work* in *Texts for Nothing and Other Shorter Prose, 1950-1976*, ed. Mark Nixon (London: Faber and Faber, 2010)

K *Krapp's Last Tape and Other Short Plays*, ed. S. E. Gontarski (London: Faber and Faber, 2009)

LO *The Lost Ones* in *Texts for Nothing and Other Shorter Prose, 1950-1976*, ed. Mark Nixon (London: Faber and Faber, 2010)

N *Not I* in *Krapp's Last Tape and Other Shorter Plays*, ed. S. E. Gontarski (London: Faber and Faber, 2009), 88.

M *Murphy*, ed. J. C. C. Mays (London: Faber and Faber, 2009).

MC *Mercier and Camier*, ed. Seán Kennedy (London: Faber and Faber, 2010)

Mo *Molloy*, ed. Shane Weller (London: Faber and Faber, 2009)

MPTK *More Pricks Than Kicks*, ed. Cassandra Nelson (London: Faber and Faber, 2010)

TN *Texts for Nothing* in *Texts for Nothing and Other Shorter Prose, 1950-1976*, ed. Mark Nixon (London: Faber and Faber, 2010)

TOT *The Old Tune* in *All That Fall and Other Plays for Radio and Screen* (London: Faber and Faber, 2009)

TT *That Time* in *Krapp's Last Tape and Other Shorter Plays*, ed. S. E. Gontarski (London: Faber and Faber, 2009)

U Samuel Beckett, *The Unnamable*, ed. Steven Connor (London: Faber and Faber, 2010)

W *Watt*, ed. C. J. Ackerley (London: Faber and Faber, 2009)

WFG *Waiting for Godot*, ed. Mary Bryden (London: Faber and Faber, 2010)

WW *What Where* in *Krapp's Last Tape and Other Shorter Plays*, ed. S. E. Gontarski (London: Faber and Faber, 2009)

DF James Knowlson, *Damned to Fame: The Life of Samuel Beckett* (London: Bloomsbury, 1996).

Foreword

what is the word

> What follows is speculation; often far-fetched speculation, which the reader will consider or dismiss according to his individual predilection.
>
> Freud, *Beyond the Pleasure Principle*[1]

In the Spring of 2017, I was fortunate enough to direct a production of *Footfalls*. My cast were both highly experienced, but were performing Beckett for the first time. From the first read-through, two persistent questions arose: What is wrong with May? and What has happened to her? These questions arose repeatedly during the question and answer sessions with the audiences after each performance. These are possibly inevitable questions from both the actors' and audience's perspectives. For the former, the best practice of creating a credible character in a theatrical context might seem to demand some form of knowledge of the character's history and, hence, her motivation; or, if not knowledge, then at least some form of working hypothesis. For the latter, the desire to diagnose May's condition is, of course, a desire to know what has been witnessed. The audience knows what it has seen and heard—a woman pacing, responding to an off-stage voice, and then creating a narrative 'sequel'—and yet seeing and hearing are not felt to be enough and the desire to know what has been witnessed leads to a diagnostic drive. If only, the thought goes, we could come to understand what is wrong with her. If only, we were told what the 'it all' is that May keeps revolving in her poor mind.

This diagnostic drive is not to be condemned (after all, much academic work has sought to do the same thing for May, or Mouth,

1 Freud, *Beyond the Pleasure Principle* in *The Standard Edition of the Complete Psychological Works of Sigmund Freud*, Vol. XVIII, trans. James Strachey et. al. (London: Vintage, 2001)

for example) but perhaps should be seen as an inevitable consequence of Beckett's work. That he was alive to such possibilities is evident long before he turned to the stage. Indeed, *Watt* could be seen as demonstrating, and possibly undermining, just such a diagnostic drive. When the Galls come to tune the piano, Watt cannot say 'Yes, I remember, that is what happened then' (*W*, 61), leaving the incident of the Galls as one of an interplay of its formal facets alone: 'a mere example of light commenting bodies, and stillness motion, and silence sound, and comment comment' (*W*, 60). Watt has not 'executed an interpretation since the age of fourteen, or fifteen,' so he find this need to know beyond the 'face values' deeply upsetting, as many an audience member faced with a late Beckett play might also feel. Indeed, 'light commenting bodies, and stillness motion, and silence sound' might serve as a fair description of Beckett's later work for the theatre in which such formal features fail to provide access to a deeper understanding that an audience might expect and seek. This is not to say that Beckett's theatre fails to provide such an understanding; rather it invites the attempt to know, to diagnose, and thus focuses the audience's attention on the processes of bearing witness, endlessly.

The plight of Watt trying to come to terms with the Galls, father and son, is but one of example in the novel of what Arsene describes as 'the unutterable, the ineffable' that demands failing attempts to utter it, to eff it (*W*, 52). 'To eff' is of course a non-existent word, despite the fact that it should, logically, be available within the language, as the word's journey from Latin to English has retained the negative form whilst disposing of the positive, *effabilis*. It seems as if Beckett makes an appeal within the logic of language to that which is not available within that language. In so doing, Beckett can not describe but only circumscribe a site of emergence. According to this logic, only a successful identification and description of the ineffable would arrest the economy of emergence. This is once again a facet of the diagnostic drive that audience and actors so often feel when encountering Beckett's work, and upon which the academic community might be said to depend.

In the present work, Rhys Tranter has circumscribed this area of emergence as that of trauma. By definition, Tranter suggests, trauma is precisely that which cannot be identified as such in Beckett's work: it is always, as it were, off stage or unsaid. If one were to identify the trauma, it could then be successfully 'disposed of,' as Freud put it. For Freud, coming to terms—and the word is loaded—is a question of mastery. The traumatized patient repeatedly suffers because there 'is no longer any possibility of preventing the mental apparatus from being flooded with large amounts of stimulus, and another problem arises instead—the problem of mastering the amounts of stimulus which have broken in and of binding them, in the psychical sense, so that they can be disposed of.' (*Beyond the Pleasure Principle,* 30) The therapeutic project would be to ensure just this mastery through the identification of the traumatic episode itself. If we transpose Freud's description into the field of literary criticism, and in particular Beckett criticism, then immediately a number of concerns become apparent. Firstly, there is a danger that we as critics wish to assume a mastery over texts that repeatedly disavow such mastery. Secondly, the act of 'binding' these texts—thereby giving them a coherence around a single focal point or related points—begs the question whether they can then be disposed of, thus silencing both those texts and future critical works. This means that care needs to be taken with whatever critical tools we bring to bear on the works, be it archival, historical or more philosophical and speculative; a care that recognises that we as critics are part of the same economy of emergence and repetition as the texts themselves.

Throughout this book, Tranter stresses that the status of 'late,' with all its connotations and complications, should be borne in mind. There might seem to be no more 'late' text than *what is the word*, the final written work, which, according to Van Hulle, was to be Beckett's last word no matter if another were to follow:

> On the first page of the manuscript of *what is the word*, [Beckett] added in the top margin 'Keep! for end', indicating that

> no matter how much longer he might live and whatever he might still write, the final word had to be this acknowledgement that he could not find the word. (*C,* xvi)

So, the last word was to be *what is the word* no matter if it was in fact the last word and, if van Hulle is correct, it was to be delayed in order for it to be the last word. Fittingly, the English translation appeared in print once Beckett was himself 'late' as it only appeared posthumously. Perhaps no less fittingly, there is some doubt about what *what is the word* is; poem or prose? Van Hulle includes it in his Faber edited collection of late prose. Lawlor and Pilling also include it in *The Collected Poems of Samuel Beckett.* Calder, who was the first to print the piece within a book, included it as prose in the volume *As the Story was Told*[2], although he describes it as Beckett's last 'literary utterance' to avoid the issue of genre (10). (As an aside, in both van Hulle's collection and *The Collected Poems*, *what is the word* is not given the position of the last word at all, as both volumes provide further texts as appendices.)

Whatever its generic status, *what is the word* exhibits the same ambiguous relation to the diagnostic drive as the incident of Watt and the Galls. Although not written as a question, the title seems to create a series of hesitant responses that approach the word that lies ineffably out of reach. The responses undergo a process of weakening as verbs are lessened in their force or hedged about with caveats. So, 'see' becomes 'glimpse' which is in turn is weakened into 'seem to glimpse' and then further into 'need to seem to glimpse'. Similarly, the identification of a site 'there' is weakened to the point where it becomes 'afaint afar away over there'(*C*, 134). As the words pile up, the object of their search recedes still further away, yet those words have been generated precisely in this need to search for *the* word at last. Even if we posit that 'what' is the word that was searched for all along (thus

---

2 *As The Story was Told: Uncollected and Late Prose* (London: Calder, 1990)

making 'what is the word' a statement rather than reading it as a question) the answer would only beg a series of further questions: what does what signify? A condition of 'whatness' perhaps? And what might that mean?

One aspect in *what is the word* that does not suffer this process of lessening is the word 'folly'. From the outset, 'folly' predicates all the various attempts towards naming the word, so, by the end, the text reads:

> folly for to need to seem to glimpse afaint afar away over there what –
> what –
> what is the word—
>
> what is the word
> (*C*, 134-5)

Folly might not be *the* word, but it is no less a crucial one. Awareness of one's own foolishness in searching does not stop one searching; after all, we '*need* to seem to glimpse' what is just 'over there.' But such an awareness mitigates against any notion of mastery as we are engaging in an inevitable yet mistaken enterprise from the very beginning. Instead of mastery, there are the steady accretions of language and those accretions might give us access to not folly, but, from the Old French, *folie* or 'delight'.

Paul Stewart
November 2017

Introduction

Travails

Trauma is one of the key concepts underscoring the writing and reception of Samuel Beckett's work. This book sets out to re-read Beckett's post-war writing as a response to, and theorisation of, traumatic experience, with a particular focus on writing and representation. Biographical readings have taken account of the role mourning has played in the writer's prose, poetry and drama. Broader historical interpretations trace allusions to the atrocities of twentieth-century cultural memory. Intertextual research has also identified latent traumatic content via the many literary, religious and philosophical texts woven into the works. The influence of trauma is difficult to overstate in relation to Beckett's texts, although it typically adopts an aesthetic of understatement, allusion, and ellipses. The status of trauma in Beckett's writing appears to resist concrete or meaningful understandings. Its appearances are, by definition, peripheral and fragmentary, making it difficult to place at the centre of a research project or a sustained critical assessment. This is because, paradoxically, trauma is never fully present in Beckett's texts, nor is it totally absent: it remains elusive, troubling the borderlines between what exists and what does not. This study will ask how cultural and historical trauma can serve to illuminate the limitations and indeed possibilities of language and representation, and how the belated deferral of written signifiers, performed rehearsals, and electronic broadcasts ask us to rethink notions of presence and agency. To put it another way, trauma manifests as the ill seen and ill said of Beckett's oeuvre: a concept that challenges the possibilities of witnessing and recording, and, as a result, prompts a revaluation of what we mean by truth, history, and identity.

Through an analysis of several novels and short prose pieces, alongside experimental works for the stage, and radio dramas commissioned by the BBC, this book addresses how trauma, with its connected themes of absence and loss, punctuates Beckett's approach to writing across different mediums. This study will not attempt to seize, or re-member, latent references within the texts, in order to restore them to some kind of rational coherence. David Houston Jones also contends that 'it is impossible to recover identifiable historical references' (Houston Jones 2011, 2) of this kind, and so an amplification of the 'muted echoes of atrocity' (2) would be redundant, an ambitious task that would clarify little. Nor is this study intended to be an addition to the already proliferous number of excellent psychoanalytic readings of Samuel Beckett's work: while it is true that this work engages with psychoanalytic criticism and theory, its primary focus is the relationship between trauma, language, and subjectivity. As a result, psychoanalytic terms have been appropriated and repurposed to explore the strange and unstable status of writing that Beckett's work so often illuminates. This project is concerned with the unstable status conferred by the term 'trauma' itself, and its implications for the way we conceive a literary work; throughout Beckett's post-war writing, trauma becomes a means by which categories of language, presence, and subjectivity are productively deconstructed. As Angela Moorjani writes *The Aesthetics of Loss and Lessness*, Beckett's canon demarcates a contradictory space 'where timelessness and selflessness, if not placelessness, abound' (Moorjani 1992, 175).

In her book *Theatre on Trial: Samuel Beckett's Late Drama*, Anna McMullan compares a moment in *Quoi où*, first written in 1983, to its English translation, *What Where*. The play, which revolves around a series of characters with alliterative names (Bem, Bim, Bom and the Voice of Bam), each an imperfect repetition that appears 'as alike as possible' (*WW*, 151) tentatively discusses the administration of torture in order to extract information from a subject. McMullan notices that the English translation 'describes the process of torture as giving him "the works" and the French text uses the verb "travailler"' (McMullan 1993, 43). In English, the term 'work' can be made 'in reference to any action requiring effort or difficult to do', a 'hard task'.[1] In its original

1 'Work', in OED (2017), accessed January 3, 2017, http://www.oed.com.

French, the word 'travailler' introduces a more direct idea of punishment or suffering. McMullan quips that the two divergent expressions might be read together to suggest 'enforced study sessions' (43), and there is a sense in which the observation is correct. Indeed, the action of working in Samuel Beckett's texts can often be suggestive of a torturous or painful process. Of course, the romantic cliché of the suffering artist is not new to literary studies; in fact, is it something of a staple in accounts by writers and journalists recalling their meetings with Mr. Samuel Beckett. As Charles Juliet puts it in *Conversations with Samuel Beckett and Bram van Velde*, the writer is perceived as a 'superior man, a man who inhabits the depths, ceaselessly questioning what is most fundamental. Suddenly it is obvious to me: he is *Beckett the Inconsolable…*' (Juliet 2009, 19). But whilst the image of Samuel Beckett as suffering artist is a potent, persistent, and no doubt lucrative one, it bears little relation to the subtleties and complexities of the work itself.

Instead, we might appropriate this canny word 'travail' as a way into Beckett's 'work' as a term that employs a multiplicity of definitions. As we have already observed, 'travail' is suggestive of a work or an exertion, such as a literary work, that makes specific demands upon an individual in its production and consumption; it might also be considered in relation to a severe pain or ordeal that one is forced to endure. In addition, there is an etymological connection between the word 'travail' and the verb 'travel'. In this case, 'travail' can be suggestive of a journey, and combines notions of work, exertion, pain and ordeal with the movement or transmission from one discrete space to the next. Together, these divergent concepts can be usefully applied to Samuel Beckett's post-war prose, poetry and drama, to initiate an engagement with some of the central precepts of contemporary trauma theory. As Roger Luckhurst has observed, the ordeal of trauma is something that

> appears to be worryingly transmissible: it leaks between mental and physical symptoms, between patients (as in the 'contagions' of hysteria or shell shock), between patients and doctors via the mysterious processes of transference or suggestion, and between victims and their listeners or viewers who are commonly moved to forms

> of overwhelming sympathy, even to the extent of claiming secondary victimhood. (Luckhurst 2008, 3)

Luckhurst goes on to posit that post-war responses to 'unbounded' events such as the Holocaust are 'extremely transmissible. Trauma works its way across generations, to the extent that the notion of "transgenerational haunting" has now become its own specialism' (69). Beckett's 'travails' appear to anticipate this movement: they are suggestive of a painful event or ordeal that literally 'works' its way from one generation to the next, transmitted through official historical records, documents and oral accounts as a troubling and unsettling form of cultural inheritance. This ongoing movement is identified in Maurice Blanchot's reading of Beckett's *How It Is*, first published in French in 1961: 'This is biblical speech: extending from generation to generation, it runs on' (Blanchot 1993, 330). The novel's affiliation with transgenerational inheritance, suffering, and religious iconography has been duly noted by other critics. Édouard Magessa O'Reilly observes that *How It Is* has been read variously 'as an allegory of earthly existence or of the writing process as such, as the description of a *Purgatorio*-like afterlife' (O'Reilly 2009, xiii), or, as critic R.-M. Albérès suggested in a 1961 review for *Nouvelles littéraires*, it can be likened to 'the Book of Job and to the works of Pascal for the lyricism of its despair' (xii).[2] As Angela Moorjani memorably puts it: 'In the French fiction of the forties, Beckett situates the writer writing within a ghostly site, the domain of the unborn and the dead' (Moorjani 1996, 83). Beckett's work appears to designate a space for the representation of trauma or traumatic experience, but it is a space that is constantly

---

2 Iain Bailey has explored Beckett's intertextual use of the Bible at length in his monograph, *Samuel Beckett and the Bible* (London: Bloomsbury, 2014). For more on the uses of the Bible in Beckett's drama and later prose, see Chapter 3 of Mary Bryden's *Samuel Beckett and the Idea of God* (London: Macmillan Press, 1998), 102-131. Finally, for an essay on the relationship between Biblical texts and Beckett's representation of pain, see Glenn Clifton, 'Pain without Incarnation: *The Unnamable*, Derrida, and the Book of Job', *Journal of Beckett Studies*, 20:2 (2011), 149-71.

shifting in tone and perspective: from pathos to irony to tragedy to humour, categories of action and being, past and present, are continually called into question.

The moment we begin to read Beckett's texts through the lens of an historical or cultural context, we attempt to place them within some form of chronological order (eg. the unfolding events of the twentieth century) or within an aesthetic lineage (noting the presence of traumatic representation in a number of modernist texts, ranging Joyce and Woolf and others). And yet, what I will argue in this study is that Beckett's work does not neatly conform to rational expectations of timeliness or tradition, but somehow resists our grasp (*maintenance*), and consequently and our ability to maintain a stable meaning. Whereas standard Freudian accounts of trauma attempt to locate or constitute an event that returns from a previous historical moment, an experience that repeats itself, Beckett's writing articulates some of the key characteristics of traumatic experience without making them fully present for the reader or the audience. The term 'travail', in this sense, suggests that Beckett's work might be considered as representing a form of traumatic experience that is perpetually on the move, imperfectly echoing past contexts in the present, whilst signalling developments that have yet to arrive in the future. This notion of the travail, echoes Said's 'late style' as an aesthetic of apartness, exile, and anachronism, not only signals a deep and abiding tension at the heart of post-war twentieth-century modernity, but connects to uncertainties about the veracity of language, meaning, and truth, across Beckett's work in radio, prose, and drama.

Methodologies

In the last two decades, there has been a marked acceleration in the number of academic interpretations of Beckett's texts assessing the impact of historical events on the writer's work. Among them, we might list Seán Kennedy and Katherine Weiss' *Samuel Beckett: History, Memory, Archive*, a 2009 essay collection that '[seeks] to restore Beckett's work to its relevant historical and cultural contexts' (Kennedy

2009, 2). Such new critical revaluations are no doubt the product of a general resurgence in Beckett interest since the public centenary celebrations of 2006, and the proliferation of new historical and archival materials that have been made available in recent years.[3] In addition to the work of Kennedy and Weiss, there have been other collections that contextualise Beckett within some form of cultural or literary heritage; *Beckett's Literary Legacies*[4] is just one example, with essays that locate affinities between Beckett and fellow post-war writers, such as Paul Celan and Maurice Blanchot, and more recent contemporary examples, including Sarah Kane, J. M. Coetzee, Paul Auster and Don DeLillo.[5]

David Houston Jones' 2011 publication *Samuel Beckett and Testimony* can also be read as part of a wider movement that contextualises Beckett's writing as a canon that engages with the cultural and historical fallout of trauma and traumatisation.[6] This bold and ambitious undertaking is not without its problems, as Seán Kennedy observes:

---

3 In 2011, Cambridge University Press published *The Letters of Samuel Beckett: 1941-1956*, the second in a four-volume series that is making a number of rare archival materials available to the public for the first time. While Beckett's correspondence is notably sparse during the war years (with letters of the second volume beginning in January 1945), the collection nonetheless sheds light on the historical aftermath of post-war Europe, and the cultural and artistic life of Paris during this period.

4 Matthew Feldman and Mark Nixon, eds., *Beckett's Literary Legacies* (Newcastle: Cambridge Scholars Publishing, 2007).

5 Two important new studies were published after this manuscript was submitted for publication, and so are not included in this work. Firstly, *Samuel Beckett and BBC Radio: A Reassessment*, eds. David Addyman, Matthew Feldman, and Erik Tonning (New York: Palgrave Macmillan, 2017); and secondly, Emilie Morin's groundbreaking monograph, *Beckett's Political Imagination* (Cambridge: Cambridge University Press, 2017).

6 Like this study, Jones' work draws upon the ideas of Maurice Blanchot and Jacques Derrida to explore issues corresponding to trauma and traumatisation. However, whereas this work is specifically concerned with exploring trauma theory through Beckett's prose, drama and radio

> Samuel Beckett's writings can seem particularly resistant to historical readings, an observation that is especially true of those written after the Second World War. Set at an anonymous crossroads, or in strange, unfamiliar cities, the major works that secured Beckett's reputation give the distinct impression that they are set 'both anywhere and nowhere'. (Kennedy 2009, 1)

Boxall elaborates on this idea in his monograph, *Since Beckett*, when he suggests that the work 'appears to inhabit a different history altogether, a history that cannot easily be slotted between 1929 and 1989. Beckett's work has seemed to belong to a world of its own, to be sealed into an historical and geographical cylinder' (Boxall 2009, 3). Nonetheless, the attempt to secure the texts within a general (or specific) historical and cultural context continues. Kennedy states that 'it has long been noted that traces of history-memory appear throughout Beckett's *oeuvre*, and their significance has yet to be fully accounted for' (Kennedy 2009, 2). It is analogous to the problem of trauma, which signals a partial presence or symptom that demands investigation and explication. Through a process of acting out or working through, a causal explanation and delineation of trauma might be revealed and attained. But, more often than not, the root or origin of trauma is just as difficult, even impossible, to ascertain. There arises a paradoxical condition, where both trauma and literary text offer a suggestion of presence and meaning, whilst simultaneously denying and deferring its final signification. As Alysia E. Garrison suggests of *The Unnamable*, 'the condition of absolute silence is nonetheless pierced by the intermittent acoustic pulse of a voice that demands, yet defies, our witness' (Garrison 2009, 91). This desire to account for the subtle echoes, references and abstractions of Beckett's theatre and prose thus becomes a condition of the texts themselves.

The recent proliferation of trauma as an operative term in Beckett scholarship is, more than likely, a product of broader devel-

---

works, Jones provides an excellent exposition of the relationship between testimony, the archive and Beckett's prose.

opments in the field of trauma studies. In 1995, Cathy Caruth published a groundbreaking collection of articles, interviews and reflections entitled *Trauma: Explorations in Memory* (1995), which included contributions from Shoshama Felman, Harold Bloom, and Georges Bataille, and which interviewed key figures in the fields of Post-Traumatic Stress Disorder and Holocaust testimony, Robert Jay Lifton and Claude Lanzmann respectively. In 1996, Caruth published *Unclaimed Experience: Trauma, Narrative, and History*, a work that traces a contemporary psychoanalytic interpretation of traumatisation via a series of literary and critical theoretical readings. Ruth Leys' 2000 work *Trauma: A Genealogy* delineates a history of trauma from its psychoanalytic origins in Freud, to recent developments in contemporary medical research. In 2001 came Dominick LaCapra's study, *Writing History, Writing Trauma*, a monograph that addresses a number of the central issues of traumatic representation, specifically those pertaining to cultural memories of the Holocaust. Finally, Roger Luckhurst's *The Trauma Question*, first published in 2008, provides both a cultural and historical context for contemporary ideas on the subject, alongside a number of literary, artistic and cinematic readings.

Jonathan Boulter has addressed the idiosyncratic representation of traumatic experience in Beckett's work in a 2004 essay entitled 'Does Mourning Require a Subject?'. The piece pays attention to Beckett's *Texts for Nothing*, a post-war sequence written after the publication of the 'Three Novels', *Molloy*, *Malone Dies*, and *The Unnamable*. Boulter notes that trauma and, by extension, the academic field of trauma studies, has become a popular way by which literary texts are investigated and understood in the late twentieth and early twenty-first century. This status as a 'key trope in contemporary culture' places it in a privileged position whereby its theorisation is regularly employed as a useful 'hermeneutic tool' (Boulter 2004, 332). For Boulter, there is something troubling about the way that trauma is so often employed to explain or decipher modernist and postmodernist literary texts. Boulter stresses that recent works celebrate 'the shattering and loss of traditional metaphysical and ontological categories such as truth, ethics, and the subject' (332-3); the irony, for Boulter, lies in the fact that trauma becomes the means by which such categories can be restored through a process of 'discovering, narrating, working-through'. For Boulter, and I am simplifying here, what makes Beckett's treatment of traumatic experience radical rather than ironical and conservative is its refusal to constitute a stable human figure at the centre of proceedings: there is no fully-constituted representation of human subjectivity, the hook on which Western metaphysics hangs. As a result, Beckett's work 'forces a rethinking of the basic assumptions of narrative and interpretive agency'. Boulter argues that this has deep implications for our understanding of trauma as it might apply to literary studies, since Beckett's work calls into question many of the concept's central assumptions. The essay concludes by suggesting that trauma studies can be said to reveal an unsettling conservative undercurrent, that in attempting to 'work back, to resurrect, and represent the originary scene of loss' (345), practitioners are in fact pursuing a 'quintessentially modernist approach' (346) to restore Western definitions of history, identity, and truth.

In his 2007 essay '*Endgame*'s Remainders', Russell Smith also addresses the traumatic content of Beckett's work, in this case by taking a close look at the writer's 1958 play. Smith takes issue with some of the lines of argument in Boulter's aforementioned essay, while acknowledging that Beckett's texts tend to 'resist explicitly historicist readings of his work' (Smith 2007, 102). For Smith, the difficulties of Beckett's texts can indeed be productively read and understood within a traumatic framework. The disagreement between Smith and Boulter is interesting: both scholars offer fascinating engagements with their chosen texts, and both demonstrate a keen and sophisticated knowledge of trauma theory and how it might relate to Beckett's work. But despite the expertise of both scholars, a divergence persists on how to address the role and status of traumatic experience in Beckett's writing. How does the traumatic symptom manifest itself in the writer's post-war texts, and in what ways does it engage with or challenge contemporary orthodoxies regarding the understanding or documentation of traumatic experience? In what ways does Beckett's work offer more than a simple case study to be noted and resolved?

And does his representation of individual traumatic experience in fact signal something broader?

Adding to the recent spate of academic works on trauma and cultural memory,[7] Beckett Studies has also accommodated a rising number of academic works that focus on physical, somatic or material analyses of the writer's prose, poetry and drama. On 24 June 2010, a 'Beckett and the Brain' seminar was held at Birkbeck College in London. The seminar aimed to address the following questions:

> Recently, archival support for Beckett's knowledge and use of neurological, psychological and psychoanalytic material, allied with an increasingly dominant cultural sense of the mind as a complex epiphenomenon of an evolved neurological substrate, has produced critical studies exploring the suggestive resemblances between Beckett's textual experiments and those neuropsychological and psychiatric disorders that illuminate the modes of functioning of the human brain. What has been less fully explored, however, are the methodological implications of reading Beckett's work alongside historical and contemporary neurology and psychology. What are the critical and ethical problems inherent in relying on a mode of 'resemblance' between Beckett's work and brain science? What

---

7 While the scholarship on Beckett and trauma is the product of the 1980s and 1990s rise of trauma theory, Beckett's texts have long been explored in relation to melancholia, loss, and related psychoanalytic concepts across a range of Freudian, Jungian, Lacanian, and Kleinian approaches. Scholars have also taken account of Beckett's own interest in psychoanalytic theory and his experience as an analysand under the care of Dr Wilfred Bion (for the latter, see Steven Connor, 'Beckett and Bion', *Journal of Beckett Studies*, 17:1-2 [2009], 9-34). For a handy summary of some of the key critical approaches to the field, see Angela Moorjani's chapter, 'Beckett and Psychoanalysis' in *Palgrave Advances in Samuel Beckett Studies*, ed. Lois Oppenheim (Basingstoke: Palgrave Macmillan, 2004), 172-93; and Lois Oppenheim's own essay, 'Situating Samuel Beckett' in *The Cambridge Companion to the Modernist Novel*, ed. Morag Shiach (Cambridge: Cambridge University Press, 2007), 224-237.

> new kinds of critical practice might be forged between disciplines? Might Beckett's work have clinical as well as critical uses?[8]

In 2012, the seminar was expanded into an AHRC-funded research project, spanning three separate workshops in Reading University (hosted by Ulrika Maude), Birkbeck College (Laura Salisbury) and the University of Warwick (Elizabeth Barry).[9] This research initiative was hailed as a 'new discovery for science and art'[10] by *The Observer*, and appears to symbolise a wider multidisciplinary engagement between medical and scientific investigation and fields such as literary criticism or theatre studies. In the same year came the publication of *Samuel Beckett and Pain* (2009), a collection of essays that takes Samuel Beckett's direct experience of 'psychical and psychological pain' (Tanaka et al 2009, 9) as its starting point for critical reflection. More recently there have been studies like Joseph Anderton's *Beckett's Creatures: Art of Failure After the Holocaust* (2016).

Informed by an engagement with emergent scientific methodologies, Beckett Studies has addressed a number of neglected aspects of the author's writing. Innovative developments in Western medicine have allowed fresh readings of Beckett's work, spanning the length of his published career. Plays, novels and short stories can now be interpreted in ways that reconfigure character behaviour and development as causally related to a range of developing scientific theories. However, this recent advancement in empirical knowledge does not stop at the body of Beckett and his protagonists, but also creates im-

---

8 'Beckett and the Brain', Birkbeck, University of London, accessed February 25, 2013, http://www.bbk.ac.uk/english/about-us/events-old/past-conferences/beckett-and-the-brain-24-june-2010.

9 The official website of the AHRC-funded project is hosted at 'Beckett and the Brain', University of Warwick, accessed February 25, 2013, http://www2.warwick.ac.uk/fac/arts/english/research/currentprojects/beckettandthebrain/.

10 Vanessa Thorpe, 'A new discovery for science and art: the cultural divide is all in the mind' in *The Observer*, 24 November 2012.

plications for the way we read and interpret drafts and alternate versions of the author's texts. The Beckett Digital Manuscript Project, launched by Mark Nixon and Dirk Van Hulle in June 2011, is an attempt

> to reunite the manuscripts of Samuel Beckett's works in a digital way, and to facilitate genetic research: the project brings together digital facsimiles of documents that are now preserved in different holding libraries, and adds transcriptions of Beckett's manuscripts, tools for bilingual and genetic version comparison, a search engine, and an analysis of the textual genesis of his works.[11]

Genetic research, as Dirk Van Hulle has stated elsewhere, aims to 'establish a chronology and reconstruct the writing history' (Van Hulle 2009, 169) of a literary text. The impulse toward scientific and empirical readings of Beckett's work can suggest a strictly causal approach to interpretation. As Van Hulle warns in his essay on genetic criticism, 'it may be tempting to project dramatic structures into the writing process in order to be able to present the published text as the dénouement or the inevitable outcome of a linear process' (169). It could be tempting to explain somatic representations of the human body according to a recognised symptom or condition; or, perhaps, reveal the finer points of Beckett's theatre and prose with recourse to psychological and physiological theories of consciousness and experience. But this would be to assume that the methodological terms employed by science and medicine are, in themselves, the stable outcomes of a completed investigative process.

This study aims to draw upon the psychoanalytic and medical term 'trauma' to complicate, rather than simplify, our understanding of Beckett's oeuvre. It offers a way to examine a body of work that is primarily concerned with the uneasy status of truth and representation across language and performance text. The promise of 'inevitable outcome' is perpetually deferred and complicated throughout the writer's

---

11 Series Preface to *The Beckett Digital Manuscript Project*, accessed February 24, 2013, http://www.beckettarchive.org/introduction.jsp.

post-war texts, and trauma is a concept that seems to articulate this quality. The term itself is the product of a long-standing process of cultural and scientific reflection and investigation, but contemporary understandings of it are framed in an awareness of its fragile meaning and delicate applications. The term 'travail' is perhaps at its most useful here to elucidate the relationship between trauma and language: it evokes not only the action and embodiment of, say, a literary work and its traumatic substance, but the inherent mobility of that work, its ceaseless transitions from meaning to meaning, and its unstable deferrals.

In early historical observations of trauma patients, physicians formulated a series of diagnostic tests and compiled a series of symptoms. Sigmund Freud's work in this area is of central historical importance, in part because his psychoanalytic work rests among the founding texts of contemporary trauma studies. Freud noted that 'patients give us an impression of having been "fixated" to a particular portion of their past, as though they could not manage to free themselves from it and were for that reason alienated from the present and the future' (Freud 1991, 313). Roger Luckhurst categorizes symptoms of this condition as 'disordered memory, disturbed sleep and frightful dreams, and various types of paralysis, melancholia, and impotence, with a particular emphasis on the sudden loss of business sense' (Luckhurst 2008, 22). On the history and development of trauma, Luckhurst identifies 'the belated onset of these symptoms' as a central characterizing symptom of the traumatized patient. It would seem, to cite physician John Erichson, that 'at the time of the occurrence of the injury the sufferer is usually quite unconscious that any serious accident has happened to him [*sic.*]'.[12] The identifying trait, here, is a sense of belatedness, of time out of joint, and, by extension, a strange logic of deferral, repetition and return.

Much contemporary discussion of trauma focuses on descriptions of a specific loss, or a recognized absence, with explicit reference

12 John Erichson, qtd. in Luckhurst, *The Trauma Question*, 22.

to an originary event. We can trace this pattern from Freud to contemporary writers such as Ruth Leys and Cathy Caruth, who both, despite divergent ideas about the construction and effects of trauma, place great focus on the specificity of an originary event. They have each discussed the difficulty with which the human mind comprehends or controls the traumatic event, and the necessary delay—or belatedness—that defines all traumatized responses. The understanding and apprehension of the traumatic event is perceived as a possible path to recovery; it is a process that prioritizes the excavation and understanding of such events as the primary means to resolve them. In this way, trauma becomes a space to explore what is not accommodated within rational Western subjectivity: that which resists traditional categories, and disrupts the coherency with which subjects attempt to understand the world around them.

Thus, trauma acts as a kind of impasse to representation. Freud himself defined traumatic neuroses by 'fixation to the moment of the traumatic accident' that 'lies at their root' (Freud 1991, 315). It is a moment that is obsessively returned to and recuperated by the trauma sufferer as an experience that cannot be adequately explained or rationalized. It cannot be grasped via conventional methods because it disrupts chronology, order and our ability to comprehend it. In the introduction to *Unclaimed Experience*, Cathy Caruth notes that each of the texts she discusses

> engages, in its own specific way, [with] a central problem of listening, of knowing, and of representing that [which] emerges from the actual experience of the crisis. If traumatic experience, as Freud indicates suggestively, is an experience that is not fully assimilated as it occurs, then these texts, each in its turn, ask what it means to transmit and to theorize around a crisis that is marked, not by a simple knowledge, but by the ways it simultaneously defies and demands our witness. (Caruth 1996, 5)

This demand to witness and record experiences is vital to our understanding of Western humanist history as a series of linear, ordered events; and, as such, it is a demand that determines our understanding of the subject as a source of agency and meaning. Yet, I would suggest, Beckett's work attests to the way that trauma problematises standard models of Western knowledge and understanding via a logic of fragmentation, dispersal and deferral.

This book is concerned with the maintenance and appreciation of such deferrals; it aims to identify and uphold the slippery perplexities of Samuel Beckett's post-war writing in the context of contemporary trauma theory. As Seán Kennedy writes, 'the post-war writings draw us back, again and again, to scenes of catastrophe that are all the more powerful for remaining inexplicit' (Kennedy 2009, 5). In Beckett's work, we can assess how, in the words of David Houston Jones, 'the authority of the witness is both undermined and, perhaps, paradoxically reinforced by the unbearable and unspeakable nature of traumatic experience, which inscribes testimony with a central indeterminacy' (Houston Jones 2011, 6). This study does not aim to offer a diagnosis or an elucidation, as such, but to remain attuned to what is indirect and unclear in Beckett's writing. Instead of categorising or rationalising passages, protagonists, or references according to a prescribed psychoanalytic or empirical explanation, this project will attest to the unclear status of traumatic reference in Samuel Beckett's writing. In an essay on Beckett and contemporary literature, Peter Boxall addresses the question of historical transmission not with an attempt to harmoniously restore the past to the present, but by preserving the possibility of impossibility, silence, and darkness:

> If Beckett has left [Don] DeLillo a legacy, if he has taught him how to think and see in the bright gloom of today, then it is this contradiction in the very possibility of historical transmission that is perhaps one of his more valuable bequests. We can understand the persistence of Beckett's spirit in DeLillo's vision of America only if we attend to the impossibility of the road that leads from him to us, from there and then to here and now; only if we hear the silence and see the darkness in which Beckett shapes his thinking and seeing. (Boxall 2007, 224)

Using the work of Cathy Caruth and Roger Luckhurst as a starting point, and drawing upon critical texts by Jacques Derrida and Maurice Blanchot, this work suggests that Beckett's work constitutes a kind of 'late stage' in his creative output, a work that engages with the status of writing and literary inheritance via a traumatic logic of belatedness, untimeliness, and deferral. Beckett's 'late stage' manifests itself in the comings and goings of the post-war prose, the spectral rehearsals of the drama, and the haunted transmissions of the wireless broadcasts, and conjures a space where time, memory, and selfhood fracture and disperse.

After Auschwitz

Speaking of Samuel Beckett as a post-war writer, the author and critic J. G. Ballard once confessed that 'I have never been able to read him'.[13] He explained that he found the writer's work 'too grey and reductive', and drew upon personal experiences of a Japanese internment camp to illustrate his point: 'I have seen hell—Shanghai 1937-45—and it is nothing like Beckett's.'[14] Perhaps ironically, Ballard's 'hell' found expression through speculative fiction during the immediate post-war period, with novels such as *The Atrocity Exhibition* (1969) and *Crash* (1973) delineating a cultural crisis, the 'marriage of reason and nightmare that has dominated the 20th century' (Ballard 1995, i). His novels and short stories utilise a number of experimental forms, from the glossary format of *The Atrocity Exhibition*, to the newsreel of 'Theatre of War' (1977),[15] travel writing in 'Having a Wonderful Time' (1978),[16] the questionnaire in 'Answers to a Questionnaire' (1985),[17]

---

13 J. G. Ballard interviewed by L. Tarantino, qtd. in *J. G. Ballard: Quotes*, ed. V. Vale and Mike Ryan (San Francisco: RE/Search Publications, 2004), 95.

14 Ibid.

15 J. G. Ballard, 'Theatre of War' in *The Complete Short Stories: Volume II* (London, New York, Toronto, Sydney: Harper Perennial, 2006), 452-472.

16 J. G. Ballard, 'Having a Wonderful Time' in *The Complete Short Stories: Volume II*, 473-478.

17 J. G. Ballard, 'Answers to a Questionnaire' in *The Complete Short Stories: Volume II*, 657-661.

and even the television schedule in 'A Guide to Virtual Death' (1992).[18]

Each of these stories, to a greater or lesser degree, contextualises traumatic subject matter via the recognisable media of the post-war information age. His fictionalised autobiographies, *Empire of the Sun* (1984) and *The Kindness of Women* (1991), are perhaps the closest he has come to a full personal account of his wartime experience, and they are written in a more conventional and accessible prose form.[19] It is striking, then, that Ballard is so critical of Beckett's writing. It is difficult to be certain of which texts Ballard is referring to, but one suspects the austere minimalist production design of *Endgame*, or perhaps *Waiting for Godot.* If this is the case, then one is inclined to ask why Ballard would place them within the context of a post-war setting, since the time and place of these, and many other Beckett texts, is decidedly vague.[20] While Ballard's reading is dismissive of the manifest content of the work as 'grey and reductive', he nonetheless traces some kind of reference, a latent content underscoring the works themselves. At the very moment he dismisses Beckett's writing, he seems to acknowledge something that permeates it in an indirect yet recognisable way. It is perhaps this uneasy status between presence and absence that troubles the writer's sensibilities.

18 J. G. Ballard, 'A Guide to Virtual Death' in *The Complete Short Stories: Volume II*, 757-759.

19 Ballard's memoir, *Miracles of Life: Shanghai to Shepperton* (London: Harper Perennial, 2008), published shortly before the author's death, devotes the first of two parts to Second World War experiences, including chapters on the attack of Pearl Harbour, his internment at Lunghua Camp and American air raids.

20 For more on the 'vague' status of representation in Beckett's work, it is worth consulting Rosemary Pountney's work *Theatre of Shadows: Samuel Beckett's Drama 1956-76* (Gerrard's Cross: Colin Smythe, 1988). Pountney explores the phenomenon of 'vaguening', a part of Beckett's writing process where historical or biographical references connected to the author's life and experience were altered or removed during the revision of manuscripts, rendering such references absent or ambiguous.

Ballard is not the only one to trace the residue of history in Samuel Beckett's writing. His prose and theatrical work has often been received as a kind of response to the Second World War and the enactment of European atrocities such as the Holocaust. And yet, in contrast to memoir, historical document, or realist fiction and theatre, Beckett's writing offers tentative engagements emphasising distance and separation, rather than realisations, re-enactments or representations. Peter Boxall notes that 'if Beckett's work might still be thought of, even "after Auschwitz", as poetry, then it is poetry in the process of consuming itself, poetry whose only task and whose only gift is to reveal the impossibility of its own undertaking' (Boxall 2007, 212). In his biography of Beckett, *Damned to Fame*, James Knowlson notes that the writer's 'challenge to naturalism' (*DF*, 636) drew a number of hostile reactions, not least from *Sunday Times* reviewer Dennis Potter:

> Would Solzhenitsyn have understood? Would the Jews on the way to the gas chamber? Question: Is this the art which is the response to the despair and pity of our age, or is it made of the kind of futility which helped such desecrations of the spirit, such filth of ideologies come into being?[21]

Potter was responding to two new television plays and a filmed version of *Not I*, aired on BBC 2 in April 1977. What is perhaps most interesting about these works[22] in the context of Potter's review is that they do not refer to, or attempt to portray, an identifiable historical event. The first presents the daily routine of a male protagonist, wandering the roads by day and attempting to recall a female face by night; the second work, *Ghost Trio*, is similarly preoccupied with the nocturnal absence of a woman who does not make an appearance; whilst the third presents a disembodied Mouth recounting a narrative in close-up at high speed. There is little doubt that the performances are each, in their own ways, unsettling. Each, too, signals some kind of traumatic absence or rupture that punctuates the lives, rhythms and

---

21 Dennis Potter, qtd. in Knowlson, *Damned to Fame*, 636.

22 *...but the clouds...*, *Ghost Trio* and *Not I*.

routines of its troubled protagonists. In his attempt to deride a method of representation that, supposedly, does not adequately address the ethical dilemmas of a post-war aesthetic, Potter conjures Solzhenitsyn and the Holocaust as though they are somehow embodied within the texts themselves. This mirrors Ballard's invocation of 'hell' and wartime Shanghai in his readings of Beckett's 'grey and reductive' works. With these examples in mind, we might ascertain in Beckett's writing a strange transmission of affect, the partial reproduction or spectral representation of traumatic content that addresses and accounts for history, whilst simultaneously resisting the problematic authority of a linear, sovereign account. As Kennedy puts it: 'There can be no doubt that Beckett's assault on representation was informed by his reading in philosophy, [and the essays of *History, Memory, Archive*] suggest it was also impelled by a realization of the complicity of concepts like "Identity" and "History" in the production of authoritarian master narratives and patterns of domination' (Kennedy 2009, 2). But how does Beckett's work achieve this effect?

In an essay exploring the relationship between art and philosophy in the writings of Beckett and Theodor W. Adorno, Jay Bernstein states that 'Art works are impossible objects' (Bernstein 1990, 180). He continues:

> Works are meaningful, they enact a synthesis, but not discursively true; they are purposeful but without practical purpose. Their meaning is semblance of truth without domination; their purposelessness an image of use value that cannot be exchanged. Their purposelessness is their form of resistance to change—a form that is harassed and subject to defeat. Their non-conceptual form is their form of resistance to identity thinking—a form that is harassed by the desire for meaning (180-1)

Bernstein finds Beckett's *Endgame* as 'central to Adorno's thought' (177), and the cultural critic's seminal essay, 'Trying to Understand

Endgame', appraises the status of Beckett's work in relation to its cultural and historical moment.[23] As Boxall notes, Adorno 'characterise[s] Beckett's writing as a writing at the ends, at the limits of expression' (Boxall 2007, 213). Michael Rothberg also addresses Adorno's take on the moral implications of a pleasure-giving art after Auschwitz, elaborating on Adorno's acceptance of writers like Franz Kafka and Samuel Beckett as artists who deliberately refuse such modes: 'Beckett's art, Adorno claims, evades this problem through its refusal of realist configuration' (Rothberg 1997, 63). *Endgame* both addresses and resists direct representation, and in doing so appears concerned with the ethical dimensions inherent to holding up a mirror to the world:

> Playing with elements of reality without any mirroring, taking no stand and finding pleasure in this freedom from prescribed activity, exposes more than would taking a stand with the intent to expose. The name of the catastrophe is to be spoken only in silence. The catastrophe that has befallen the whole is illuminated in the horrors of the last catastrophe; but only in those horrors, not when one looks at its origins. [...] Part of what is absurd in [Beckett's] writing is that it hides its face. (Adorno 2003, 267)[24]

In this way, Beckett's texts 'intervene in the affirmative postwar cultural politics of Western [...] society' (Rothberg 1997, 68). In light of the idea of Beckett as a poet of 'mute expression' (Boxall 2009, 14), the writing that hides its face might be considered as a condition of literature itself. In Maurice Blanchot's *The Infinite Conversation*, the essay 'Words Must Travel Far' reflects on the indirect voice of literature in its treatment of Beckett's 1964 work, *How It Is*. Blanchot writes:

---

23 David Cunningham offers a useful outline of Adorno and Beckett in 'Trying (Not) to Understand: Adorno and the Work of Beckett' in *Beckett and Philosophy*, ed. Richard Lane (Basingstoke: Palgrave Macmillan, 2002), 125-39.

24 For more information on Adorno's appreciation of Beckett's play, see Dirk Van Hulle, 'Adorno's Notes on *Endgame*', *Journal of Beckett Studies*, 19:2 (2010), 196-217.

> — Aren't you attributing too much importance to the qualifying terms that the critic avails himself of? And who still says a book is good or bad; or if he does, does not know that he speaks without having the right to? In truth, what can one say of a work? In praising Beckett's *How it is*, would we dare promise it to posterity? Would we even wish to praise it? Which does not mean that it surpasses, but rather discredits all praise, and that it would be paradoxical to read it with admiration. We have, then, a category of works that go unrecognized more through praise than through disparagement: to deprecate them is to come into contact with the force of refusal that has rendered them present and also with the remoteness that gives them their measure. If the strongest attraction, the deepest concern could be expressed through indifference, then indifference would indicate to what level these lead. (Blanchot 1993, 328)

There is, for Blanchot, an ethical problem attached to the formal appraisal of a work, whether it takes the form of rejection or commendation.[25] As Leslie Hill writes, 'criticism [becomes] disabled, forced to carry on, if at all, only by enduring through its own interruption' (Hill 2012, 19). Blanchot's essay encapsulates an alternative through a conversation, or exchange, between two distanced positions. As in the exchanges between Vladimir and Estragon in *Waiting for Godot*, Hamm and Clov in *Endgame*, and, to some degree, Winnie and Willie in *Happy Days*, the end is forestalled via a continuous series of transactions—a fragmentation or discontinuation of monologue through the eternal back and forth of multiple voices.[26] For Blanchot,

---

25 Jacques Derrida adopted just such a position with regards to Beckett's work by deliberately choosing not to engage with it critically. Derek Attridge addresses Derrida's refusal to formally appraise the 'signature' of Beckett's work in his essay, 'Taking Beckett at His Word: The Event of *The Unnamable*', *Journal of Beckett Studies*, 26:1 (2017), 10-23. Asja Szafraniec extensively deals with the relationship between Derrida and Beckett in his monograph, *Beckett, Derrida, and the Event of Literature* (Stanford: Stanford University Press, 2007).

26 Daniel Katz cites Adorno's essay as emblematic of Beckett's statement in *Three Dialogues with Georges Duthuit*: 'the liberating vitality of Beckett's work in relation to the death camps derives from its *refusal* to express,

the role of the critic is, in some sense, anathema to literature. It attempts to impose or encapsulate the complexities and subtleties of a literary text within the framework of a final judgement:

> — he is the last to arrive, the one who speaks last.
>
> — Having the last word is an advantage that may please those engaged in argument; others would step back from such an unfortunate privilege. Moreover, if there is this back and forth of words between us—we who are ourselves nothing but the necessity of this back and forth—perhaps it is to avoid the arrest of a last word. (Blanchot 1993, 326)

The operation of latent traumatic content within Beckett's texts once again obeys the principle of the 'travail', an account or a work that is continually on the move, resisting a final signified, or the 'unfortunate privilege' of a last word. As Boxall argues,

> a form of literary possibility does meet its limits in Beckett's writing [and his work] does constitute an encounter with the impossible, and with the impassable. But whilst Beckett's writing situates itself as a writing at the end or at the limit—like Malone's narrative, a writing in the impossible process of dying—it is nevertheless the case that it continues to go on, that it continues to "exert" an "influence" on our culture, making and shaping it. (Boxall 2007, 207)

The texts convey a process of continual and partial transmission from one site to another, a series of discontinuous echoes and fragments that undermine the security of a final resting place, or the broad stroke of a critic's pen. Voices, in Beckett, do not emanate from a single, historical point of origin, nor are they directed toward a single, teleological end. Their sources are multifarious and difficult to determine. Blanchot phrases this concept in the dialectical form of a question and

---

within the clear sense of an *obligation* that has no name.' See Daniel Katz, 'What Remains of Beckett: Evasion and History' in *Beckett and Phenomenology*, eds. Ulrika Maude and Matthew Feldman (London: Continuum, 2009), 144-57 (145).

answer, of multiple voices that continue but do not finally resolve themselves:

> — Then why does he not speak directly?
>
> — Because, I imagine, he cannot: in literature there is no direct speech. (Blanchot 1993, 327)

As we shall see in the chapters that follow, Samuel Beckett's writing works obliquely, refusing the consolation of a direct or full re-presentation. Instead, it follows the traumatised logic of the 'travail', continually moving from one place to another, transgressing boundaries of here and there, past and present, via a spectral logic that unsettles and defers Western presence.

In summary, this book aims to address the concept of trauma in two distinct ways. Firstly, it identifies the works themselves as texts that imply a latent traumatic content, perhaps responding to a wider cultural and historical post-war shift, whilst drawing attention to the very problem of its representation. While secondly, the book explores how Beckett's work challenges and undermines the value of trauma as a point of diagnostic certainty; instead, the study attempts to remain attuned to how Beckett's texts across radio, prose and theatre unravel and deconstruct Western understandings of time, place and the self in a number of subtle ways.

Selecting the Texts

The process of selecting texts for a research project charts a series of omissions; it implies an opposition between critical or literary texts that are vital to an argument, and those that are dispensable. During a period in Beckett Studies where various biographical and historical materials have been made publicly available for the first time, the question of engaging with these documents has been a central methodological concern of the project. However, since it is not the intention of this study to map 'real' or biographical trauma upon the characters of Beckett's prose, a detailed reading of the author's correspondence, notebooks or other personal archival materials has been unnecessary. In fact, since the study aims to stress the unstable status and unreliability of traumatic representation in Beckett's writing, it would seem counterintuitive to explain the literary texts with recourse to letters, notebooks, memoirs or biographies. With that in mind, however, certain biographical details have been employed throughout the work to offer historical context, or simply for anecdotal enjoyment.

This study is limited to texts that Beckett either wrote in (or translated into) English, with only occasional references to other language versions. Lamentably, since Beckett was a writer who employed French, German and a number of other languages during his career, this has resulted in the omission of a number of worthy passages that, I am sure, are ripe for analysis. The book adheres to texts published via the Faber and Faber reissue series (2009-), edited and introduced by a number of prominent and upcoming Beckett scholars. Due to considerations of space and time available for the project, the study does not engage with manuscripts of texts that are available at archives throughout the world. This is unfortunate for a number of reasons, not least because it subsequently forbade readings of early drafts of the texts discussed herein—but also because it rules out a number of noteworthy unpublished texts, such as the 1967 work 'Medical Monologue', 'a woman's monologue about medications' (Cohn 2001, 302).

But even within the range of texts readily available in English, there are large areas of Beckett's output that this study has not addressed. With space as a prominent concern, many of the better known plays (*Waiting for Godot*, *Endgame*, *Happy Days*) have been set aside in favour of later works that are not so often addressed in Beckett criticism. With regard to prose, the first chapter charts a trajectory from a late pre-war text, *Murphy* (1938), to the four post-war novellas that predate Beckett's "*Three Novels*", or "*Trilogy*" (*Molloy*, *Malone Dies* and *The Unnamable*). The study also explores Beckett's use of radio as a medium of artistic expression, with a particular focus on *All That Fall*, but there is no corresponding section devoted to film productions or his plays for television. These omissions were necessary to the structure of the book, which economises on space to explore three tightly focussed areas of Beckett's published output. But, for future research and exploration, I believe it would be highly productive to assess television productions such as *Eh Joe* for their relation to concepts of traumatic repetition and return, not to mention the dimensions of Beckett's closed-place prose works, such as *The Lost Ones* and *Lessness*.[27] These omissions are undoubtedly productive threads for further research and exploration, which I believe can be usefully employed in the future to expand and develop some of the principal aims of this research project.

Chapter Outline

The first chapter, 'Coming and Going', explores the motif of walking and wandering in Beckett's prose as a traumatic symptom of belatedness, exile, and loss. Walking is conventionally understood as an act that conveys agency and purpose, a movement that directs the individual from a specific point of departure to a final point of arrival. Drawing upon the work of Rebecca Solnit and others, the chapter reads Beckett's wanderers against dominant cultural associations associated with walking, such as rational thought, linear progression, and teleological resolution. Through discussions of *Murphy*, *Watt,* the *Three Novels* and post-war *Nouvelles*, the chapter elides walking with Beckett's wandering prose style to examine how traumatic symptoms disrupt familiar boundaries of public and private, movement and stasis, past and future. Walking and wandering thus becomes part of a literary mode that traumatically conveys a crisis of time, place, and the self.

The second chapter, 'Late Stage', which gives this book its title, is similarly concerned with the way human presence is deferred

27 Daniel Katz's has offered a concise analysis of critical works by Antoinette Weber-Caflisch and Jean-Michel Rabaté, respectively, which link *Le Dépeupleur* (*The Lost Ones*) to historical descriptions of concentration camps and the writing of Holocaust survivor, Primo Levi. See 'What Remains of Beckett: Evasion and History' in *Beckett and Phenomenology*, eds. Ulrika Maude and Matthew Feldman (London: Continuum, 2009), 144-57 (145).

or denied in Samuel Beckett's late dramatic works. Returning to the difficult and uncertain status of the word 'late', the chapter assumes a range of possible definitions: firstly, the term can denote a point in the author's career when a play was written, positioning it after some of Beckett's initial successes; secondly, the term suggests a temporal relationship between a theatrical performance and the text which it seems to follow; thirdly, the texts are late in the sense that they seem to address belated traumatic symptoms that return to haunt a principal character; and, in addition to these definitions, the protagonists themselves appear to be 'late' in the sense that they are not of this world, their status as living beings becoming something that is impossible to determine. The chapter suggests that the texts themselves operate in a way that recalls the belated return of the traumatic symptom: something that is perpetually late, that never completely manifests itself to us, but which resists categorical attempts to impose or delineate a complete meaning or account.

In the third and final chapter, 'The Voice Breaks', Beckett's radio plays are addressed with particularly close attention to the BBC production of *All That Fall*. The broadcasts are placed within the context of the nineteenth-century invention of wireless radio and its longstanding associations with superstition and spiritualism. Radio is read as a ghostly medium that signals the cutting edge of twentieth-century communications technology, while simultaneously forging associations that unravel and deconstruct distinctions between now and then, presence and absence. By surveying Beckett's deployment of loss and departure in his work for radio, the chapter traces a traumatic symptomology which precedes the Second World War, and in doing so addresses the role of technology in constituting the 'traumatic modernity' of the nineteenth and twentieth centuries.

1. Prose: Coming and Going

Preamble

The act of walking suggests a steady and progressive forward movement towards a fixed point or goal. In Samuel Beckett's immediate post-war prose, characters and narrative voices all proceed towards some unspecified end, but a final resolution is difficult to establish. The straightforward transition from beginning to end is complicated as protagonists lose their way in dense forests, or narrators retrace long familiar paths. Starting points never seem to be clear or straightforward, and it is often difficult, if not impossible, to identify a specific origin or point of departure. The journey itself, towards a set destination, also falls prey to a seemingly endless series of discursions, digressions and deferrals. Characters are propelled forward by unknown and obscure causes, and find no refuge or sanctuary in the routes ahead of them. Our presuppositions about walking, that it offers a coherent and linear method to transport a subject from one fixed point to another, are gradually unraveled through the journeys Beckett's narrators take. Some go in search of their origins; some follow circuitous routes; others follow strange assignments; and there are still more that stray from familiar, established courses altogether. Walking is a rich theme throughout Beckett's work, and I suggest that an examination of the trope in his fiction can reveal associations with ideas about traumatic experience and subjectivity. From the modernist inheritance of the flâneur in his pre-war novel, *Murphy*, to his post-war narratives *Mercier and Camier*, the *Nouvelles* and *The Three Novels*, we can trace how the act of walking is coupled with the writer's stylistic wandering to form a traumatic aesthetic of belatedness, exile,[1] and loss.

---

1 In 1961-2, English professor Lawrence E. Harvey had an opportunity to question Beckett about the theme of exile in his work, and was told that such motifs were oversimplifications. Harvey writes: 'When I mentioned the Eden-Exile tension that I found in his work, Beckett objected and

In accounts of Samuel Beckett's life, walking is repeatedly equated with traumatic memories and psychological disturbances. Deidre Bair recalls Beckett 'spending most of his time walking' (Bair 1990, 159) during a period in 1933, following the death of his cousin Peggy Sinclair, and his father, William Beckett, from a heart attack. Bair suggests the writer 'would use these long frustrating walks [...] in his writing, in descriptions of the countryside or of his thoughts while pacing' (159-60). Walking, here, is adopted as a romantic motif by the biographer, allowing the artist to find creative inspiration while wandering the countryside. Bair embellishes the image further when reporting a period in 1935 when 'Beckett's shabby figure was often seen shuffling along the quays in the darkening winter afternoon. He began to make restless forays through the countryside, walking from five to ten miles each day' (215). Walking, for Bair, becomes a physical manifestation of the writer's inner psychological turmoil: for example, on one occasion, after an unhappy exchange with theatre director Roger Blin, Beckett reportedly 'took to chain-smoking and pacing at the back of the theater' (423). Authorised biographer and Beckett scholar James Knowlson also lists walking as one of the writer's 'regular pastime[s]' (*DF*, 12). In 'A Writer's Homes—A Writer's Life', he states: 'Above all, Beckett adored walking, sometimes covering as many as 10, even, very occasionally, 20 kilometers a day on the quiet roads and footpaths around Molien and Meaux' (Knowlson 2010, 20).[2] Knowlson suggests that walking becomes an important theme throughout much of the author's late work:

> After just such a lengthy walk he made clear to Pamela Mitchell in a letter written in December 1954, only a few months after the death of his brother, 'the real walk is elsewhere, on a screen inside,

---

described life as being "just a series of movements".' See *Beckett Remembering Remembering Beckett: Uncollected Interviews with Samuel Beckett and Memories of Those Who Knew Him*, eds. James Knowlson and Elizabeth Knowlson (London: Bloomsbury, 2006), 136.

2 Knowlson is referring here to Beckett's rural retreat at Ussy-sur-Marne, a tranquil alternative to his city apartment in Paris.

> old walks in a lost country, with my father and my brother, but mostly with my father, long ago' (SB, letter to Pamela Mitchell, December 27, 1954). (Knowlson 2010, 21)

Walking was a prominent theme for Beckett throughout his writing career, and can be found in all kinds of places, from early poems and prose texts, to dramatic work for stage, television and radio. While conventionally it is an act that suggests purpose and direction, it also becomes emblematic of the romantic country wanderer, or the modernist urban navigator. Beckett himself described the task of the artist as the expression of being, suggesting that being is 'chaotic', 'the opposite of ordered form', and is in fact 'a collection of meaningless "movements"'.[3] But walking is also strongly associated with issues of grief, memory and traumatic loss in Beckett's writing: an action that signals compulsive repetition and return.

Rebecca Solnit's *Wanderlust: A History of Walking* demarcates the important role that walking plays in Western cultural history. Solnit designates walking as an action that confers political agency and fulfillment, something that is justified and purposeful; but she also identifies the strange temporality that walking can develop, 'the time of walking to or from a place, of meandering, of running errands', or 'the time inbetween' (Solnit 2011, xiii); in this way, walking 'strikes a delicate balance between working and idling, being and doing' (5). In Solnit's view, walking is characterized precisely by its tendency to accommodate a diverse range of contradictions, and as such cannot be aligned with any one methodology. It is an 'amateur act' that

> trespasses through everybody else's field—through anatomy, anthropology, architecture, gardening, geography, political and cultural history, literature, sexuality, religious studies—and doesn't stop in any of them. (4)

---

3 From Laurence E. Harvey's notes on meeting Beckett, included in *Beckett Remembering Remembering Beckett: Uncollected Interviews with Samuel Beckett and Memories of Those Who Knew Him*, eds. James Knowlson and Elizabeth Knowlson (London: Bloomsbury, 2006), 134.

As though to emphasise this point, Solnit includes a wide range of writers, thinkers and historical figures who have described, discussed or theorized walking in their separate works.[4] Walking can thus be defined as a kind of undisciplined discipline: a concept that appropriates familiar orthodoxy, but which is not limited to any single method, routine or practice.

Throughout this first chapter, I address the ways in which Samuel Beckett's early post-war texts present walking and wandering through their protagonists and narrative voices. In the first section, I explore how walking is unsettled as an instrument of Western progress, and outline the implications this holds for conventional understandings of time, place and identity. In the second section, representations of walking are linked to the language of loss and departure, and its consequences for our grasp of rational humanist subjectivity. In each case, walking is interwoven with theories of trauma and traumatic experience, and becomes a site of logical order and radical ambiguity. Steven Connor has previously observed 'a compulsion in the act of walking'[5] in Beckett's work, which I suggest we might read walking as a kind of traumatic symptom, belatedly staging and restaging a cultural and historical crisis in the post-war European landscape. The related concepts of walking and wandering can provide new ways to engage with issues of trauma, language and identity, and, in this way, can aid the elucidation of a post-war crisis in Western humanism.

---

4 The list ranges from Sigmund Freud to Henry David Thoreau, from Emily Post to Beckett himself.

5 Steven Connor, 'Shifting Ground', accessed December 3, 2012, http://www.stevenconnor.com/beckettnauman. The essay was originally published in German as 'Auf schwankendem Boden', in the catalogue of the exhibition *Samuel Beckett, Bruce Nauman* (Vienna: Kunsthalle Wien, 2000), 80-7.

Traumatic Progress

Walking as Thinking

In Jean-Jacques Rousseau's *Confessions*, the Genevan writer and philosopher states: 'For, as I think I have said, I can only meditate when I am walking. When I stop, I cease to think, my mind only works with my legs' (Rousseau 1983, 382). Similarly, in John Thelwall's *The Peripatetic* (1793) the writer reveals: 'I pursue all my meditations on foot'.[6] Walking, here, is a bodily action that complements and improves the operation of the mind. It is the rational act *par excellence*, linear, coherent, and progressive. But both examples are deceptively simple for the straightforward relationship they convey between walking and thinking. Rousseau (in J.M. Cohen's translation) and Thelwall both refer to 'meditation', a term that is not limited to the process of rational thought but can encompass the spiritual or religious contemplation of a truth or mystery.[7] The term 'meditation' can also refer to a textual work, usually religious in nature, which presents a discourse on some matter or argument. This chapter shall begin by exploring the assumed connections between walking and thinking within the history of Western culture, but with an acknowledgement that walking is often linked to a particular kind of thinking and, indeed, writing: a meditative practice that is prone to wander outside and beyond prescriptive limits. If we look again at the opening of Rousseau's comment, 'as I think I have said', we can trace an attempt to recall some previous moment which comes across not as certainty but as hesitation, a moment where a straightforward statement reveals some form of doubt or ambiguity.[8]

---

6 John Thelwall, qtd. in Solnit, *Wanderlust*, 14.

7 'Meditation', in OED (2017), accessed January 3, 2017, http://www.oed.com.

8 Indeed, as Russell Goulbourne notes in his translation of Rousseau's digressive and meditative *Reveries of the Solitary Walker* (Oxford: Oxford University Press, 2011): '[Rousseau] was not afraid to take on dearly held Enlightenment convictions—such as the belief in progress—and show the to be mere assumptions and unproven contentions.' (x)

Many of our foundational Western texts connect the process of learning or the acquisition of knowledge to walking from one place to another. We might consider a 'course of study' or a 'step-by-step guide' as further examples of this enduring tendency to link walking with the accumulation of knowledge. There is also the concept of the encyclopaedia, literally a 'circle of learning'[9] that confers a general education; the infinite image of the circle conveys an individual along a long a track or course before returning them to the point at which they began, transformed by the process of learning.

Solnit states that 'the link between thinking and walking recurs in ancient Greece' (Solnit 2011, 16),[10] alluding to Aristotle's habit of pacing back and forth while he lectured: 'The colonnade or walk (peripatos) gave the school its name […] The philosophers who came to it were called the Peripatetic philosophers or the Peripatetic school, and in English the word *peripatetic* means "one who walks habitually and extensively"' (15). Walking has been adopted as a somatic metaphor for the abstract and unseen process of rational thought; it holds superficial connotations of regularity, familiarity and predictability, while the notion of travelling implies a mastery of the surrounding landscape, and a broad, encompassing vantage point. It also offers a convenient method of structuring and understanding the rational humanist pursuit of knowledge. For example, the OED defines the term 'discourse'[11] as both a process of passing 'from premises to conclusions' and the action 'to move, or travel over a space [or] region'. Through this walking metaphor, the individual is coded as an independent and objective scientific agent, seeking to follow a path from

---

9 'Encyclopaedia', in OED (2017), accessed January 3, 2017, http://www.oed.com.

10 Solnit observes that walking was a favoured pastime of a number of Western philosophers, including Jeremy Bentham, John Stuart Mill, Thomas Hobbes, Immanuel Kant, Friedrich Nietzsche and Ludwig Wittgenstein.

11 'Discourse', in OED (2017), accessed January 3, 2017, http://www.oed.com.

ignorance to knowledge.[12] The journey is divided into stages, or steps, whereby discoveries are made incrementally, and end with the arrival at a new level of knowledge or illumination.

In his 2013 work, *The Old Ways*, Robert MacFarlane makes a salient observation about the way that walking informs our understanding of writing and consciousness:

> The relationship between thinking and walking is [...] grained deep into language history, illuminated by perhaps the most wonderful etymology I know. The trail begins with our verb *to learn*, meaning 'to acquire knowledge'. Moving backwards in language time, we reach the Old English *leornian*, 'to get knowledge, to be cultivated'. From *leornian* the path leads further back, into the fricative thickets of Proto-Germanic, and to the word *liznojan*, which has a base sense of 'to follow or to find a track'. (MacFarlane 2013, 31)

The etymological roots of walking reveal a longstanding symbiosis. And, as a result, the notion of walking and wandering is not only embedded in representations of figures traversing a landscape, but in the very act of writing itself: walking is thus embedded into contemporary notions of discourse and narrative progression.

And yet, the cultural history of walking across literary and philosophical traditions remains complex. One of the signature European texts on walking and thinking is Rousseau's 1782 work, *Reveries of a Solitary Walker*, a collection of ten essays (walks) which deliberately '[eschew] chronology and a narrative stressing cause and effect in favour of reflection, self-analysis, and meditation' (Goulbourne 2011, xiii). Solnit's *Wanderlust* follows this tradition into the twentieth century, where narratives of individual enlightenment are complicated by

12 Of course, this metaphorical structure is not limited to Western culture, but can be observed in various cultural and historical contexts throughout the world. It would also be a mistake to assume that the metaphor is only applicable to scientific narratives of exploration or discovery; most notably, it has often been applied to accounts of religious enlightenment, where embodied actions are transformed into incorporeal spiritual experience.

new literary representations. Through the conventions of literary modernism, 'the recounted walk encourages digression and association, in contrast to the stricter form of a discourse of the chronological progression of a biographical or historical narrative' (Solnit 2001, 21). For Solnit, Beckett's modernist predecessors James Joyce or Virginia Woolf use the act of walking to explore the interior, psychological terrain of individual thought and experience, an '[attempt] to describe the workings of the mind' (21). Samuel Beckett's work responds to this counter-tradition in the cultural history of walking, where it is represented as an act or a literary device that encourages divergence and ambiguity.

Seamus Deane outlines Joyce's portrayal of Stephen Dedalus' perambulations in his introduction to *A Portrait of the Artist as a Young Man*: 'The walk is itself one of the novel's most effective rhetorical devices, allowing for conversation, flashbacks, meditations, and aligning these in a variety of ways to the geography of the city' (Deane 1992, xiv). Whilst Joyce's novel is defined via a series of sophisticated and innovatory narrative techniques, Deane suggests that the act of walking stabilises the wandering mind of Stephen Dedalus by locating him within a specific cultural and historical context. Walking defines an intersection between individual experience and national history:

> The geography implies a history. Insofar as it is public, referring to public buildings and monuments, the history that accompanies it is 'official', national history. Insofar as it is private—hoardings, provision shops, a dairy with a clock—it is 'personal', the history of Stephen, his friendships, his reading and his thoughts. (Deane 1992, xiv)

In Joyce's novel, walking becomes a stylistic motif that enables a complex renegotiation of private and public space, individual memory and shared history, and the position of the individual within broader society.

The wayward protagonists of Beckett's pre-war writing are keen to follow the trail of their Joycean predecessors, and the texts frequently marry the act of walking to moments or opportunities for personal enlightenment. In his 1934 short story 'Walking Out' (an Irish expression, similar to the English 'stepping out', that denotes a courting ritual), the protagonist connects his habitual strolling with the contemplation of the divine: 'It was one of those Spring evenings when it is a matter of some difficulty to keep God out of one's meditations' (*MPTK*, 95). The walker, in this context, is suggestive of the romantic artist, deep in reflection. Walking becomes not only a symbol of personal freedom, but a retreat into an interior landscape that holds the potential of deeper insight: 'I went out to walk it off. [...] the best thing to do was to go to the wood for a little sursum corda' (100). Wandering becomes akin to religious or spiritual pilgrimage, a ceremonial ritual or prayer that leads to a mystical harmony between self and surroundings.[13]

Beckett's 1938 novel *Murphy* is more directly reminiscent of the Joycean setting.[14] In a gesture that recalls Joyce's 1922 novel *Ulysses*, the eponymous Irish protagonist, Murphy, navigates the roads and pathways of 1930s London as a kind of modernist flâneur,[15] with Dublin's River Liffey substituted with London's River Thames. The construction of space through references to other literary and historical texts is another thing *Murphy* appears to consciously emulate. As Ackerley and Gontarski have recorded: 'The Chelsea Embankment is invested with elements of Dante's *Purgatory*; Tyburnia suggests Magistrate Fielding; Hyde Park invokes a pastoral tradition; and the Bethlam

13 Due to lack of space, I shall not explore how these notions are parodied or undermined in Beckett's early texts, but am simply using them to explore the connections between certain modernist conventions and previously established romantic motifs.

14 *Murphy* also draws upon 'the tradition of philosophical comedy from Cervantes and Rabelais to Fielding and Joyce'. See C. J. Ackerley and S. E. Gontarski, eds., *The Grove Companion to Samuel Beckett* (New York: Grove Press, 2004), 387.

15 Raymond Mullen offers a lively overview of Beckett's engagement with the figure of the flâneur in '"Stalking about London in a Green Suit": Beckett's *Murphy*, London and Flânerie', *Studies: An Irish Quarterly Review*, 95:379, 301-11.

Royal Hospital enacts a drama of Bedlam.'[16] The themes of belonging and exile that echo throughout both *Portrait* and *Ulysses* also find a counterpoint in Beckett's sketch of an Irishman abroad:

> Regress in these togs was slow and Murphy was well advised to abandon hope for the day shortly after lunch and set off on the long climb home. By far the best part of the way was the toil from King's Cross up Caledonian Road, reminding him of the toil from St. Lazare up Rue d'Amsterdam. And while Brewery Road was by no means a Boulevard de Clichy nor even des Batignolles, still it was better at the end of the hill than either of those, as asylum (after a point) is better than exile. (*M*, 48)

Walking is the method by which Murphy slowly navigates the urban sprawl of London. The layout of the city is clearly identified by the listing of specific streets and notable landmarks, which, in turn, trigger a series of other locations and associations. We might observe a kinship between Murphy's ambulation and Michel de Certeau's observations about walking in the city: the layout of the urban centre orders Murphy's spatial orientation, and yet the character's movements are shaped by personal choices and involuntary memories that cannot be predetermined. Murphy recalls, in de Certeau, those walkers he named as 'unrecognized producers, poets of their own acts, silent discoverers of their own paths in the jungle of functionalist reality', that is to say, wanderers of '"indirect" or "errant" trajectories obeying their own logic' (de Certeau 1984, xviii). As the protagonist wanders from one road to the next, past memories are summoned and similarly navigated. At this moment in the text, walking implies a stable vantage point on Murphy's surroundings, but also evokes images of regression and return. It cannot be read straightforwardly as an action or discourse of personal progress or enlightenment, but becomes something

---

16 For more intertextual references, see *The Grove Companion to Samuel Beckett*, 323. Notice how Dante's epic journey narrative is subtly echoed through the use of Homer's echo journey narrative, *The Odyssey*, in Joyce's *Ulysses*.

more complex. As we shall see in the texts of Beckett's post-war period, walking becomes both an emblem of personal discovery and, at times, a troubling signal of traumatic return.

Watt and Traumatic Temporality

Beckett's later texts hint towards a crisis or impasse in the post-war European landscape. Traditional ideas about Western civilisation as a progressive cultural and historical power were challenged in the aftermath of the Second World War and the uncovering of the Holocaust. Movements in science, philosophy and the arts responded to these and other events through an attempt to reevaluate ideological narratives of history, progress and modernity; this coincided with a growing suspicion of the role and reliability of language, and the dangerous implications of utopian politics.

In *Beckett and Poststructuralism*, Anthony Uhlmann remarks that 'in modern European history time has most commonly been conceptualized as an arrow' (Uhlmann 1999, 124-5). This image, an impressionistic emblem of direction and violence, configures time according to an idea of *Chronos*; Uhlmann defines *Chronos* with an extract from Gilles Deleuze and Félix Guatarri's *A Thousand Plateaus*: 'it is the time of measure that situates things and persons, develops a form, and determines a subject'.[17] Time is thus the foundational basis upon which human subjectivity is formed, managed and eventually resolved. The delineation of an empirical, chronological order allows individuals to construct coherent historical narratives with which to understand themselves and their surrounding landscape. Uhlmann suggests that this common consensus becomes complicated in the wake of the Second World War:

> The notion of the progress of history has only recently been challenged; and, I would suggest, it was the events of World War Two

17 Gilles Deleuze and Félix Guattari, qtd. in Uhlmann, *Beckett and Poststructuralism*, 125.

> in particular which threw this conception of time into crisis. 'Progress' was (is), of course, tied to science and technology: to the *accumulation* of knowledge. Progress was (is), like judgment, a matter of accounting, of credits and debits […] In the order of time as an arrow, progress as accumulation was equated with telos. In general terms the telos was one of the will to dominate, to conquer or convert the rest of the world to Western values and Western civilization (Uhlmann 1999, 125)

The metaphors of historical evolution are mapped out, according to Uhlmann, in adherence to a pervasive cultural narrative of dominance and mastery. Progress accumulates power through the expansion of political and territorial boundaries. Progress is consolidated through the Western humanist subject, a figure who embodies dominant cultural and societal values, and whose presence enables the reproduction and dissemination of ideological discourse. And so, narratives of teleological maturation, of personal growth and discovery, traditionally stabilise the prevalent cultural orthodoxy of the time.

Trauma unsettles and undercuts such discourses. As D. Horvitz suggests, 'Narrative representations of trauma […] expose the need for social transformation; they target for disruption such bureaucratic institutions as the legal and medical systems or […] capitalism and consumerism'.[18] Whilst representations of trauma in Beckett's writing do not form the basis of political manifestos, or ideological treatises, they nonetheless critique certain Western humanist ideals, and deconstruct manifestations of those ideals. In *Watt* and the texts that follow, traditional assumptions are parodied and unsettled. Modernity defines and shapes the landscape of Beckett's fiction, but instead of connection and efficiency the texts dwell on deferral, delay and disappointment.

Written in the wake of James Joyce's death, *Watt* marks a point of transition between Beckett's pre-war modernist writing and the late modernist stage that would follow. The novel was produced in Occupied France during the Second World War, and responds, albeit indirectly, to the broader cultural traumas of the time. Working as

---

18 D. Horvitz, qtd. in Luckhurst, *The Trauma Question*, 89.

a member of the French Resistance in a cell that was betrayed by one of its members, Beckett narrowly escaped Nazi capture and was forced to flee Paris to the small rural village of Roussillon d'Apt. It is in Roussillon that Beckett writes the manuscript of *Watt*, a dark but humorous book that playfully critiques the project of modernity. While acknowledging its humour, Ruby Cohn describes *Watt* as 'above all a very painful and demanding work' (Cohn 2001, 123). James Knowlson describes it as a 'comic attack on rationality', and suggests that while the main protagonist 'may demonstrate some of the conventional symptoms of schizophrenia or obsessional neurosis', Watt is simply applying 'the causality of the rationalists to problems that eventually lead only to paradox' (*DF*, 334). This confluence of rationality with psychological trauma is significant, and is a motif that finds many forms in Beckett's post-war representations of walking and wandering.

Watt begins with a tram that has not yet arrived, and ends with the isolation of a remote railway station. Seán Kennedy suggests that *Watt* reflects anxieties that arose during the Second World War, while signaling broader concerns about the role and purpose of modernity (Kennedy 2011). Progress as accumulation, or what Uhlmann refers to above as the 'will to dominate', triggers an association with deeply rooted historical traumas in Ireland's past. In Kennedy's reading, *Watt* can be treated as a reinterpretation of the traditional Big House narrative, where established social and political institutions are implicated in a widespread form of cultural exploitation. The Big House, an imposing ideological infrastructure, is haunted by the trauma of what he refers to as 'famine memory'.[19] Historical narratives of ritual, ceremony and tradition are not markers of humanist progress or mastery, in this context, but the embodiment or return of transgenerational traumas, passed down through familial lines. In *Watt*, this is presented, perhaps surprisingly, with a dark, playful humour through the existence of the Lynch family. Illness, tragedy and death befall each Lynch family member in turn, suggesting a legacy of traumatic experience that snakes through the genealogical map of Ireland: 'Five generations,

19 Author correspondence with Seán Kennedy, 21 November 2012.

twenty-eight souls, nine hundred and eighty years, such was the proud record of the Lynch family, when Watt entered Mr Knott's service' (*W*, 87).

Walking in *Watt* is presented satirically as an act which undermines Western narratives of tradition, knowledge and advancement. Jonathan Boulter interprets the protagonist's bizarre movements as symptomatic of a traumatic event in the text (or, rather, the traumatic absence of an event that should have been): 'Watt's encounter with Knott, I would argue, begins *and ends* in trauma, in a realization that no contact is possible' (Boulter 2008, 106). Watt is unable to reach or communicate with his employer, despite numerous efforts, and this inability manifests itself in compulsive repetitions. Boulter suggests that the 'dialogue that should have taken place between Watt and Knott is displaced into the narrative *of* that failure, the narrative that Sam receives from Watt years after the fact' (106). The novel presents the 'image of a dark mind stumbling through barren lands', where 'questions of the efficacy of narrative to translate experiences of absence and nothingness [...] become central to the trajectory of *Watt*' (107). Trajectory, in this sense, marks a progressive course or path that is broken, ruptured or reversed. At times, the protagonist's movement is a caricature of progress, breaking the flowing and cohesive motion of the body into a fragmented series of jerks, leanings and repetitions:

> Watt's way of advancing due east, for example, was to turn his bust as far as possible towards the north and at the same time to fling out his right leg as far as possible towards the south, and then to turn his bust as far as possible towards the south and at the same time to fling out his left leg as far as possible towards the north, and then again to turn his bust as far as possible towards the north and to fling out his right leg as far as possible towards the south, and then again to turn his bust as far as possible towards the south and to fling out his left leg as far as possible towards the north, and so on, over and over again, many many times, until he reached his destination, and could sit down. So, standing first on one leg and then on the other, he moved forward, a headlong tardigrade, in a straight line. (*W*, 23-4)

Watt's movements inflict violence on his body, while denying the subject control or mastery of himself or his surroundings. Watt is contextualized with reference to Western geographical values (East, North, and South), but his limbs appear to move in many different directions at once. Whilst Watt's limbs move 'as far as possible' toward empirical markers, we are continually reminded of the character's bodily limitations. Even as Watt progresses onward in a direct line, his body appears as a split and disharmonious collection of parts and gestures. Walking, as a series of straightforward and logical steps, is reconceived as the result of continual and repetitive physical struggle.

The traditional Western association between walking, language, and thinking is similarly subverted in the text through Watt's disturbed and troubling actions. As Steven Connor points out in his analysis of the above passage, 'the fanatically intense description both exceeds its object and also lags behind it' (Connor 2007, 32).The narrator, Sam, describes events from a fixed and objective viewpoint: 'Continuing my inspection, like one deprived of his senses, I observed, with a distinctness that left no room for doubt' (136-7). The enquiring narrative voice mimics the omniscience of traditional realist fiction, while drawing attention to its limitations. The narrator describes Watt 'advancing backwards towards me':

> His progress was slow and devious, on account no doubt of his having no eyes in the back of his head, and painful too, I fancy, for often he struck against the trunks of trees, or in the tangles of underwood caught his foot, and fell to the ground, flat on his back, or into a great clump of brambles, or of briars, or of nettles, or of thistles. But still without a murmur he came on, until he lay against the fence, with his hands at arm's length grasping the wires. Then he turned, with the intention very likely of going back the way he had come, and I saw his face, and the rest of his front. (136)

The passage is playfully comic, but once again conveys traumatizing violence being inflicted upon Watt's body: Watt's front becomes his back, while his back becomes his front. As a result, progress becomes regression and vice versa. Watt's walk denaturalises the ordered subject's engagement with its environment, and unsettles progressive

Western narratives of humanist mastery. The surrounding landscape cannot be seen or conquered, but impedes advancement through a series of unseen and insurmountable obstacles. Progress is 'devious' in the narrator's description, a word the OED defines as 'a winding or straying course' (although the term is also suggestive of moral or ethical ambiguity).[20] Sam's reversed perspective also conceals a wound on Watt's face. When he finally becomes visible, his face is compared to a 'striking' (136) representation of Christ by Hieronymus Bosch: 'Then he turned, with the intention very likely of going back the way he had come, and I saw his face, and the rest of his front. His face was bloody, his hands also, and thorns were in his scalp' (136). Watt thus becomes a kind of perverted Christ-like figure, an icon of traumatic bodily suffering and holy martyrdom. We might, perhaps, read Watt's distorted identity as an ironic comment on spiritual leadership or utopian narratives of redemption and fulfilment. If Watt is a martyr, it is for an unknown cause: the origin of his suffering remains obscure, and his authority as a leader is dubious.

The 'devious' progression of Watt's walk leads to further idiosyncrasies, such as the reversed order of his speech:

> Why, Watt, I cried, that is a nice state you have got yourself into, to be sure. Not it is, yes, replied Watt. This short phrase caused me, I believe, more alarm, more pain, than if I had received, unexpectedly, at close quarters, a charge of small short in the ravine. This impression was reinforced by what followed. Wonder I, said Watt, panky-hanky me lend you could, blood away wipe. Wait, wait, I am coming, I cried. (136)

As Watt's gait[21] and speech are both inverted, walking and thinking become emblematic not of progress and communication, but of regression and incoherence: 'These were sounds that at first, though we walked face to face, were devoid of significance for me' (141). Sam

---

20 'Devious', in OED (2017), accessed January 3, 2017, http://www.oed.com.

21 Incidentally, the OED makes etymological connections between the word 'gait' and the noun 'gate', which suggests not just a characteristic manner of walking, but also 'a way, road, or path'.

confesses that communication with Watt at this point becomes increasingly difficult, even meaningless. The narrative voice attempts to retain objectivity through the exposition of identifiable periods of development (or disintegration). The result is a careful transcription of Watt's disordered and incoherent speech patterns:

> The following is an example of this manner:
>
> *Lit yad max, ot oh. Ton taw, ton tonk. Ton dob, ton trips. Ton vila, ton deda. Ton kawa, ton pesa. Ton das, ton yag. Os devil, rof mit.*
>
> This meant nothing to me. (143)

Admitting that the speech 'made little or no sense to me', (143) Sam subjects Watt's language to careful and rational enquiry. While, 'at first', (141) Watt's inversions are impenetrable, the novel's transcriptions objectify them in a way that allows for logical examination and decoding. By following the narrator's instructions, we might approximately translate Watt's above speech as follows: til day xam, to ho. Not Wat, not knot. Not bod, not spirt. Not aliv, not deda. Not awak, not asep. Not sad, not gay. So lived, for time (Til day xam, to ho. Not Watt, not Knott. Not body, not spirit. Not alive, not dead. Not awake, not asleep. Not sad, not gay. So [I] lived, for [a] time). This—ironically—straightforward reversal of walking and thinking then deteriorates further into an even more complex pattern: 'So all went well until Watt began to invert, no longer the order of the words in the sentence, but that of the letters in the word' (141). Another period of confusion and perplexity is followed by a pattern of enquiry and enlightenment, with the narrator eventually affirming that 'in the end I understood' (143). Sam's ability to explain Watt's speech reveals a strict internal logic at work that can be rationalised and accommodated within a more traditional Western framework.

In a monograph exploring intertextual links between Beckett and the work of Dante Alighieri, Daniela Caselli builds on the work of Katherine Travers Gross and Ruby Cohn to explore the function of walking in *Watt*. Caselli's points out that Watt as a 'figure of inversion' resembles 'the damned [that] are forced to walk backwards by having their faces turned towards their loins' (Caselli 2005, 96).[22] Dante's distorted human forms are found in canto XX of the *Inferno*, 'Their faces were reversed upon their shoulders / so that they came on walking backward, / since seeing forward was denied them'.[23] These 'submerged' diviners walk along in a procession that is silent, solemn, and slow, with tears their only form of expression. Robert Hollander suggests that in Dante's text, the diviner's inability to speak reflects 'the fact that their voices, announcing their false prescriptions, were the instruments of their deception'.[24] Hollander goes further to suggest that the contortion of their heads is also punishment for 'having looked, with wrongful intent, into the future'.[25] And so what we see in Watt's inverted walk is an uncanny and traumatic reworking of Dante's twisted figures, creatures who signify the unreliability of language and a prohibition on harnessing the future for one's own gain. Composed in Nazi Occupied France, Beckett's novel adapts Dante's *Inferno* with comic irony to interrogate the authority of written and spoken truths, and the totalizing project of a progressive, future-leaning modernity. Watt's physical and verbal ramblings remain ambiguous and elusive. Their final meaning is unclear to the reader, hovering between distinct definitions or values (being neither awake nor asleep, or neither alive nor dead, implies in-between states that cannot be definitively categorised). Beckett's traumatic representations of walking in *Watt* ultimately lead to the estrangement, or denaturalisation, of language and meaning.

---

22 Caselli also notes that the same figures are mentioned in Beckett's radio play, *All That Fall*.

23 Dante Alighieri, *Inferno*, trans. Robert Hollander and Jean Hollander, intr. Robert Hollander (New York: Anchor Books, 2002), 361.

24 Robert Hollander in Dante Alighieri, *Inferno*, trans. Robert Hollander and Jean Hollander, intr. Robert Hollander (New York: Anchor Books, 2002), 371.

25 Hollander, *Inferno*, 371.

Walking as Traumatic Symptom

Taking *Watt* as a point of departure, walking in Beckett's work might be read productively through the lens of the traumatic symptom. If we define the effects of traumatisation as the 'piercing or breach of a border that pits inside and outside into a strange communication' (Luckhurst 2008, 3), walking is an action that disrupts familiar boundaries of public and private, movement and stasis, past and future. Rebecca Solnit notes that 'the subject of walking resembles walking itself in its lack of confines' (Solnit 2001, 4), and suggests inevitable associations with trespassing. Roger Luckhurst, in his elucidation of traumatic experience, continually draws on metaphors of movement and transmission, infringement and transgression: 'Trauma violently opens passageways between systems that were once discrete, making unforeseen connections that distress or confound. Trauma also appears to be worryingly transmissible: it leaks between mental and physical symptoms' (Luckhurst, 2008, 3). The tramping protagonists of Beckett's post-war writing ceaselessly roam from one space to another, present everywhere but belonging nowhere. The metaphor of the walker is a convenient symbol for what Luckhurst names the 'mysterious processes of transference or suggestion' (3) that trauma enacts.

Dominick LaCapra has warned that 'there is no such thing as writing trauma itself if only because trauma, while at times related to particular events, cannot be localized in terms of a discrete, dated experience' (LaCapra 2001, 186). This notion chimes with Michel de Certeau's observation that 'to walk is to lack a place. It is the indefinite process of being absent and in search of a proper' (de Certeau 1984, 103). The walker is thus a figure who cannot be assigned a fixed locality. This notion, too, can be linked to Beckett's melancholic representation of walking as an historical and embodied experience that effects a breaking or fragmentation of the humanist subject, and progressive narratives that structure experience. LaCapra describes trauma in terms of 'a shattering break or caesura in experience which has belated effects' (186), an event reminiscent of the many halts, breaks and stops of Beckett's vanished and misplaced wanderers. If we consider trauma as something that 'in effect, issues a challenge to the capacities of narrative knowledge' (Luckhurst, 2008, 79), walking, in Beckett's writing, simultaneously affirms and unsettles such capacities.

Mercier and Camier, Beckett's first novel in French, was begun on 5 July 1946 (Kennedy 2009, vii).[26] In much the same way as *Watt*, *Mercier and Camier* uses comedic devices that ironise and distort conventional literary representations of reality. The novel opens with a teasing, playful claim to narrative omniscience: 'The journey of Mercier and Camier is one I can tell, if I will, for I was with them all the time' (*MC*, 3). The reader is welcomed into a traditional and familiar narrative convention, but conditionally; the tentative 'if I will' emphasises our reliance upon a specific narrative viewpoint and inclination, while also accentuating our lack of access to pertinent information.[27] The text challenges our expectations, and drawing attention to the possible limitations of its language. The narrator's presumed mastery is juxtaposed with a distinct lack of purpose and direction among the lead characters. The first meeting of Mercier and Camier is presented as a routine in the literal and comic sense, for its exaggerated predictability and its comedic, farcical elements. Mercier and Camier are walkers who arrange to meet at a specific time and place. But their mutual destination (an endpoint that, paradoxically, marks the beginning of their journey) becomes a space of non-meeting, of perpetual absences, arrivals and subsequent departures:[28]

26 The novel was not published in French until 1970, and the English translation did not follow until 1974.

27 The expression 'if I will' could also be interpreted according to the verb form 'to will', or 'to go astray'. See 'Will', in OED (2017), accessed January 3, 2017, http://www.oed.com.

28 The idea of a meeting place where the act of meeting is deferred or denied is, of course, echoed in Beckett's later work, *Waiting for Godot*. In the case of the later play, which builds on many of the themes and motifs of *Mercier and Camier*, a consensus regarding time and place becomes a source of unsettling ambiguities as Vladimir and Estragon anticipate a man named Godot who never arrives, despite promises and assurances from a messenger boy.

> Camier was first to arrive at the appointed place. That is to say that on his arrival Mercier was not there. In reality Mercier had forestalled him by a good ten minutes. Not Camier then, but Mercier, was the first to arrive. (*MC*, 3)

The adjustment of temporal perspectives generates alternative truths or realities. The narrator's claim to empirical certainty is undermined with the introduction of an alternative perspective. Linear chronology, which structures events in an ordered and progressive way, is not only playfully undermined in the narration, but seems to be the very thing that prevents two things happening at once: in other words, the description of events, one after another, generates a series of absences that prevents the two protagonists from meeting.

Walking appears to promise an eventual resolution to the farce, bringing characters closer step-by-step, but it is also the act that drifts them away from their agreed meeting-point:

> He possessed himself in patience for five minutes, with his eye on the various avenues of approach open to his friend, then set out for a saunter destined to last full fifteen minutes. Meantime Camier, five minutes having passed without sight or sign of Mercier, took himself off in his turn for a little stroll. On his return to the place, fifteen minutes later, it was in vain he cast about him, and understandably so. For Mercier, after cooling his heels for a further five minutes, had wandered off again for what he pleased to call a little stretch. Camier hung around for five more minutes, then again departed, saying to himself, Perhaps I'll run into him in the street. It was at this moment that Mercier, back from his breather, which as chance this time would have it had not exceeded ten minutes, glimpsed receding in the morning mist a shape suggestive of Camier's and which was indeed none other. Unhappily it vanished as though swallowed up by the cobbles, leaving Mercier to resume his vigil. But on expiry of what is beginning to look like the regulation five minutes he abandoned it again, feeling the need of a little motion. (*MC*, 3-4)

In the novel, these arrivals, lapses and departures are arranged into the grid of a timetable. The narrator observes a 'stink of artifice' (4) in this deliberate, chronological structure.[29] The timetable imposes strict positive values and empirical order upon the disordered occurrences described in the prose. In this artificial way, Mercier and Camier's course becomes determined by the inevitability of standardised time, its ceaseless advancement, and the limits it defines: 'So short that it is not worth their while beginning, too long for them not to begin, that is the time they are pent up in, as cruelly as Balue in his cage' (*MC*, 62).[30] Whereas walking is traditionally a marker of temporal order and linearity, in *Mercier and Camier* it creates the possibility of digressions, absences and the reevaluation of timetables and geographical limits. Beckett's text unsettles modernity's claim on linear order and presence by evoking the absence that lies behind its signifiers.

Blurring National Boundaries

Walking signals ambiguity in *Mercier and Camier*. The protagonists' tendency to wander and stroll through their surroundings unsettles the stability of chronological order and the predictability of events. Their wandering seems without purpose or direction, and the journey they take seems little more than 'a scurrying to and fro to no avail' (*MC*, 62). It is difficult to read the text without considering the mass displacement of people in the aftermath of the Second World War, or indeed Beckett's own exiled status as an Irish expatriot now living per-

---

29 This is also parodied through the use of chapter summaries throughout the novel, which attempts to reduce the protagonists' circumstances to a straightforward, chronological list of events.

30 The reference to Balue, the bear of Rudyard Kipling's 1894 collection of short stories, *The Jungle Book*, introduces an unmistakable traumatic element into the text. Whilst the allusion to Kipling's novel is brief, it connotes an image of cruelty and confinement that, in turn, connects to ideas of Western colonial rule and a history of cultural trauma and repression.

manently in France. Ruby Cohn describes the setting as 'vaguely Ireland',[31] but it is the adverb 'vaguely' that is significant, and not necessarily the designated place-name. Ackerley and Gontarski suggest that Beckett's

> deeper significance to Irish writers may be as an exemplary figure who raises such issues as translation, exile, estrangement, and dispossession, themes at the heart of plays [and other texts] that occupy a recognizably Irish setting. (Ackerley and Gontarski 2004, 277)

While this point is certainly valid in the context of Irish literary culture, it overlooks the way that *Mercier and Camier* both constructs and undermines notions of a 'recognizably Irish setting'. The novel's representation of landscape unsettles Western notions of a limit, a border, or a place. There are, for example, references to Irish culture and history that echo throughout the novel, that imply a stable context for the characters; but the text's lack of specificity suggests a geographical space that shifts and roams unreliably. The narrative is notably sparse,[32] delineating a modest journey undertaken by two virtually rootless wanderers:

> Can you walk? said Camier.
>
> I'll walk, never fear, said Mercier. He got up and took a few steps. How's that? he said. (*MC*, 52)

---

31 Ruby Cohn, qtd. in Seán Kennedy's 'Preface' to *Mercier and Camier*, x.

32 Fintan O'Toole has drawn connections between 'austere forms of Irish naturalism and [Samuel Beckett's] minimalism', according to Ackerley and Gontarski. Writing about *Waiting for Godot*, O'Toole observes that the play 'bears an uncanny relationship to the kind of jokes that people in Ireland were making about the rather bleak nature of the place in the 1950s, when isolation and emptiness had a literal resonance in the depopulation of the countryside'. For more, see Ackerley and Gontarski, *The Grove Companion to Samuel Beckett*, 277.

But the landscape creates a tension between mastery and impotence, progress and regression, motion and stasis:

> It is no longer possible to advance. Retreat is equally out of the question.
>
> He added, some moments later:
>
> What are you musing on, Mercier?
>
> On the horror of existence, confusedly, said Mercier. (*MC*, 16)

The 'horror of existence' is an unexpected response to Camier's question, comic in its hyperbole, but we can trace in it a hint of the novel's status as a cultural product of the Second World War. Its grim allusion to living and existing in post-war Europe does not evoke a specific trauma, but is understood as a general and revolted reaction against the modern world. This generalised trauma is evoked 'confusedly', at a point where the characters' onward advancement is hopelessly stalled. The connection between walking and humanist mastery of the landscape, or the purposeful movement towards a specific aim or destination, is continually undermined and parodied. At one point, the two advance along 'the edge of the sidewalk' as a 'crowd pressed on as towards some unquestioned goal' (15); the protagonists trace a border between the pavement and the road on 'slippery streets' (15), where an unnamed and anonymous mass progress onward without apparent reason or purpose. The word slippery is suggestive of the wet climate, but carries the added resonance of a place or a truth that is difficult to grasp or maintain. 'Where do our feet think they're taking us?', asks Camier, suggesting that it is the body, rather than the mind, that is doing the thinking: they decide to follow a towpath 'till boredom doth ensue' (15), a resolve that, strangely, defers the moment of decision to some unspecified future point. As Kennedy describes in his Preface to the 2010 Faber and Faber edition, '[*Mercier and Camier*] is in some obvious sense a quest narrative, albeit one in which no progress is made and the purpose of the quest remains elusive' (Kennedy 2010, ix).

The relationship between walking and landscape is elucidated in Steven Connor's essay, 'Shifting Ground', which explores the work of Samuel Beckett and the artist Bruce Nauman. Connor describes the ground as something that 'is temporal first of all in the sense that it is closely associated with the here and the now',[33] but which 'can also shift, as we make shift upon it'.[34] In *Mercier and Camier*, the act of wandering shifts and alters the ground beneath the characters' feet, making it difficult to establish a sense of time, place or continuity. For the two fugitive characters that are possibly misplaced or exiled, the landscape of the text remains 'vague', ambiguous, and strangely resistant to attempts to traverse it:[35]

> We advance painfully—.
>
> Painfully! cried Mercier.
>
> Laboriously... laboriously through the dark streets, dark and comparatively deserted, because of the late hour no doubt, and the unsettled weather, not knowing who is leading, who is following, whom. (*MC*, 70)

Walking is once again a symptom of some broader cultural trauma, but in the text the act itself coincides with violence done to the human

---

33 Steven Connor, 'Shifting Ground' <http://www.stevenconnor.com/beckettnauman/> [Accessed on 3 December 2012]. The essay was originally published in German as 'Auf schwankendem Boden', in the catalogue of the exhibition *Samuel Beckett, Bruce Nauman* (Vienna: Kunsthalle Wien, 2000), 80-7.

34 Connor, 'Shifting Ground'.

35 Kennedy's Preface outlines several differences between the French language edition of the novel and its eventual English translation. Among those differences, there appear to be several attempts by Beckett to evoke the Irish landscape more directly, and several other attempts to make references to Ireland less clear. In his discussion, Kennedy draws upon Steven Connor's '"Traduttore, traditore": Samuel Beckett's Translation of *Mercier and Camier*' in the *Journal of Beckett Studies*, 11/12 (1989), 27-46.

body: to walk is to suffer physical pain and psychical uncertainty. The representation of landscape in Beckett's novel can be connected to the representation of Western humanist subjectivity; when the land is resistant to stable and empirical limits, characters are represented as rootless and changeable. Whereas in Deane's interpretation of Joyce, geography marks an empowering engagement with shared public space, in Beckett's novel geography is always uncertain: 'What does it matter, said Mercier, where we are going? We are going, that's enough' (*MC*, 73). Considered in the wider context of post-war European landscape, the text evokes the displacement of national boundaries and the redeployment of political and ideological divisions. Mercier and Camier's exile or displacement within the European landscape (we remain unsure whether they are in a version of Ireland, France, or some other place) presents both a figurative and literal embodiment of a crisis in cultural, political and ideological values. The novel's seventh chapter opens with a description of desolate and abandoned surroundings, stating that the landscape 'leads to nothing any more' (*MC*, 81). As old soil is upturned, cultural histories are reformed or lost according to new geopolitical limits. This, in turn, forms a break in the continuity of the humanist subject, and a defamiliarisation of time, place and supposedly natural or eternal ideological values. Walking in *Mercier and Camier* becomes a traumatic symptom of this strange condition.

A similar motif recurs in Beckett's *Four Nouvelles* (*The Expelled, The Calmative, The End* and *First Love*). *The End*, first published as *Suite* ('What Follows') in 1946, recounts the return of a narrator to a place that was once familiar:

> In the street I was lost. I had not set foot in this part of the city for a long time and it seemed greatly changed. Whole buildings had disappeared, the palings had changed position and on all sides I say, in great letters, the names of tradesman I had never seen before and would have been at a loss to pronounce. (*FN*, 40)

Whilst the first-person narrative voice affords a sense of intimacy with the reader, the lack of a proper name also confers distance through anonymity, and prevents us from making any immediate assumptions (based on, for example: gender, race, age, national identity). The street is similarly anonymous: its orderly arrangement of buildings and edifices is just one configuration of many in a dense urban landscape. Setting foot in a space is commensurate with experience, in the extract, and the distance between two steps appears to span years, if not longer. In the interim, a number of visible changes have occurred, altering a familiar sight into something that is now unfamiliar, breaking the narrator's sense of history or continuity. Buildings have altered, while others have disappeared. But the change is most clearly articulated by references to language: 'great letters' spell the names of tradesman and shop owners that the narrator cannot understand or repeat. The new letters imply a momentous cultural shift has occurred, the recession or expansion of geopolitical borders, but this possibility is not further explained and so remains ambiguous:

> There were streets where I remembered none, some I did remember had vanished and others had completely changed their names. The general impression was the same as before. It was true I did not know the city very well. Perhaps it was quite a different one. (*FN*, 40)

The suggestion of change, movement and transition is undermined by the 'general impression', implying stasis and stability. But the meaning of the store names and their respective purposes are sources of confusion and disorientation. This condition recalls Anne Whitehead's discussion of Anne Michaels' work, *Fugitive Pieces*, in which she suggests that

> the traumas of the recent past profoundly change our ability to position ourselves in relation to them or to find our bearings. The question of positioning that landscape evokes can be regarded as crucial within the current discourse of trauma. (Whitehead 2004, 48)

Whitehead is focussing upon an ethical issue surrounding the role we might play as investigators or recorders of past traumatic events, attempting to uncover evidence in a landscape that evades or disorientates us as observers. Yet, for the protagonist, or witness, our inability to to apprehend the past is mirrored by his inability to recognise the present. As Beckett related to Lawrence E. Harvey, his own work is characterised by a certain 'restlessness, of moving about at night'.[36] The protagonist of *The End* finds himself lost, without purpose or direction, confessing that 'I did not know where I was supposed to be going' (40). The civilian becomes an exile in surroundings that were once familiar, but now seem uncanny and distant. James Knowlson notes that the text does not rest 'on any specific localities', but instead 'focuses on the experience of change [and] estrangement that his protagonist feels' (*DF*, 374).

Even when the narrator is capable of distinguishing between two different kinds of public space, their altered aspect yields the same general result: 'I don't know how long I wandered thus, resting now in one place, now in another, in the city and in the country. The city had suffered many changes. Nor was the country as I remembered it. The general effect was the same' (*FN*, 45). Whilst the text clearly distinguishes between the rural landscape and the urban environment, both spaces are reduced to an experience of alteration and adjustment. Another of Beckett's *Nouvelles*, *The Expelled*, continues the motif through its narrator's description of his origins:

> I did not know the town very well, scene of my birth and of my first steps in this world, and then of all the others, so many that I thought all trace of me was lost, but I was wrong. I went out so little! [...] I felt ill at ease with all this air about me, lost before the confusion of innumerable prospects. (*Ex*, 6)

Familiarity is replaced by confusion and bewilderment. Here, walking not only presents a marker of developmental progress (a child's first

---

36 Samuel Beckett, qtd. in notes by Lawrence Harvey in *Beckett Remembering Remembering Beckett: Uncollected Interviews with Samuel Beckett and Memories of Those Who Knew Him*, eds. James Knowlson and Elizabeth Knowlson (London: Bloomsbury, 2006), 136.

steps), but a symbol of aimlessness, since ensuing steps lead the narrator away from a stable and unified sense of identity. The navigation of an altered landscape leads to a break or disjunction in the subject's experience of cultural and historical narratives, and, as such, focusses not on the mastery but on the disempowerment of the humanist subject.

Going Nowhere

For Hugh Kenner, the narrators of Samuel Beckett's *Four Nouvelles* mark 'a descent from middle-class somnambulistic orthodoxy to the fluid expedients of beggardom'.[37] The characters are ejected, exiled or otherwise removed from a position within an established social hierarchy, and become vagrant trampers, defined by the OED as those 'who [travel] from place to place on foot'.[38] These narratives of departure, and the identities of the narrators themselves, are mediated via continuous references to walking, shoes, boots, steps and feet:

> I must have read somewhere, when I was small and still read, that it is better not to look back when leaving. And yet I sometimes did. But even without looking back it seems to me I should have seen something when leaving. But there it is. All I remember is my feet emerging from my shadow, one after the other. My shoes had stiffened and the sun brought out the cracks in the leather. (*FN*, 42)

At this moment in *The End*, the image of the narrator's feet emerging from the shadows is suggestive of freedom, agency and illumination. But, while the narrator moves in the light of day, his figure simultaneously obstructs the sun's rays. He remains, despite his onward progression, a shadowy and obscure figure. The light, when it falls upon the cracked leather shoes, does not suggest harmony or direction, but rather fracture and imperfection. The wanderer's identity remains unclear, and casts a similarly troubling shadow on orderly public spaces.

---

37 Hugh Kenner, qtd. in Christopher Ricks' Preface to *The Expelled, The Calmative, The End with First Love*, xiv.

38 'Tramper', in OED (2017), accessed January 3, 2017, http://www.oed.com.

When describing the river that runs through the city, the narrator observes that it 'still gave the impression it was flowing in the wrong direction' (*FN*, 40). The image is, perhaps, contrary to the streaming current of the Thames in Beckett's earlier novel, *Murphy*, or the reliability of Joyce's River Liffey as a familiar landmark in *Ulysses*. The direction that the river runs becomes an emblem of regression and a breakdown of the natural order. But the narrator's outsider perspective appears to accommodate this slippage. The fact that the river 'still gave the impression' it was running backwards implies a familiarity with its strange motion, which, in effect, serves to stabilise it.

Michel de Certeau describes the city walker as a follower of the 'urban "text" they write without being able to read' (de Certeau 1984, 93); later in his essay, 'Walking in the City', he outlines a grid of 'urbanistic systematicity' (105), a constellation of proper names and street numbers that structures the subject's relationship to his or her surrounding environment. For the individual, walking through a public space inevitably demands a negotiation with social norms and expectations. In *The Expelled*, for example, there are areas designated for walking that are governed and policed. The narrator's wandering transgresses these boundaries and, in doing so, disrupts certain cultural codes of conduct and social order. The wandering narrator is both a subject of and subject to these unspoken but strictly governed limits of the urban space:

> A policeman stopped me and said, The street is for vehicles, the sidewalk for pedestrians. Like a bit of Old Testament. So I got back on the sidewalk, almost apologetically, and persevered there, in spite of an indescribable jostle, for a good twenty steps, till I had to fling myself to the ground to avoid crushing a child. (*Ex*, 8)

The policeman conveys authority by evoking one of Western culture's founding texts. Yet despite his stern direction, policing the public space by delineating its appropriate boundaries, the narrator's navigation is perpetually disrupted by chaos and disorder. In *The Calmative*, walking also runs in opposition to accepted convention, and does not—or cannot—observe the customs of Western standardised time.

The narrator's restless wandering during the night reveals a deeper uncertainty about the distinction between the real world and an imagined, dream world:

> How tell what remains? But it's the end. Or have I been dreaming, am I dreaming? No no, none of that, for dream is nothing, a joke, and significant what is worse. I said, Stay where you are till day breaks, wait sleeping till the lamps go out and the streets come to life. But I stood up and moved off. (*FN*, 31-2)[39]

The compulsive and traumatized act of walking does not affirm social convention in Beckett's work, nor does it consolidate the narrator's identity; instead, it ruptures or absents dominant cultural codes and values. To draw once again on de Certeau, walking in the city is a spatial practice that resists the 'all-seeing power' of a totalising urban space, with walkers and wanderers 'down below' that cannot be fully accounted for, or accommodated within a single, unified narrative (de Certeau 1986, 92-3).

Throughout Beckett's texts, walking is closely tied to the historical narratives and myths that structure identity and culture. At the close of *The Expelled*, the narrator describes a habitual routine that is followed whenever he is away from his homeland: 'When I am abroad in the morning I go to meet the sun, and in the evening, when I am abroad, I follow it, till I am down among the dead' (*Ex*, 16). The narrator is compelled to follow the trajectory of the sun as it hovers over

39 The motif of the nocturnal walker as an emblem of disordered modernity, historical trauma and personal exile recurs in W. G. Sebald's 2001 novel, *Austerlitz*, trans. Anthea Bell (London: Penguin Books, 2011), 178-9: 'It is a fact that you can traverse this vast city almost from end to end on foot in a single night, said Austerlitz, and once you are used to walking alone and meeting only a few nocturnal spectres on your way, you begin to wonder why, apparently because of some agreement concluded long ago, Londoners of all ages lie in their beds in those countless buildings in Greenwich, Bayswater or Kensington, under a safe roof, as they suppose, while really they are only stretched out with their faces turned to the earth in fear, like travellers of the past resting on their way through the desert.'

the landscape: walking, here, appears to trace a path towards a greater natural order, or balance. But, as the sun falls, evening presents an in-between state that is neither day nor night; instead, it signals a period of transition from light to dark, or, in this case, from life to death. The passage continues: 'I don't know why I told this story. I could just as well have told another. Perhaps some other time I'll be able to tell another. Living souls, you will see how alike they are' (*Ex*, 16). The idea of testimony, or of recounting a personal narrative, is introduced at this point of transition in the text. When the guiding light of the sun is finally lost, walking begins to lose direction, and the development of the narrative becomes aimless and confused, before finally breaking off altogether. The story does not quite resolve itself, but ends on a tentative note. There might be other stories that will bring greater illumination, at some point in the future, but the promise is deferred for another time, another story.

The Calmative also dramatises the tension between movement and inactivity: 'I thought I could go no further, but no sooner had the impetus reached my legs than on I went, believe it or not, at a very fair pace' (*FN*, 27). The narrator's compulsive movement and advancement confers physical exertion and excess, and the very act of walking appears to imply other, deeper certainties: 'I wasn't returning empty-handed, not quite, I was taking back with me the virtual certainty that I was still of this world, of that world too, in a way' (27). But at the very moment that walking forward connects to a truth, or a certainty, about the subject's position and identity in the world, there is an additional consideration, or an additional 'way', that creates an alternative route or origin. And so, even as walking allows the narrator to advance along a meaningful path, it also gives rise to an excess of possibility, even to the accommodation of many, seemingly contradictory, options. The environments are vague and ambiguous in the sense that they cannot be readily identified or categorised, but in the additional sense that they generate other confusions regarding categories of identity, of purpose, and of difference. Walking is emblematic here of a belated and traumatized subjectivity that roams and wanders the fields and towns of Beckett's later writing.

The post-war European landscape becomes increasingly abstracted in Samuel Beckett's trilogy of novels, *Molloy*, *Malone Dies* and *The Unnamable*. Beckett's traumatised narrators struggle to navigate vague and cryptic environments, and the texts themselves become increasingly concerned with interior spaces and psychological ruminations (they were described by one reviewer as a 'running commentary on experience').[40] Humanist mastery of the environment falls prey to aimless wandering, while the representation of subjectivity, through the recounting of narrative and memory. Crucially, the physical act of walking in these texts is mirrored and elided with Beckett's stylistic wandering, where the prose moves and transitions restlessly from one scene or subject to another, often disregarding conventional linear order. Rambling through an ambiguous and 'vague' landscape takes the form of linguistic or verbal detours, a series of incoherent talks or writings that digress from the point rather than progress towards it. Toynbee's review of *Molloy* described the eponymous character as a 'scatological tramp—a Wandering Jew combined with a Tom o'Bedlam'.[41] Tom o'Bedlam is familiar as a 'mad', 'insane' and institutionalised figure cast adrift as a beggar, or vagrant; while the Wandering Jew is a motif that evokes the exile of Exodus in the Old Testament tradition, and eerily evokes the displacement of European Jewry in the aftermath of the Holocaust. The tramping figure of Molloy is a wanderer that evokes the trauma of canonical texts and the historical traumas of the post-war moment, without being identical with them: his compulsive movement, whether through the physical act of walking or the text's discursive wandering, undermines the novel's quest narrative as it strays across forests and topics. The abstraction, or vaguening, of the Beckettian landscape is thus a traumatic symptom that troubles the stability of meaning and value, of time, place, and identity.

Throughout the three novels, the relationship between walking, language and humanist subjectivity is perhaps most keenly represented by their digressive and meandering prose. (In a dismissive 1955

40 Anon., 'Prince of Darkness', *Times Literary Supplement*, 17 June 1960.

41 Philip Toynbee, 'Going Nowhere', *The Observer*, 18 December 1955.

review of *Molloy* for *The Observer*, Philip Toynbee adopted the headline: 'Going Nowhere'.)[42] Steven Connor has suggested that *The Unnamable* 'remains at the enigmatic heart of Beckett's writing, and of critical writing about Beckett'.[43] In the text, it is precisely the concept of locating the humanist subject on a road towards unity or resolution that deconstructs and unravels the narrator—between departure and arrival, the road or pathway marks a kind of non-space where one's position becomes difficult to finally determine:

> All this business of a labour to accomplish, before I can end, of words to say, a truth to recover, in order to say it, before I can end, of an imposed task, once known, long neglected, finally forgotten, to perform, before I can be done with speaking, done with listening, I invented it all, in the hope it would console me, help me to go on, allow me to think of myself as somewhere on a road, moving, between a beginning and an end, gaining ground, losing ground, getting lost, but somehow in the long run making headway. All lies. I have nothing to do, that is to say nothing in particular. (*U*, 25)[44]

Once again, the text describes movement in terms of a travail, a work of suffering that compels the subject to continue along an ambiguous and tormented path. The notion of a truth that can be discovered through progression is presented in the text as a kind of misdirection. (Maurice Blanchot goes so far as to describe the novel itself as 'An experiment without results' (Blanchot 1993b, 86), suggesting

---

42 Toynbee, 'Going Nowhere'. Bamber Gascoigne appears to rephrase Toynbee's headline in another review for *The Observer* published nine years later, this time for Beckett's *Play*: 'How far can Beckett go?' in *The Observer Weekend Review*, 12 April 1964.

43 Steven Connor, Preface to *The Unnamable*, xxiii.

44 On the subject of business, Roger Luckhurst states the following on surgeon John Erichsen's 1866 observations on 'railway spine': 'The case histories presented offered portraits of disordered memory, disturbed sleep and frightened dreams, and various types of paralysis, melancholia and impotence, with a particular emphasis on the sudden loss of business sense.' See Luckhurst, *The Trauma Question*, 22.

that the text emulates the pursuit of knowledge but resists the pretension of a conclusive solution.) The use of words such as 'business' and 'labour'[45] are suggestive of economic demands 'imposed' upon the individual, but the word 'truth' attempts to consolidate these terms as natural and right. The narrators have deconstructed the apparent naturalness of their surroundings, and appear to occupy a kind of no man's land between two distinct and steadfast points: the beginning and end of a journey. This finds an echo elsewhere in *The Unnamable*, with the demand to 'Set aside, once and for all, at the same time as the analogy with orthodox damnation, all idea of beginning and end' (108).

Beckett's post-war characters attempt to navigate environments that were once familiar, but which have since become strange or unstable. Walking as navigation, as understanding of and mastery over a landscape, gives way in Beckett's writing to unsettlement and deferral. Walking, in his prose texts, is not a logical act that leads to a concrete destination, but an exercise that seems to lead nowhere. As the narrator of one of Beckett's later works describes it, 'I have never in my life been on my way anywhere, but simply on my way' (FAW, 57). The text in question, *From an Abandoned Work*, designates a tension between the conscious aim and purpose of a work, and the lack of aim and purpose indicated by the act of abandonment. Walking, throughout these texts, both symbolises and unsettles Western expectations of presence, agency and the progression towards truth.

Coming and Going

Fort-Da

In *Beyond the Pleasure Principle*, Sigmund Freud recounts an anecdote about a child playing. The child in question did not yet have a strong grasp of language, but drew upon 'a small repertoire of expressive sounds comprehensible to those around him' (Freud 2003, 52). He

45 The word 'labour' is perhaps also significant in its connection to ideas of 'works' and 'travails'.

had established 'a good rapport with his parents' and a strong emotional bond with his mother, although he 'never cried when his mother left him for hours at a time'. To explain this, Freud observes that the child established a habit of flinging small objects within his grasp as far away from him as possible. This activity would coincide with an appearance of contentment, accompanied by what Freud describes as a 'long-drawn-out "o-o-o-o" sound, which in the unanimous opinion of both his mother and myself as observer was not simply an exclamation but stood for *fort* ("gone")' (53). It is assumed, on the basis of repetition and the apparent happiness of the child, that the process represented a kind of game. Freud continues:

> Then one day I made an observation that confirmed my interpretation. The child had a wooden reel with some string tied around it. [...] keeping hold of the string, he very skillfully threw the reel over the edge of his curtained cot so that it disappeared inside, all the while making his expressive 'o-o-o-o' sound, then used the string to pull the reel out of the cot again, but this time greeting its reappearance with a joyful *Da!* ('Here!'). That, then, was the entire game—disappearing and coming back—only the first act of which one normally got to see; and this first act was tirelessly repeated on its own, even though greater pleasure undoubtedly attached to the second. (53)

For Freud, the actions of the child can be readily explained. The *fort-da* game reflects 'the child's immense cultural achievements in successfully abnegating his drives [...] by allowing his mother to go away without his making a great fuss' (53). Whereas the disappearance of the mother was beyond the child's control or ability to anticipate, the game allowed the subject to repeat and reenact the disappearance using objects that could be easily controlled and manipulated. In this context, Freud suggests, hurling the object away and declaring it gone, before returning it to view, stages the disappearance and reappearance of the item in a way that the child can successfully control. The game compensates for the loss, and succeeds in bringing comfort to the child. But, crucially, there is also a sense in which the child's actions could be construed as a 'defiant statement' (54), whereby the game creates an opportunity to consciously determine and execute the disappearance in a way that asserts personal dominance. What begins as a distressing loss for the child becomes an act of empowerment: 'Alright, go away! I don't need you; I'm sending you away myself!' (54). Freud observes a similar behavioural process in the same child later in life. On the second occasion, disappearance is personified by an absent father who is away at war: 'This same child whose game I had observed when he was one and a half had the habit a year later of flinging down any toy that had made him cross and saying "Go in war!"' (54). From this case, Freud infers a general principle: 'children repeat everything in their play that has made a powerful impression on them, and that in doing so they abreact the intensity of the experience and make themselves so to speak master of the situation' (55). The *fort-da* game offers the child an opportunity to convert a passive role that cannot be predicted or controlled into an active and participatory one

Cathy Caruth draws upon Freud's anecdote in her study, *Unclaimed Experience: Trauma, Narrative, and History*. In her reading, Caruth evaluates to what extent the *fort-da* game is about departure and return: 'What strikes Freud as he tells the story of the *fort-da* is that the game of departure and return is ultimately, and inexplicably, a game, simply, of departure' (Caruth 1996, 66). At a later point in the book, Caruth summarises the game as follows:

> In discussing the general phenomenon of traumatic repetition, Freud moves from the example of the nightmares of the soldiers who have come back from the war, to the repetition he observes in a child's game: the game of saying, alternately, *fort* and *da* while throwing a wooden spool back and forth, which symbolizes, in Freud's reading, the departure of the mother and the child's anxiety that she might not return. Freud's biographers have taught us that this game was in fact played by Freud's own grandchild; it was indeed the son of Freud's own daughter, Sophie, who was, through this game, coping with the suffering of the possible protracted absence or loss of his mother, by repeating or reenacting her departure. (109)

The *fort-da* game is a response to an original trauma, or departure, in a child's development; yet, this trauma appears to be remedied through a language that grants stability and control to the subject. What is most significant about the game, for the purposes of this study, is the way disappearance and reappearance is mastered. In addition to the control and manipulation of available objects, the presence conferred by language and speech plays a vital role. It is language that makes explicit differentiations between presence (there) and absence (gone), and language that allows the child to transition from a passive, silent and helpless observer to a defiant and active subject position.

Analysis of the *fort-da* game in relation to Beckett's work is a well-rehearsed theme in Beckett studies. As Steven Connor points out in his work, *Samuel Beckett: Repetition, Theory, and Text*, Freud's account of the *fort-da* game offers a rich avenue for interpretation across the gamut of Beckett's texts:

> Beckett's work [...] repeatedly produces that duality demonstrated in Freud's work in which repetition and the death-instinct do not stand against the pleasure principle in simple opposition, but enfold the pleasure principle within them, affirming life at the very moment of death, openness within the jaws of closure. (Connor 2007, 11)

Elaborating further, Connor writes that

> for Beckett, we will see, the centrality of death and the repetition compulsion which draws near to it is not a matter of a simple instinct for negation. The forms of repetition that proliferate in his work establish death not as the mere absence of life, but rather as the place where the natures of life, death, difference and repetition are concentrated and problematized. (12)

And so, as we shall see, in Beckett's texts we can trace a complex engagement with the *fort-da* formulation of psychoanalytic theory, an engagement which erodes standard binary oppositions of life and death, pleasure and pain, and presence and absence.

Coming and Going

Angela Moorjani identifies the influence of *Beyond the Pleasure Principle* as 'one of the most important of Beckett's Freudian intertexts', and notes the writer's 'fondness [...] is apparent from the direct and indirect references to the pleasure principle in *Murphy* and *Molloy* and from repeated textual performances of the *fort-da* game in his work' (Moorjani 2004, 174). Beckett's post-war texts, and to some degree his earlier writing, undermine the assumption that language can formulate an appropriate and effective response to traumatic events or experiences. In Freud's description of the *fort-da* game, language signifies absolute markers of presence and absence, allowing the subject to restage (and master) the trauma of absence or loss in a way that comforts and consoles. Language itself also implies a presence that is as available to the subject as the objects within the young child's grasp. In Beckett's prose, language unsettles the oppositions of presence and absence, whilst enacting its own form of traumatic departure via deferrals, detours and digressions. The absolute distinction between 'there' and 'gone' is compromised by the motif of 'coming and going'. If the term 'there' marks an ability to distinguish presence, 'coming' is neither fully present nor fully absent; similarly, whereas 'gone' unambiguously marks a point of departure, the sense of 'going' is, quite literally, neither here nor there. This condition is articulated in a passage from *Watt*:

> Or is there a coming that is not a coming to, a going that is not a going from, a shadow that is not the shadow of purpose, or not? For what is this shadow of the going in which we come, this shadow of the coming in which we go, this shadow of the coming and the going in which we wait, if not the shadow of purpose, of the purpose that budding withers, that withering buds, whose blooming is a budding withering? I speak well, do I not, for a man in my situation? And what is this coming that was not our coming and this being that is not our being and this going that will not be our going but the coming and going in purposelessness? (*W*, 48-9)

Coming and going is perhaps one of the central motifs of walking and discursive wandering in Beckett's prose, and indeed across all his work. The 'situation' of the subject that is coming and going is that of one whose status is radically uncertain: the stability of identity is dispersed across many different times, spaces, and personas, as a form of being that is perpetually on the move. The presence of shadows suggest darkness, obscurity, and the unknown, while also a shape cast by some other figure, perhaps a truer and more reliable self. Blooming, a process of development or maturation, becomes a site of ambiguity and contestation. Despite the narrator's attempt at systematic enquiry, the 'purposelessness' of the coming and going reflects the apparent, meandering purposelessness of the text itself, the final meaning of which remains unclear.

This inability to establish presence via the continual disruption of chronology and linearity through breaks, interruptions and repetitions are common tropes in traumatic narratives. In *The Unnamable*, coming and going forbids the possibility of a final resting place, and insists on a continuing sense of restless motion, 'like bodies in torment, the torment of no abode, no repose, no, like hyenas, screeching and laughing, no, no better, no matter' (109). As David Houston Jones states, 'Beckett's characters seek their place in language with anguish, and their narratives suggest a prior event which can never satisfactorily be recovered' (Houston Jones 2011, 5). The trope does not confer mastery or purpose in the text, but precisely a lack of coherent direction or motivation. This ceaseless movement transgresses and contaminates traditional boundaries, and renders conventional Western understandings of time, place and difference problematic. The narrator of *The Unnamable* states that 'I feel the end at hand', suggesting either death or the promise of resolution, 'and the beginning likewise' (117), articulating a position whereby two mutually exclusive definitions intersect at the same place, and so contradict each other. The narrator of an earlier text, *The Calmative*, expresses it another way: 'All I say cancels out, I'll have said nothing' (*FN*, 19). The lack of presence or embodiment in language frees it from any one specific context, and disables the maintenance of fixed definitions; as a result, the subject's ability to identify itself and the world around it falls into crisis.

Coming and going becomes the means by which we can understand walking and stylistic wandering as not just emblematic of some latent traumatic symptom, but as an unsettling deconstruction of Freud's *fort-da* (there-gone/presence-absence) binary opposition. While traditionally, walking denotes presence through its suggestion of a physical, embodied act, its representation in Beckett's work mirrors the digressive structure of the prose texts themselves, and signals a narrative voice that cannot be quantified, tracked or located. They are akin, in some sense, to de Certeau's urban walkers, 'ordinary practitioners' who live 'below the thresholds at which visibility [of the outlay] begins' (de Certeau 1986, 93). Whilst following specific pre-determined routes, there is room for the unexpected gesture through variation and improvisation. In this way, Beckett's narrators resemble what de Certeau refers to in German as *Wandersmänner*, 'whose bodies follow the thicks and thins of an urban "text" they write without being able to read it' (93). In Beckett's writing the language of subjectivity is simultaneously constructed and disassembled through the process of wandering:

> There's going to be a departure, I'll be there, I won't miss it, it won't be me, I'll be here, I'll say I'm far from here, it won't be me, I won't say anything, there's going to be a story, someone's going to try and tell a story. Yes, no more denials, all is false, there is no one, it's understood, there is nothing, no more phrases, let us be dupes, dupes of every time and tense, until it's done, all past and done, and the voices cease, it's only voices, only lies. Here, depart from here and go elsewhere, or stay here, but coming and going. (*TN*, 11)

While *Texts for Nothing III* anticipates the staging of a traumatic departure in a way that implies assurance and mastery, there are contradictions from the very beginning. In the opening phrase, there is a marked disparity in the attempt to locate (there is) something that is absent (departure) in a future that has not yet occurred (going to be). The text asserts the presence of the narrator as a reliable witness to the upcoming departure, but as this supposed proximity is challenged, the lack of presence prohibits accurate testimony. The story itself becomes a kind of promise, a narrative that is always anticipating its own arrival, and so never really belongs to the present in any reliable sense. The narrative voice, divided between 'here' and 'there', is indicative of a wider instability in language: a deferral or delay of meaning along a chain of linguistic signifiers, with no possibility of full presence, and so no possibility of truth or resolution.

Wandering plays an interesting role in Beckett's collection of *Texts for Nothing*, published after the completion of *The Unnamable*. The collection troubles the 'universal human activity' (Solnit 2001, 16) of walking, and its association with the supposed coherence and universality of rational thought. The title itself is something of a contradiction, designating a body of work toward no particular aim or cause; as James Knowlson and John Pilling have pointed out, 'Beckett's aesthetic at this time was predicated upon failure and the unavoidability of failure' (Knowlson and Pilling 1979, 42). Both academics agree that they are 'not his most brilliant or compelling works' (42), and that they 'do not escape from the *impasse* of *The Unnamable*' (42). But I would suggest that the texts are rich in topics for discussion, and that impasse is a dominant and important theme. John Fletcher has compared the original French title of the collection, *Textes pour rien*, with the musical expression *mesure pour rien*, which translates as 'a bar's rest' (Fletcher 1964, 196).[46] The notion recalls the tension between the 'wandering' and the 'still', and Solnit's description of walking as 'the time inbetween' (Solnit 2001, xiii). Beckett's *Texts for Nothing*, then, are comparable to a space between origin and destination, a space that implies movement and presence but does not confirm it: an unregulated space that accommodates contradiction.

This tension between 'here' and 'there' is repeated throughout the thirteen short texts that comprise the collection, and indeed recurs in Beckett's later work in prose and drama. The narrator of the first

---

46 Alternatively, Neil Badmington suggested to me that the 'pourri' (meaning 'rotten') can also be heard in *Textes pour rien*, suggesting 'Rotten Texts'.

story cannot settle in any one place: 'I couldn't stay there and I couldn't go on' (*TN*, 3). In the second text, the narrator addresses another in a similarly restless manner: 'You are there, there it is, where you are going will never long be habitable' (*TN*, 7). In the ninth text of the series, the concept of 'coming and going' disrupts all possibility of tense, location, and subsequently of narrative itself:

> There's a way out of there, no no, I'm getting mixed, I must be getting mixed, confusing here and there, now and then, just as I confused them then, the here of then, the then of there, with other spaces, other times, dimly discerned, but not more dimly than now, now that I'm here, if I'm here, and no longer there, coming and going before the graveyard, perplexed. (*TN*, 39)

The wandering prose does not allow a specific vantage point, and denies the subject the possibility of mastery. This lack of agency in the subject is revealed through deeper instabilities of language and definition. Meanings shift and adjust according to their context; the narrator confuses 'the here of then, the then of there, with other spaces, other times', and when terms are repeated in different places and locations throughout the passage, their significations multiply and disperse.

Whereas traumatic repetitions of the *fort-da* game suggest a mastery of departure, in Beckett's texts the very terms that define the game are suspect, and it is language that enacts a process of departure. In *The End*, the assumed temporal and spatial presence of the narrator is undermined and vacated:

> One day I witnessed a strange scene. Normally I didn't see a great deal. I didn't hear a great deal either. I didn't pay attention. Strictly speaking I wasn't there. Strictly speaking I believe I've never been anywhere. (*FN*, 31)

The traumatic texts articulate a crisis in representation, unsettling the presumed grip of language on concrete notions of time, place and identity:[47]

47 For more on trauma and subjectivity in Beckett's *Texts for Nothing*, see Jonathan Boulter's 'Does Mourning Require a Subject? Samuel Beckett's

> See what's happening here, where there's no one, where nothing happens, get something to happen here, someone to be here, to put an end to it, have silence, get into silence, or another sound, a sound of other voices than those of life and death, or lives and deaths everyone's but mine, get into my story in order to get out of it, no, that's meaningless (*TN*, 14)

The narrator of *Text for Nothing III* once again articulates the problem of presence and absence that language seems to generate. Definitions of time, memory, and place are each called into question. There is a demand for the reader to see what cannot be seen, to witness an event that the text does not or cannot define, in order to seek a final resolution, a stable silence. But there is no one to witness or be witnessed, and no occurrence to observe or record. Instead, there are other voices that give expression to alternative possibilities. These possibilities appear to destabilise traditional Western oppositions of life and death, and operate in some other, unknown way. We might read this as some kind of post-war philosophical or epistemological crisis, or perhaps a crisis of individual identity, but the problems suggested by the extract each seem to lead back to the problem of language and representation.

Writing 'About' Trauma

Samuel Beckett's status as a modernist writer remains a source of debate among critics, although there is no doubting the influence that the movement holds on his earlier work. What is significant, however, is the way in which modernist devices are exploited in Beckett's writing. In his book *The Trauma Question*, Roger Luckhurst suggests that the 'epiphanies of Modernism could be suggestively rewritten through traumatic temporality' (Luckhurst 2008, 121); I would suggest that there is no better place to look for such a reconfiguration than the wandering subjects of Beckett's post-war fiction. The writer and literary critic Maurice Blanchot takes these implications further by suggesting that the complexities that arise when reading are not limited to

---

Texts for Nothing', *MFS Modern Fiction Studies*, 50:2, Summer 2004, 332-350.

literature, but can make us question 'what is of concern in a situation that is not fictional, that refers to the real torment of a real existence' (Blanchot 2003b, 88).

It is tempting to read terms like 'real' or 'existence' hyperbolically in this context, since novels such as Beckett's *The Unnamable* appear to have no stable referent outside the text itself. One 1960 review of the novel for *The Observer* ironically observed that

> From internal evidence, the nearest I can come to a rational explanation of *The Unnamable* is that, in Mr. Beckett's part of our Montparnasse, there is a slaughter-house and that, nearby, in a real Rue Brancion there is a café-restaurant, called, possibly, *Ali Baba*, outside which stands a big jar, twined with fairy-lamps and bearing the bill of fare and from the top of which emerges the plaster head of one of the forty thieves.[48]

The reviewer's wry attempt to stabilise the meanings of the text by recourse to a traditional realistic method of reporting emphasises both the complexity and the irreducible strangeness of the novel.

Samuel Beckett's prose works do not define traumatic events in any specific or explicit way. Even when at their most straightforward, such descriptions remain brief, obscure or abstracted. Both *Malone Dies* and *The Calmative* present characters who have received some kind of physical blow that has disrupted a linear understanding of their surroundings, but violence does not fall into a rational or predictable schema. *Molloy* begins with its eponymous narrator locating himself in his mother's room, but the reason or logic behind his arrival alludes to some kind of unspecified medical emergency: 'I don't know how I got there. Perhaps in an ambulance, certainly a vehicle of some kind. I was helped. I'd never have got there alone' (*Mo*, 3). *Malone Dies* ends with the slaughter of several characters on a small boat, and the narrative closes with an ambiguous breakdown in the structure and regularity of the prose. In *The Unnamable*, the narrators are held captive by anxieties about events that, while they seem to occur concurrently with the inscription, remain strangely deferred by the text itself.

48 Rayner Heppenstall, 'Unnamed, At Last' in *The Observer*, 10 April 1960.

Trauma does not occur in this passage, but it is present in the form of a belated and terrible promise:

> fear of sound, fear of sounds, the sounds of beasts, the sounds of men, sounds in the daytime and sounds at night, that's enough, fear of sounds, all sounds, more or less, more or less fear, all sounds, there's only one, continuous, day and night, what is it, it's steps coming and going, it's voices speaking for a moment, it's bodies groping their way (*U*, 104)

There is little doubt that Beckett's writing is concerned with the issue of trauma and the way traumatic events impact upon conventional understandings of time, place and identity. Trauma disrupts the fixity of a stable narrative voice: 'since that day it's not I anymore' (*U*, 125). If language is the means by which the humanist subject defines and understands itself as an active and present agent, in Beckett it is also the source of traumatic disruption and untimely deferral.

In *Writing History, Writing Trauma*, Dominick LaCapra identifies Beckett as one of a number of writers who may be 'working over and through trauma whether personally experienced, transmitted from intimates, or sensed in one's larger social and cultural setting' (LaCapra 2001, 105). The idea that Beckett's work matured in Europe in the aftermath of the Second World War is significant in this context. LaCapra goes on to suggest that Beckett's texts, alongside those of Maurice Blanchot, Franz Kafka and Paul Celan, might be conceived 'as a writing of terrorized disempowerment as close as possible to the experience of traumatized victims without presuming to be identical to it' (105-6). Such writers appear to be exploring issues surrounding trauma and testimony without presumption of an identification with the thing in itself. Whilst this could offer a number of productive possibilities, LaCapra remains cautious of what he labels 'emulative writing', a form of writing that

> becomes especially open to question when it takes an unmodulated orphic, cryptic, indirect, allusive form that may render or transmit the disorientation of trauma but provide too little basis for attempts to work it through even in symbolic terms. (106)

Whilst the title of LaCapra's study demarcates a separation between narratives of trauma and standardised narratives of history, there is still a requirement, in his view, that works that implicate or allude to trauma provide some form of concrete representation, whether it is literal or symbolic. Samuel Beckett's writing—and, arguably, the texts of Celan, Kafka and Blanchot—appear to resist this logic, and in doing so prompt an important question: are Beckett's prose texts concerned with the concept of trauma itself as a cultural and historical phenomenon, or do they simply emulate its effects without reason or purpose?

But there is a subtle binary logic at work in LaCapra's assessment of 'emulative texts'. Since Beckett's work operates from what he calls 'a *relatively* safe haven compared with actual traumatization' (105), a distinction is made between texts that explicitly (or symbolically) address trauma, and those that do not. The idea of 'actual traumatization' becomes a marker of legitimacy and authenticity through its implications of presence and deliberate action. The term 'actual', as defined by the OED, is 'used to emphasize the authentic or archetypal status of [a] specified thing'; the word carries connotations of something 'relating to acts or action', something 'existing in fact' and 'real'.[49] One less common use of the term defines 'actual' as something 'in operation or existence at the time; present, current'. Whilst each of these meanings establishes a stable and convenient way to define traumatisation, they simultaneously establish LaCapra's expression as oxymoronic; trauma cannot be defined according to agency or presence, but operates via a logic of partial absence and belated return. Cathy Caruth asserts that the return of traumatic experience 'is not the signal of the direct experience but, rather, of the attempt to overcome the fact that it was *not* direct, to attempt to master what was never fully grasped in the first place' (Caruth 1996, 62).

What distinguishes Beckett's texts is the way they acknowledge the problem of presence and absence as a key attribute of traumatic experience. In each case, we have the implication of trau-

49 'Actual', in OED (2017), accessed January 3, 2017, http://www.oed.com.

matisation without an 'actual' attempt to represent it, or make it present. Beckett's work is about traumatisation of one kind or another, but in a way that implies motion, repetition and circularity; the OED defines the term 'about' as an adverb suggesting something that is: 'all over or around; in various directions; in a circuitous course; to and fro; (also referring to things scattered over a surface) up and down, here and there.'[50] Language, in Beckett's texts, cannot actualise trauma with reference to absolutes, such as 'here', 'there', or 'gone', but infers or suggests traumatisation as a process that resists such definitions. The wandering protagonists of Beckett's post-war fiction do not approximate traumatic events, but circle about them, coming and going via routes that are devious, obscure or, to adopt Caruth's term, 'indirect'.

Language and Dis-Orientation

Wolfgang Iser, in his outline of trauma narratives, suggests that via the process of reading 'we uncover the unformulated part of the text', a part of the text that reveals some kind of fragmentary or partial characteristic, and that the resulting sense of 'indeterminacy is the force that drives us to work out a configurative meaning'.[51] Representations of walking in texts such as *Molloy*, or wandering in *Malone Dies* and *The Unnamable*, give the prose an outward appearance of progressive conformity, whilst confounding attempts to accumulate or consolidate a final conclusion or resolution: 'it's visions, shreds of old visions, that's all you can see' (*U*, 124). As Luckhurst notes, 'Trauma fictions work with and against this phenomenological description of reading' (Luckhurst 2008, 93). Drawing upon the example of Toni Morrison's *Beloved*, a book that he argues 'helped establish some of the basic narrative and tropological conventions of trauma fiction' (90), Luckhurst establishes the form as a genre that continually resists attempts by the reader to master or understand it:

---

50 'About', in OED (2017), accessed January 3, 2017, http://www.oed.com.

51 Wolfgang Iser, qtd. in Luckhurst, *The Trauma Question*, 93

> In [Toni] Morrison, trauma takes discordance to the very limits of coherence. If concordance is possible, this grasping together of fragments into story is far from unifying. The reader is jarred by belated recognitions of events that are barely supportable in novelistic discourse. It may be that such a reading presents us with what 'seemed to elude our consciousness', but this is not an act of completion or closure so much as a confrontation with a violent history that has been held outside national history or collective memory. *Beloved* aims to de-stabilize subjectivity; it disarms the reader with narrative and figurative techniques that force a confrontation with traumatic material. (93)

Trauma, in Luckhurst's view, not only destabilises the conventions of familiar literary forms, but also mounts a challenge to the linear constructions of subjectivity itself. Drawing upon the work of Kali Tal, Luckhurst 'asserts vigilance' against what Tal describes as the risk of 'reducing a traumatic event to a set of standardized narratives', whereby 'traumatic events are written and rewritten until they become codified and narrative form replaces content as the focus of attention'.[52] I would suggest a slight adjustment to Tal's outline, whereby an attention to the language and form of a literary text could provide a way not to reinforce, but to avoid the standardisation of traumatic narratives. The literal and digressive wandering form of Beckett's work is a narrative motif that questions the status and the reliability of content in conventional trauma fiction.

In *The Writing of the Disaster*, Maurice Blanchot offers a number of fragmentary reflections or ruminations on the nature or definition of the disaster: its definition, its capacity, its origin, its result. Whilst Blanchot's text continues to resist straightforward attempts to explain or decode its meaning, the concept of the disaster becomes a wandering emblem of catastrophe, trauma and disruption. I would suggest that there are certain family resemblances between the aporetics of disaster and representations of walking in Samuel Beckett's work. Both resist the actualisation of trauma that is codified by standardised

---

52 Kali Tal, qtd. in Luckhurst, *The Trauma Question*, 89.

narratives, and both address traumatisation via indirect means. Blanchot writes:

> I will not say that the disaster is absolute; on the contrary, it disorients the absolute. It comes and goes, errant disarray, and yet with the imperceptible but intense suddenness of the outside, as an irresistible or unforeseen resolve which would come to us from beyond the confines of decision. (Blanchot 1995, 4)

Rather than orientating the subject in relation to a position or direction, the Beckett's literary representation of walking dis-orientates the landscape and subjectivity. As part of a lineage of literary inheritance, Beckett's restless wanderers and journeymen nod to Dante, Rousseau, and Joyce, but in the post-war context become symbolic of the rational Western subject gone awry: they are figures that disintegrate into emblems of disruption, disorder and repetition.

Maurice Blanchot's essay on Beckett's trilogy of novels, *Molloy*, *Malone Dies*, and *The Unnamable*, relates the tension between movement and stasis to a question about identity. The essay, entitled 'Where now? Who now?', explicitly connects the problem of place and presence with the question of subjectivity. Blanchot suggests that motion is intrinsic to the novel's style: 'It is this treadmill movement that strikes us first' (Blanchot 1993b, 86). The metaphor of the mechanical treadmill blends ideas of movement and stasis with technological images of circularity and repetition.[53] In *Molloy*, Blanchot notes, the wanderer 'who already lacks the means to wander' (86) is defined according to a series of 'halting, jerky movements [that] occur in a space which is the space of impersonal obsession, the obsession that eternally leads him on' (87). Movement, here, progresses according to a

53 The notion that we; as readers, are 'struck' is also suggestive of a break in narrative linearity; as the movement 'strikes us', one is easily reminded of the traumatic blows received by Beckett's characters during various intervals in the texts.

logic of neurotic compulsion. Blanchot asserts that '*Malone Dies* evidently goes further still' (87), before speculating whether the protagonist is

> merely going round in circles, obscurely revolving, carried along by the momentum of a wandering voice, lacking not so much sense as center, producing an utterance without proper beginning or end, yet greedy, exacting, a language that will never stop, for then would come the moment of the terrible discovery: when the talking stops, there is still talking; when the language pauses, it perseveres; there is no silence, for within that voice the silence eternally speaks. (86)

The qualities of momentum, revolution and disarray can be identified in a particular passage of *The Unnamable*, where testimony is deferred by the continual alteration of subject positions:

> I wait for my turn, my turn to go there, my turn to talk there, my turn to listen there, my turn to wait there and my turn to go, to be as gone, it's unending, it will be unending, gone where, where do you go from there, you must go somewhere else, wait somewhere else, for your turn to go again, and so on, a whole people, or I alone, and come back, and begin again, no, go again, go on again, it's a circuit, a long circuit, I know it well, it's a lie, I can't stir (*U*, 129)

Momentum carries forward the narrative voice via logic of disarray and disorientation. It 'proceeds without sophistry and without subterfuge [...] exhibiting the same jerky movement, the same tireless, stationary tread' (Blanchot 1993b, 89). Freud's *fort-da* game suggests a framework that restages departure through the active and purposeful use of language, whereby trauma is both repeated and worked through by the subject; but this framework is dependent upon the assumption that linguistic terms represent (or make present) fixed meanings. Beckett's language hovers on the borderlands of speech and inscription, of presence and absence: it is precisely at the moment that language appears to offer a fixed perspective that it continues to progress or persevere in one of many separate directions.

This traumatic configuration of language and writing as a system that belatedly restages departure and embodies it holds implications for our understanding of representations of the humanist subject. For Blanchot, the novel evokes a subject 'fallen out of the world, eternally hovering between being and nothingness, henceforth as incapable of dying as of being born, haunted by his creatures, meaningless ghosts he no longer believes in' (91). This inability to establish a fixed sense of place or location results in a destabilisation of personal identity. Orderly progression and purposeful action are also called into question, as binary oppositions of 'there' and 'gone' or 'living' and 'dead' lose their power to signify accurately or meaningfully. Ideas, concepts and values formed through the reliable arrangement of words become, at best, suspect, at worst, deconstructed altogether; words imply a spectrality, and exist in the text as ghosts that signal only a partial presence.

Nouns and pronouns are traditionally places where humanist subjectivity gathers and collects itself; they constitute a kind of landscape of identity, whereby speech from outside addresses a specific position, while emissions can be identified according to a specific source, or origin. Names locate the subject within a particular time and space, and allow progress to develop according to a series of fixed points. But this logic is continually undermined in Beckett's texts. The name 'Murphy', in Beckett's 1938 novel, marks the protagonist as an exile in a foreign land; at the time the novel is set, 'Murphy' was a generic derogatory term applied to Irish immigrants, and so is not only a marker of individuality, but a signal of national stereotypes and xenophobic prejudice. 'Watt' is a name that could suggest confusion or indecision when heard aloud. Mercier and Camier suggest French natives uprooted in a 'vague' landscape of indeterminate status, and exist as an inseparable couple: one protagonist's identity is formed in direct relation to the other (the names 'Mercier' and 'Camier' do not, in some sense, exist independently). Molloy is replaced in the second part of his narrative with the detective who goes in search of him, Moran—a character who, in many ways, could be seen as his uncanny double.

Finally, *Malone Dies* dramatises the dissolution of identity through a gallery of grotesque characters and fanciful anecdotes.

In *The Unnamable*, this crisis of naming deteriorates further. Blanchot observes that there 'is no longer any question of characters under the reassuring protection of a personal name', and, as such, 'no longer any question of a narrative, even in the formless present of an interior monologue; what was narrative has become conflict, what assumed a face, even a face in fragments, is now discountenanced' (Blanchot 1993b, 88). The traumatised discursive wandering of the text dis-orientates the subject in relation to language, and the promise of fixed meanings and truths.

The Wandering 'I'

In *The Trauma Question*, Roger Luckhurst draws upon Shari Bernstock's *The Private Self* for its use of poststructuralist themes and ideas. The role language plays in the construction of selfhood is examined and undermined in Bernstock's work, which, Luckhurst goes on to suggest, undermines 'the monolithic "I" of the male autobiographical canon' (Luckhurst 2008, 121). Traditionally, the thinking and speaking 'I' is a stable icon of presence and identity, and as such establishes a secure foundation from which to communicate, spread and even impose ideological values. The 'I' implies individuality, coherence and unity, and promotes the Western humanist subject as a disciplined agent of established modes of thinking and being. In addition to Bernstock's narratives, I would suggest that Samuel Beckett's use of traumatic themes also interrogates the authority and position of the 'I' of dominant ideological discourse.[54] Whilst one can identify the author

---

54 The 'I' occupies an uneasy status as a referential indexical sign (or 'shifter'), which is to say that it is prone to variations of meaning, dependant upon the context. In some ways, this runs contrary to expectations of the 'I' as a marker of identical stability. The flexibility of the first person pronoun as a 'shifter' is something of a theme in Beckett's work, and is perhaps one of the defining characteristics of his post-war prose (*The Unnamable* springs to mind as a prominent example).

within the orthodoxy of the white male European literary canon, traumatized walking and wandering continually challenges the notion of a stable, unmoving subject, along with privileged claims toward truth or social authority. As Anthony Uhlmann asks in *Beckett and Poststructuralism*:

> What if even the truth of your own voice were brought into question, or further still the existence of your *own* voice? Your own voice as source that is, the source of your own story. How could the voice be said to be your own when it merely recounts stories which may concern you, but always at one remove? One begins to feel the ground fall away. Such a groundless homeland, resembling, perhaps, a sojourn in war-torn France, is traversed by Beckett in *The Unnamable*. (Uhlmann 1999, 155)

Even the notion of Beckett as a fixed and stable author of the text is called into question. Maurice Blanchot, when trying to establish who is speaking in the text, suggests that 'We might try to say it was the "author" if this name did not evoke capacity and control, but in any case the man who writes is already no longer Samuel Beckett' (Blanchot 1993b, 88). Blanchot refers to the novel as a kind of 'word experiment', where the reader is constantly attempting 'to recover the security of a name, to situate the book's "content" at the stable level of a person' (88). If what occurs in the text can be related back to the 'guarantee of a consciousness' (88), then the text will simultaneously secure both historical testimony and the position of the humanist subject. To lose the security of the name, Blanchot suggests, leads to the 'worst degradation, that of losing the power to say *I*' (88).

In Beckett's work, language enacts a traumatic departure. At the moment that 'I' is spoken, written, or thought, the individual becomes anonymous to itself. The 'I' marks the removal of individual identity, and the partial, spectral return of others who have used and repeated it. This might be read as characteristic of what Roman Jakobson calls 'the peculiarity of the personal pronoun and other shifters [that were often] believed to consist in the lack of a single, constant, general meaning' (Jakobson 1990, 388). *The Unnamable* roams from one narrative voice to the next - Basil transforms into Mahood, Mahood becomes Worm, which must, in turn, 'be rejected as the Unnamable seeks the voice more truly his own' (Ackerley and Gontarski 2004, 652). The notion of the self as a source of truth is undermined by its ceaseless search for presence and stability:

> It's the fault of the pronouns, there is no name for me, no pronoun for me, all the trouble comes from that, that, it's a kind of pronoun too, it isn't that either, I'm not that either, let us leave all that, forget about all that, it's not difficult (*U*, 123)

The Unnamable forbids the possibility of a fixed subject position, and so denies an authoritative space from which to speak. Daniel Katz discusses this problem in detail in his study of Beckett's prose, *Saying I No More*:

> The effect of narration in *The Unnamable*, however, not only has no name by which 'it' could be referred to, or refer to itself, but in addition *it cannot even refer 'itself' through the use of a pronoun.* That is why Beckett's prose so relentlessly attacks the implicit deixis of the implicit 'I' which lurks behind any utterance, no matter how 'neutral'. The effect of narration in *The Unnamable* could not even *hypothetically* speak 'in its own name'. (Katz 1999, 80)

Proper names and pronouns, along with ideas of origin and authorship, are deconstructed by the text. Language perpetually shifts toward and away from any apparent goal, and the narrative voice is continually misplaced. What remains, Blanchot suggests, is the paradoxical spectral entity of The Unnamable itself:

> a being without being, who can neither live nor die, neither begin nor leave off, the empty site in which an empty voice is raised without effect, masked for better or worse by a porous and agonizing *I*. (Blanchot 1993b, 88)

The physical act of walking, as described in Beckett's immediate post-war fiction, conveyed the problems of Western narratives of progress. Here, in his later novel, the instability of a post-war European landscape can be felt in the instability of language itself. Language is presented not as a transparent system that allows power, control and the elucidation of truth; rather, it is an ambiguous space where beginnings and endings blend and collide, and subjectivity disperses:

> our concern is with someone, or our concern is with something, now we're getting it, someone or something that is not there, or that is not anywhere, or that is there, here, why not, after all, and our concern is with speaking of that, now we've got it, you don't know why, why you must speak of that, but there it is, you can't speak of that, no one can speak of that, you speak of yourself, someone speaks of himself, that's it, in the singular, a single one, the man on duty, he, I, no matter, the man on duty speaks of himself, it's not that, of others, it's not that either, he doesn't know, how could he know, whether he has spoken of that or not, when speaking of himself, when speaking of others, when speaking of things, how can I know, I can't know, if I've spoken of him, I can only speak of me, no, I can't speak of anything, and yet I speak, perhaps it's of him, I'll never know, how could I know, who could know, who knowing could tell me, I don't know who it's all about, that's all I know, no, (*U*, 123)

The evocation of 'the man on duty' implies not only a sense of vigilance, but an ethical imperative to record, or take account. Yet the man cannot be distinguished between first and third person pronouns ('he, I'), a fact that seems of little relevance to the narrator, who perhaps playfully casts doubt on the figure's corporeal existence ('no matter'). The concern, or imperative, to speak of something, is perpetually delayed or confused by an inability to finally establish the context, status or identity of that 'something'. With this in mind, if the speaking subject is an emblem of individual agency and mastery over one's surroundings, then the inability to stabilise the self through language signals the loss of that power. The 'man on duty' becomes a symbol of powerlessness in the face of endless deferrals and ambiguities.

In Maurice Blanchot's account, it is the concern of literature itself to mediate a point between vigilance and impossibility, a limit or boundary where all possibilities become untenable. Speaking of *The Unnamable*, he writes:

> We will find it rather in the movement which, as the work tries to reach its conclusion, bears it toward that point where it is at grips with impossibility, where the flux and reflux of the eternal recommencement draws it on: excess of impotence, sterile prolixity, a spring, a source which somehow must be dried up in order to become a *resource*. Here the voice does not speak, it *is*, in itself nothing begins, nothing is said, but it is always new and always beginning again. (91)

The literary text progresses according to an accumulation of statements, but their relation to a final truth, or final signified, remains unclear. There appears to be no final marker of stability that will resolve the meaning of the text; instead, the status of the work lies precisely in the interrogation of fixed meanings and significations. And so, the shifting and unstable status of language and meaning in Blanchot's notion of the literary text reveals a troubling portrait of the Western humanist subject. As Steven Connor writes of *The Unnamable*, the text attempts to 'press through, beyond or behind the first person, to the anonymous, tormented space of writing itself' (Connor 2010, xx-xxi). Beckett's prose demarcates a space which animates questions of language and meaning, dissolving the assumption of a literary text as 'a single, bounded work' (xx-xxi), and in doing so, fragments concrete notions of a rational humanist subject.

Literature presents us with worldly objects in an unworldly context, making it hard to determine or impose empirical standards of truth or certainty. Just as walking is an outwardly observable act that cannot be properly determined as such (since the act means precisely to move, roam and ramble), then literature, too, in the words of Maurice Blanchot, 'by its very activity, denies the substance of what it represents. This is its law and its truth' (Blanchot 1995, 310). Samuel Beckett's work appears to capitalise on these paradoxes. In his preface to the early post-war novel *Molloy*, Shane Weller notes that Beckett compared writing it to 'taking a walk' (Weller 2009, ix).[55] This, in part, refers to the spontaneous way the text was composed: 'I hadn't planned it, or thought it out at all', the writer revealed (ix). In this

---

55 Beckett related his experience to John Pilling.

sense, walking is invoked as an act that is random, unplanned and impulsive. But the comparison could also refer to the qualities that define the paradoxical language of Beckett's post-war literature: its disorientation, its disarray, and its strange, traumatic temporality. As the text splits, fragments, and diversifies, so too does the construction of the rational humanist subject. This is not a process of reaction or confrontation, where a text plots or arranges a systemised critique: the deconstruction occurs within the representation itself, through the act of inscription or enunciation of language.

This chapter has limited itself to Beckett's immediate post-war writing and "*The Three Novels*" that followed, but walking is a symbol that recurs throughout the writer's lengthy career. In *Texts for Nothing*, nameless protagonists wander through landscapes surrounded by 'heath up to the knees, faint sheep-tracks, troughs scooped deep by the rains' (*TN*, 3). *From an Abandoned Work* retraces memories during the course of a morning walk: 'I have never in my life been on my way anywhere, but simply on my way' (*FAW*, 57). Even the closed-place narratives of Beckett's later work adopt motifs of roaming and wandering in ways that challenge definitions of presence, absence and identity; *The Lost Ones* is a good example of this, outlining an 'Abode where lost bodies roam each searching for its lost one' (*LO*, 101). And that is to say nothing of the role walking plays in Beckett's final extended prose works, *Company*, *Ill Seen Ill Said*, *Worstward Ho* and *Stirrings Still.* The trope of walking is a connecting pathway through Beckett's work, from his lengthy prose texts to his late avant-garde minimalist theatre. It is suggestive of shadowy figures haunting country roads, and the troubled ghostly voices that roam from memory to reflection to speculation, before seeming to disappear altogether.

2. Theatre: Late Stage

Late Words

Beginning to End

Is Samuel Beckett a writer of last words? His work is certainly preoccupied with what we might call 'last things': there are the last pain-killers and sugar-plums of *Endgame*, the last of the toothpaste in *Happy Days*, to say nothing of his 1958 play, *Krapp's Last Tape*. The word 'last' also carries a certain currency in critical interpretations, and appears to be the last word on the writer. John Banville's essay on Beckett's final prose works was published as 'Beckett's Last Words' (Banville 2006). Anthony Cronin's weighty biography of the writer was entitled *The Last Modernist* (Cronin 1999). In each case, the word seems intended to denote authority, even a sense of grandeur or stateliness—and perhaps with good reason. Beckett's texts could be read as critical or even philosophical reflections on last words or last things: an engagement with what remains, of what is left when all else has disappeared. Jacques Derrida considers remains as the signature theme of Beckett's oeuvre, the embodiment of the 'remainder which remains when the thematics are exhausted' (Derrida 1992, 60). What do we mean by the 'last' if not that which remains at the very end? Christopher Ricks makes an incisive point in his monograph, *Beckett's Dying Words*, by signalling the two meanings of the word: 'last' can signify either 'finality and extinction or, rather the reverse, endurance and continuance' (Ricks 1993, 113). If last words really do last, in an indefinite sense, perhaps this accounts for Beckett's longevity in the public sphere, and the continuing proliferation of academic debates. Last words, after all, suggest both resolution and disharmony; they begin to make an end but resist the final closing gesture.

This attribute, common to many of Beckett's texts, is, in itself, worthy of close inspection. Beckett's prose and drama experiment with conventional ideas of temporality, and raise a number of questions for our understanding of language, representation and the humanist subject. But, before continuing, I would suggest that the term 'last' is perhaps not entirely appropriate. The word complicates our understanding of time in one way, but unavoidably privileges a linear historical narrative. Last words remain because they are deemed culturally and historically significant: they present the culmination of a dialectical[1] struggle, a resolution or conclusion that Western society purposely preserves as guiding signifiers of knowledge and wisdom. Not to mention the fact that no sooner are so-called last words written or spoken than they are replaced or superseded. In *Specters of Marx*, Jacques Derrida noted that 'the media parade of current discourse on the end of history and the last man looks most often like a tiresome anachronism' (Derrida 2012, 16). The word 'last' signifies a system of standardized order, a hierarchy of meaning and significance that Beckett's texts often radically undermine. As Mark Nixon describes, the 'tension between beginning and ending, the beginning that already always incorporates an ending, and the ending that is always a new beginning, is of course a well-rehearsed theme in Beckett Studies' (Nixon 2009, 22). While the word 'last' can be useful to us, I would stress that it does not go far enough. Instead, I shall adopt an alternative term. The word 'late' might help us to engage with Samuel Beckett's writing in the aftermath of the Second World War in new and interesting ways. It is a word that invokes the radical temporality of the writer's works, whilst stressing their strange resistance to a final interpretation, authority, or resting place.

---

1 I use the expression 'dialectic' here in relation to Hegel's notion of the term: that is to say, that the progression of Western history is characterised by a relationship formed by a dialectical struggle between opposing events or ideas (thesis and antithesis) that combine to move civilisation forward in a state of unity (synthesis) towards a fixed and harmonious ideal state.

Lateness

One of the most influential contemporary accounts of lateness is Edward Said's *On Late Style: Music and Literature Against the Grain*. The work first emerged into public light in 2006, Samuel Beckett's centenary year, but its final compositional arrangement was agreed three years after Said's death in September 2003. Miriam C. Said recounts the circumstances in a moving foreword, noting that the author had amassed a 'tremendous amount of material' towards the end of his life which allowed Miriam Said and others to 'finish it and produce posthumously a version of what he had in mind' (Said 2007, vii). *On Late Style* stands as a reminder (remainder) of the way lateness can prompt an examination of timely assumptions.

Samuel Beckett does not appear within the pages of Said's study, but his work nonetheless exerts a kind of spectral influence over the proceedings. *On Late Style* is largely inspired by the work of 'a theorist of late style and of endgames' (Said 2007, 20), namely the Frankfurt School cultural critic Theodor W. Adorno and, specifically, his writing about the music of Beethoven. Beckett exerted a strong influence on Adorno's thinking during crucial periods of his life, and it is notable that Adorno intended to dedicate his magnum opus, *Aesthetic Theory* (1970), to the Nobel laureate;[2] this landmark study of the aesthetics and Western capitalist modernity was, like *On Late Style*, published posthumously from various drafts and fragments. As it happens, Michael Wood's introduction to *On Late Style* begins with a line from Beckett's literary study, *Proust*: '"Death has not required us to keep a day free," Samuel Beckett writes with grim and intricate irony' (Wood 2007, xi). The theme of death and an artist's mature work are key motivators in Said's book, but more importantly, the notion of

---

2 SB to Adorno, 15 February 1969: 'So glad your work has been going well and look forward keenly to *Ästhetische Theorie*. I am at an utter standstill on all fronts.', qtd. in Beckett, Samuel, *The Letters of Samuel Beckett, Volume IV: 1966-1989*, eds. George Craig, Martha Dow Fehsenfeld, Dan Gunn, and Lois More Overbeck (Cambridge: Cambridge University Press, 2016), 151.

'late' style' as Said conceives it can help us to reexamine our abiding assumptions about autonomy and self-mastery.

In 'Samuel Beckett and the Contingency of Old Age', Elizabeth Barry assesses the writer's personal conception of ageing, maturity, and late style:

> Beckett had been anticipating and identifying with the experience of old age for most of his life—not for the wisdom, philosophical or aesthetic maturity of even rancorous energy that it might popularly be expected to afford, but, imaginatively at least, for a diminishing of powers that might force upon a writer the qualities he had in fact been seeking all along. (Barry 2016, 206)

Barry identifies a kind of ironic inversion of popular expectations of the maturing artist, where the progression of time marks a decrease in one's powers, skills, and abilities. Beckett's writing is thus a body of work that deliberately undermines and unsettles authorial authority, alongside any notions of a proper time or place.

Said's first essay in *On Late Style*, 'Timeliness and Lateness', explores a temporal opposition between that which belongs to order and linearity, and that which does not. The essay opens by suggesting an admittedly 'irrelevant and perhaps even trivial' relationship 'between bodily condition and aesthetic style' (Said 2007, 3). To put it another way, Said poses a question: 'are there unique qualities of perception and form that artists acquire as a result of age in the late phase of their career?' Said points out that we commonly assume a correspondence between an artist's life and their work, but narrows his focus to what the correspondence might signify towards the end of an artist's life, or period of creativity. Said seeks to investigate the cultural tendency to connect age with wisdom and understanding, or maturity with mastery. The study plays out this dynamic in a number of interesting ways, but what is most poignant to a reading of trauma and subjectivity in Samuel Beckett's work is the way Said addresses some of the assumptions that we bring to our understanding of time and timeliness.

Said notes that when we consider the grounded origins of an event or an artistic work, there is an element of undecidibility inherent to the process: 'To locate a beginning in retrospective time is to ground a project (such as an experiment, or a governmental commission, or Dickens's beginning to write *Bleak House*) in that moment, which is always subject to revision. Beginnings of this sort necessarily involve an intention that is either fulfilled, totally or in part, or is viewed as totally failed, in successive time' (4-5). This uncertain starting point subsequently gives rise to a series of efforts, creations, or events that develop or evolve towards a logical endpoint or resolution. Said borrows the expression 'dialectic of incarnation' to define the timely movement from birth to reproduction and maturity, and identifies it as central to many Western aesthetic traditions:

> there is the bildungsroman or novel of education, the novel of idealism and disappointment [...], the novel of immaturity and community [...]. Other aesthetic forms, in music and painting, follow similar patterns. (5)

In contrast, Said directs our attention to aesthetic works that buck the trend of timely progression, providing a stark 'deviation from the overall assumed pattern to human life' (5). Works such as Jonathan Swift's *Gulliver's Travels*, Fyodor Dostoevsky's *Crime and Punishment*, and Franz Kafka's *The Trial*. These works, for Said, 'break away from the amazingly persistent underlying compact between the notion of the successive ages of man (as in Shakespeare) and aesthetic reflections of and on them'. To put this another way, Said identifies a category of texts which somehow unsettle, undermine, or refract conventional understandings of appropriate temporal progression, and the cultural expectations we attach to such progression. Samuel Beckett's post-war writing can also be characterised in terms of its deviation, its aesthetic break, its unsettling of the successive ages of man. In fact, for Franz Kafka's acclaimed biographer Reiner Stach the Irish writer goes far beyond what the Prague insurance clerk could bear in his own writing; as he began writing *The Castle* (yet another posthumously published work), Stach describes Kafka as 'standing at the threshold of Samuel Beckett, and unprepared to endure it' (Stach 2013, 422).

Beckett's texts unsettle the typical pattern that Said identifies whereby 'late works crown a lifetime of aesthetic endeavour', and instead explore notions of helplessness, lessness, and impotence. They embody, in their own spectral way, Said's reclaiming of artistic lateness as 'intransigence, difficulty, and unresolved contradiction' (Said 2007, 7). A state whereby age and ill health do not produce serenity, in Said's phrase, but a 'contradictory, alienated relationship' (8) to the established social order. Beckett's post-war writing for page and stage can be read alongside Said's description of Beethoven's late style, as a 'bristling, difficult, and unyielding—perhaps even inhuman—challenge'; as works that 'remain unreconciled, uncoopted by a higher synthesis'; and, finally, as compositions that are 'in fact about "lost totality", and are therefore catastrophic' (12-3). As we shall see throughout Beckett's texts, the traumatic symptomology that haunts his later work often revolves around some kind of break in a totalizing modernity, a catastrophe that prompts a crisis of knowledge and values. It is work that stresses 'apartness and exile and anachronism' (17). Its style is '*in*, but oddly *apart* from the present' (24).

While Beckett's late period is most commonly bracketed to the last two decades of his life (1970s-1980s),[3] I would like to make the case that we can read all of those works written and published after 1945 as 'late'. They are late in the sense that they typify what we commonly characterize as late modernism; they are late insofar as they mark a transformation in Beckett's approach to writing;[4] and they are

---

3 See Steven Matthews' fascinating reading of Said and the 'late style' of Beckett's final decade in 'Beckett's Late Style', *Samuel Beckett and Death*, eds. Steven Barfield, Matthew Feldman, and Philip Tew (London: Continuum, 2009), 188-205.

4 For a lengthy discussion of the biographical influences for Samuel Beckett's artistic transformation, which was precipitated by a number of personal, historical and cultural factors, see James Knowlson's excellent biography *Damned to Fame: The Life of Samuel Beckett* (London: Bloomsbury,

late in the way that they unravel the orderliness of linear histories, and utilize disharmony and anachronism to shed new light on the status of identity in the era of (late) modernity. And so, what I choose to call Beckett's 'late stage' comprises elements of Adorno and Said's 'late style'; these texts can help to elucidate Beckett's complex representation of traumatic experience in the post-war era.

Stage Presence

Even Beckett's earliest plays are late. The earliest, *Eleutheria*, is perhaps the latest of all: first published by Les Éditions de Minuit in 1995, some six years after the writer's death in 1989. To date, the play has never been produced for the theatre, making it—in some sense—later than all of Beckett's last works. We are still waiting for it. The same can be said for Beckett's second play, *Waiting for Godot*, an inventive and engaging dramatization of lateness itself: two men wait on a country road for a man who never arrives. Vivian Mercier famously described the two-act work in a review entitled 'The Uneventful Event' as 'a play in which nothing happens, *twice*'.[5] Of course, Mercier's remark is hyperbolic: there is conversation between characters, punctuated by various arrivals and departures. But the eponymous Godot does not appear, and the introduction of other characters does little but accentuate his absence. Theatre critic Kenneth Tynan described the play as a 'dramatic vacuum', a production with 'no plot, no climax, no *dénouement*; no beginning, no middle and no end'.[6] As Dominick LaCapra points out in his essay, 'Trauma, Absence, Loss': '[works by Beckett] tend not to include events in any significant way and seem to be abstract, evacuated, or disembodied. In them "nothing" happens, which makes them devoid of interest from a conventional perspective'

1996). Of particular interest is Knowlson's chapter, 'Aftermath of War, 1945-6', 340-55 (351).

5 Vivian Mercier, 'The Uneventful Event' in *The Irish Times*, 18 February 1956.

6 Kenneth Tynan, 'New Writing', *The Observer*, 7 August 1955.

(LaCapra 1999, 701). The play's non-arrivant destabilizes the conventions that structure dramatic productions: the temporal present in *Godot* cannot denote presence in the traditional sense, but only an absence and anticipation of what is still to come:

> ESTRAGON: We are happy. [*Silence.*] What do we do now, now that we are happy?
>
> VLADIMIR: Wait for Godot. [estragon *groans. Silence.*] Things have changed since yesterday.
>
> ESTRAGON: And if he doesn't come?
>
> VLADIMIR: [*After a moment of bewilderment.*] We'll see when the time comes. (*WFG*, 55)

Other earlier plays are late, too, in their ways. *Endgame* and *Happy Days* dramatize worlds that orbit around last words and scant remains: they present post-apocalyptic worlds that are almost but not-quite apocalyptic. The plays curiously refuse endings or conclusions, with the end of each production hinting towards what has been left unsaid, undone or unresolved. Beckett's plays evoke landscapes that never quite belong to the present, but hover indeterminately between a past that is forever lost and a future resolution that is never realized. Beckett's writing for the stage calls into question the possibility—or impossibility—of live theatre as such: an art-form structured around traditional Western assumptions of time, presence and resolution.

To understand how the term 'late' unsettles our understanding of dramatic theatre, it is worth taking a closer look at the vocabulary that defines it. The word 'stage', for instance, signifies the physical edifice and platform that mediates the dramatic spectacle: it is literally the thing on which performance rests. The OED defines a stage, quite unambiguously, as 'something to stand upon',[7] and in this sense is the solid, material foundation of traditional theatre. But the word holds another popular usage, relating explicitly to temporality. A stage can

[7] 'Stage', in OED (2017), accessed January 3, 2017, http://www.oed.com.

denote a fixed moment, or period, of time; it can also mean a point, or step, in a process or journey. In this other sense, the word is positively linked to standardized notions of empirical certainty: a stage is both observable and graspable as a unit or component of time and space. Thus, our expectations of theatre rest on the foundation of an assumed temporal accountability, of live presence. And yet, Samuel Beckett's productions act to disrupt and confound this expectatation. The opening stage direction of *Krapp's Last Tape*, for instance, renders the play impossible: 'A late evening in the future' (*K*, 3). Notably, the stage direction binds the word 'late' to a notion of a not-yet-present future, emphasizing the impossibility of either beginning or ending. Evening, too, signals an indeterminate period of temporal transition between day and night, light and darkness. The promise of conclusion, resolution and final unity so common to traditional dramatic performance is deferred from the outset.

Beckett's disorderly treatment of time is often linked to traumatic events. Dominick LaCapra, in his book *Writing History, Writing Trauma*, suggests that we can understand Beckett's creative output, alongside the work of Paul Celan, as a 'relatively safe haven in which to explore post-traumatic effects' (LaCapra 2001, 180). Beckett's texts engage with the issue of trauma in a distinctive and complex way. In this light, the term 'late' is analogous to Sigmund Freud's concept of 'belatedness', conceived of by psychoanalyst Jean Laplanche as a condition of 'afterwardsness'.[8] The traumatic symptom is defined as a late repetition, the belated return of an obscure past event that was once repressed by the subject. Accordingly, traumatic narratives and testimonies can never approximate a source or root cause; they are late, and so are always positioned at a temporal distance from their object. In Cathy Caruth's account, trauma is a shock that resembles a physical threat, which is inassimilable in the present: it can only be observed belatedly, in the future, and as such forces 'a break in the mind's experience of time' (Caruth 1996, 61). Roger Luckhurst suggests that this

8 See Jean Laplanche, 'Notes on Afterwardsness' in *Essays on Otherness*, trans. J. Fletcher (London: Routledge, 1999), 260-5.

temporal disruption is the principal condition of all traumatic accounts: 'No narrative of trauma can be told in a linear way: it has a time signature that must fracture conventional causality' (Luckhurst 2008, 9). Trauma ruptures established understandings of time, linearity, and cause and effect. This chapter traces the implications of such issues in *Not I*, *That Time* and *Footfalls*, while examining problems inherent in the representation of traumatic accounts.[9] Utilizing a space outside standard historical time, troubling the distinction between beginnings and endings, the plays explore the relationship between language, live representation and the traumatic event.

9 For the purposes of this discussion, I have narrowed my focus to three 'late' texts in Beckett's oeuvre. I should stress that the themes I discuss are applicable to many of the writer's dramatic works, both major and minor.

Not I

Acting Out

Not I, first published by Faber and Faber in January 1973, is perhaps one of the most distinguished traumatic stage-works of the twentieth century. James Knowlson and John Pilling describe it as a play of 'scalding intensity and [an] overpowering nature' (Knowlson and Pilling 1979, 195). In Jonathan Boulter's reading, the play is the testimony of an assault, a trauma that 'has propelled [its protagonist] into speech, into language' (Boulter 2008, 73). For Eileen Fischer, the play responds to troubling events in the protagonist's personal history by finally articulating 'what should have been said in the past' (Fischer 1979, 101). The speaker in *Not I* appears as a disembodied mouth, presented in the context of a darkened stage. Early productions of the play also included an Auditor figure, 'sex undeterminable', standing 'enveloped head to foot in [a] loose black djellaba' (*NI*, 85). Beckett's text unfolds through the implementation of a winding and fragmented monologue, punctuated by short pauses, longer silences, laughs and screams. First performed by Billie Whitelaw on 16 January 1973, Mouth's speech was delivered at a rapid rate, describing circumstances surrounding an ambiguous traumatic event in a female protagonist's past. *Not I* conforms in this way to Caruth's identification of the traumatic story as 'the narrative of a belated experience' (Caruth 1996, 7). In *Not I*, the audience is invited to witness a form of traumatic testimony, where a partially forgotten violence from the past stages a return in the present.

In Cathy Caruth's writing on trauma, she evokes a parable of the wound and the voice: 'trauma seems to be much more than a pathology, or the simple illness of a wounded psyche', she writes, 'it is always the story of a wound that cried out, that addresses us in the attempt to tell us of a reality or truth that is not otherwise available' (4). It might be possible to interpret the mouth, in this context, as a kind of wound, an open wound that articulates a trauma to an Auditor, or listeners in the audience. The analogy, after all, is not new in Beckett's work. In *Molloy*, for instance, we find the line 'eyes and mouth and other wounds' (*Mo*, 155), drawing an explicit connection between traumatic physical injury and the means by which events are witnessed or articulated. Caruth is careful to point out that the voice issuing from the wound is not a guarantor of truth, *per se*, but guides our attention toward an unspecified incident: 'The truth, in its delayed appearance and its belated address, cannot be linked only to what is known, but also to what remains unknown in our very actions and our language' (4). Notions of truth and certainty become complex and thorny issues in traumatic narratives, made thornier still by our attempts to secure them.

But what makes *Not I* exemplary for a discussion of trauma? How are we to understand the play in accordance with contemporary trauma theory? Paradoxically, what makes Beckett's dramatic text illuminating to us is its refusal to represent the very events at the heart of its narrative. The play never directly addresses, approaches, or approximates trauma as such, but accentuates our distance and separation from it. Referring once again to Caruth's research in this area, what 'returns to haunt the victim [...] is not only the reality of the violent event but also the reality of the way that its violence has not yet been fully known' (6). In *Not I*, the reality of the event remains unclear, and seems permanently obscured by incomplete descriptions and vague inferences. It is not a complete and reliable account, but only the assertion of what is not yet fully known, perhaps what will never be known. In one section of the text, Mouth describes a scene where the hitherto silent female protagonist is overwhelmed by an urgent need to speak while waiting in line at a busy shopping centre. The voice begins to utter at a speed incomprehensible to the speaker:

> … and now this stream … not catching the half of it … not the quarter … no idea … what she was saying … imagine! … no idea what she was saying! … (*NI*, 89)

The protagonist is overpowered by a compulsion to speak to the point where utterance seems independent of either free will or conscious awareness. The speech is delivered rapidly, without form or clarity, and disfigures the distinction between the present - as it occurs - and memories of the past:

> ... straining to hear ... piece it together ... and the brain ... raving away on its own ... trying to make sense of it ... or make it stop ... or in the past ... dragging up the past ... flashes from all over ... (90)

In correspondence, Beckett stressed to directors and actresses that he was not concerned with the intelligibility of Mouth's dialogue, but wanted the performance 'to work on the nerves of the audience'.[10] This, in turn, would make the production a simulation of the traumatic experience itself, playing on unintelligibility and psychological distress. But while the play might enact a simulation of trauma for its audience,[11] the text is equally concerned with the problem of its representation. This neatly coincides with Caruth's assertion that 'trauma is not locatable in the simple violent or original event in an individual's past, but rather in the way that its very unassimilated nature—the way it was precisely *not known* in the first instance—returns to haunt the survivor later on' (Caruth 1996, 4). And so, while productions of *Not I* might simulate or dramatize a certain kind of traumatic experience, the event, or 'assault', does not fully resurface. The historical trauma that Mouth attempts to articulate does not manifest itself as action on the stage, but remains strangely absent from the scene: while the forceful violence of Mouth's performance is traumatic for the performer and spectator alike, the deeper trauma of the narrative remains unseen, unheard, and irretrievable.

I would consider *Not I* as a dramatic demonstration of what is referred to in trauma theory as the 'working-through' process. The

10 Samuel Beckett, qtd. in *The Grove Companion to Samuel Beckett*, ed. C. J. Ackerley and S. E. Gontarski (New York: Grove Press, 2004), 411.

11 Johnathan Boulter: 'What the audience primarily feels—and I speak from personal experience here—is anxiety' in *Beckett: A Guide for the Perplexed* (London: Continuum, 2008), 72.

production proceeds by 'acting out' a narrative that attempts to name and classify events, and, in doing so, seeks resolution. The concept of 'working through' is psychoanalytic in origin, devised by Sigmund Freud as a method of treating traumatized patients under analysis. In a therapeutic context, the process is gradual, where a patient discovers enlightening information through acts of remembrance, or where a situation is created allowing the patient to resolve a conflict, absence or loss. This method, which aims to 'fill the gaps in the patient's memory' allows the subject, in one and the same moment, 'to overcome the resistances brought about by repression' (Freud 2003, 34). When successful, working-through enacts a process of revelation, enabling the patient to realize the 'full implications of some interpretation or insight'.[12] This may include, but is not limited to, overcoming 'a loss or painful experience', as in the process of mourning, 'since it involves the piecemeal recognition that the lost object is no longer available in a host of contexts in which he [*sic.*] was previously a familiar figure'.[13] These processes of remembering, repeating, and acting out, for Freud, offer a 'means of controlling the patient's compulsion to repeat, and turning it into a means of activating memory' (Freud 2003, 40). *Not I* enacts several principles of the procedure. By staging the return to a latent traumatic episode in the protagonist's memory, the speech operates as a method of making-present, or re-presenting, the past: 'something she had to … tell …' (*NI*, 91).

Claude Lanzmann has expressed the importance of working-through as a way to approach the traumatic after-effects of historical atrocity. Discussing his 1985 documentary film, *Shoah*, an oral history of the Holocaust recounted by witnesses and survivors, Lanzmann describes the working-through process as a way 'to connect, to link up, to accomplish the whole work of rememoration' (Lanzmann 1995, 211). Dominick LaCapra also seizes on the practical applications of the method to the treatment of post-traumatic effects:

---

12 'Working through' in *A Critical Dictionary of Psychoanalysis*, 2nd edition, ed. Charles Rycroft (London: Penguin, 1995), 199-200.

13 Rycroft, ed., 'Working through', 199-200.

> working through does not mean avoidance, harmonization, simply forgetting the past; or submerging oneself in the present. It means coming to terms with the trauma, including its details, and critically engaging the tendency to act out the past and even to recognize why it may be necessary and even in certain respects desirable or at least compelling. (The latter is especially the case with respect to a fidelity to trauma and its victims, that there is something in the repetition of the past—that amounts to dedication or fidelity to lost loved ones and is a kind of memorial that is not based on suppression or oblivion.) (LaCapra 2001, 144)

In LaCapra's account, working-through requires an active and participatory engagement with the circumstances of the traumatizing event. He describes this process as a 'coming to terms', likening the treatment to a pursuit for correct vocabulary: a search for the terms that best describe or accommodate what is inconceivable about the event itself. *Not I* is a theatrical adaptation of this impossible search, where empirical markers and temporal certainties are no sooner uttered than they seem unreliable, or slip out of reach. Place names such as Croker's Acres, or the description of a distant bell, cannot return the protagonist to the original scene, and do little to concretize the events described. Working-through is problematized in *Not I*. The play's traumatic narrative is unresponsive to rational investigation, temporal logic, or the meaning of linguistic terms. Instead of accomplishing a 'whole work' of memory and considered reflection, the text emphasizes difference, disorder and confusion.

At first glance, the play appears to offer a straightforward exemplification of the process. Mouth's speech, for example, can be interpreted as a form of 'acting out', described by LaCapra as a repetitive process 'whereby the past, or the experience of the other, is repeated as if it were fully enacted, fully literalized' (LaCapra 2001, 148). In this way, Mouth's narrative appears to enact, or make-present, the force and shock of a traumatic event:

> In acting out, one relives the past as if one *were* the other, including oneself as another in the past—one is fully possessed by the other or the other's ghost: and in working through, one tries to acquire

> some critical distance that allows one to engage in life in the present, to assume responsibility—but that doesn't mean that you utterly transcend the past. It means that you come to terms with it in a different way related to what you judge to be desirable possibilities that may now be created, including possibilities that lost out in the past but may still be recaptured and reactivated, with significant differences, in the present and future. (148)

According to this understanding, we might infer that Mouth is identifiable as the female protagonist described in the monologue. Mouth's disavowal of the first-person singular, and the lack of identification with the female protagonist, is a necessary step towards working-through, as LaCapra conceives it. There are four points in the text where such a disavowal explicitly occurs, provoking a gesture of 'helpless compassion' from the silent Auditor (*NI*, 83).[14] The refrain runs: '… what? … who? … no! … she! …' (92), climaxing in the final moments of the play with '… what? … who? … no! … she! … she! …' (92). The exclamations may be ascribed, as suggested in a note by Beckett, as a 'vehement refusal to relinquish third person' (83). This form of disassociation allows a sense of critical distance in the mind of the patient, or narrator, and affords a greater opportunity to describe (come to terms with) events by using an objective, objectifying method.

However, whilst *Not I* exemplifies the 'acting out' process (and its characteristic disassociation), it simultaneously calls it into question. If the narrative is attempting a discourse of objectivity, or at least attempts to claim distance from the event, it still does not seem

14 The role of the Auditor in *Not I* is significant as the anonymous listener who may be prompting Mouth to speak, perhaps fulfilling a therapeutic function. In this light, we might consider the figure of the Auditor as analogous to the psychoanalyst, a listener who allows a traumatic narrative to be heard, and in such a capacity is able to guide the working-through process towards a therapeutic end. I shall not focus explicitly on the Auditor in this study, as the role was removed from later productions of the play, and the 1973 television adaptation overlooked by Beckett himself.

to offer any great clarity or insight. The monologue is a testimony insofar as it attempts to recall the past, but it is a recall that is only ever partial. The speech is fragmented and incomplete, punctuated (punctured) throughout with ellipses, silences, and ambiguous gestures. Punishment and suffering are alluded to, but are defined in passing by irrationality, by the lack of a causal relationship. Each emotional response seems to occur 'for its own sake', prompted by 'some sin or other … or for the lot … or no particular reason' (86-7). In many cases, a symptom of sadness or suffering is presented without any apparent cause. For instance, Mouth recounts the protagonist on her way home one evening, 'sitting staring at her hand … there in her lap … palm upward … suddenly saw it wet … the palm … tears presumably … hers presumably …' (90). Allusions are made to an incident one April morning, but not enough information is disclosed to attempt an understanding: the protagonist is said to be grabbing at the straw, straining to hear, or make sense, of some 'odd word' (91). There are also references to a judicial procedure, 'that time in court', where she had waited to be led away 'guilty or not' (91). Themes of sin, guilt and punishment become meaningless without the presence of causality, in a narrative that corrupts all expectations of conventional time. The traumatic event itself seems condemned to remain in the past, forbidding any hope of satisfactory closure. It is too late to accurately recount the traumatic event, to explain it, to resolve it.

It is in this way that *Not I* both elucidates and complicates our understanding of the working-through process. The suggestion that events and possibilities once lost might be, in LaCapra's terms, recaptured and reactivated 'with significant differences' (LaCapra 2001, 148), is rendered problematic by Mouth. The monologue attempts to return to the past in a way that is continually unsettled and undermined, while the possibility of enacting a semblance of the original event with 'significant differences' is not viable without an original observable event with which to compare. What we are left with, it seems, is an impasse to understanding. Why is the project of working-through or acting out not a success in *Not I*? The problem seems to lie in assumptions surrounding the method and its dependence upon a linear chronological narrative. Working-through is reliant on the idea of return, of reappearance, of acting out or staging a comeback—ideas that hinge on a stable and corresponding relationship between the present and the past. This assumption also informs and stabilizes Western ideas of presence, individual agency, and the ability to decide or determine one's circumstances. In other words, working-through assumes that by re-locating past events within a graspable present, they become subject to our assumed control, and can thus be rendered benign, or at least instructive in some way. Beckett's treatment of time in *Not I* illustrates a limit to this understanding, destabilizing the correspondence between the present and the past by opening up a possibility of the 'late', the late that comes after all else, the late that has not yet arrived, the late that is an idea of the future.

The stage, in its most basic sense, is structured around the literal process of acting out. We have already observed etymological links between the stage and the assumption of a temporal present, making it an ideal space for the practice of working-through. And yet, the stage, as a foundation on which to stand in the present, rests upon a paradox. All stage presentations are necessarily structured in relation to a rehearsal: the organized repetition of a show (or 'recital'), in preparation for a later performance. Even when presentations comprise spontaneous and improvisational gestures, their presence remains rooted to this logic of repetition and rehearsal. Jacques Derrida observes in an interview with jazz musician Ornette Coleman that even 'the unique event that is produced only one time is nevertheless repeated in its very structure [...] there is repetition, in the work, that is intrinsic to the initial creation—that which compromises or complicates the concept of improvisation' (Derrida 2004, 322-3). For any action to be undertaken, it must pre-exist within the realms of the possible: with this in mind, spoken and written words become quotations or variations of previous words, while gestures conform to the limitations of the human body, while recalling or echoing movements and poses that have come before. The live stage performance, then, is traditionally perceived as a guarantor of presence, but there can be no performance without prior rehearsal; in this sense, the theatrical event is never contemporaneous, never present, but always alludes to a previous moment. Theatre is always late, and stage presence is always belated. In addition, the live performance itself—if such a thing exists at all—is always a repetition, or rehearsal, of an event that promises to take place in the future. Thus, working-through as a performance on the stage belongs neither to the past, present, or the future. It is a process that lacks any origin or telos, confounding explanation by existing outside the grasp of an observable, empirical present.

The play begins with a hermeneutic impasse, opening with the words: '… out … into this world …' (85). For the audience, the expression 'out into this world' might make sense in the narrative as an evocation of birth, or a linear movement from an interior space to an exterior space. But if we preserve the ellipses of the text, the pause or gap that structures the spoken performance, the play opens with two separate verbal statements that contradict each other, and seem to cancel each other out. What the audience might hear as an evocation of birth, perhaps signaling the beginning of the protagonist's life (and the start of the narrative), is a statement denoting two separate descriptions ('out' and 'into this world') of two distinct spaces, actions and times. And so, birth, in *Not I*, signals both a movement toward the realm of the world, of observable reality, and, simultaneously, an exile to an absolute outside, an exteriority that is unknown and undeterminable. The idea of beginning, from this perspective, is an origin that cannot be accurately established or surveyed.

Time is continually evoked in the opening moments of the play. The protagonist arrives 'before its time', 'before her time', prematurely born eight months into term, 'almost to the tick' (85); paradoxically, the child arrives before its own time, but arrives early almost exactly on time—almost to the tick. The monologue evokes a loveless life, 'nothing of any note' at 'any subsequent stage' (85) until the age of sixty. Sixty years of human life are compressed into a brief, fractured opening statement before, suddenly, a field is described. Mouth develops the narrative in the present tense, where 'a few steps then stop' (85-6) offers both an impression of ordered progression through time and space, and simultaneous negation.[15] Some thoughts occur 'oh long after' (87) the present of the narrative, corrupting its claim on the present tense, whilst other experiences occur 'all the time', denoting an inability to distinguish between past, present and future. Working-through in *Not I* is not simply an attempt to reconcile oneself with the past, but to rehearse a traumatic experience of disorientation and temporal suspension.

Coming to Terms

The word 'rehearsal' is etymologically rooted to terms that determine contemporary understandings of trauma; the same origins, in fact, also shape certain Western processes of grief and mourning. 'Rehearsal' derives from the French word 'herse', a noun that refers in English to an agricultural tool, or 'harrow', designed to divide and stir the soil. It is from this term that we derive the adjective 'harrowing', defined in the OED as something 'that harrows or lacerates the feelings', or something that is 'acutely distressing or painful'.[16] The signifier, 'rehearsal', is a term that is always already structured by associations with physical and psychological trauma; the act of rehearsal, then, can be considered as the staging or working through of an action that is, to some degree, inherently traumatic.[17]

Rehearsal shares its etymological roots with another word, 'hearse':[18] a term that denotes the placing of a corpse within a bier or coffin, transporting a dead body to a gravesite, or the burial of a body during a funeral ceremony. The term defines a social process that facilitates mourning: the performance of a coherent narrative where certain rites and passages are enacted, enabling closure for grieving family and friends. Rehearsal, in its theatrical sense, might also be considered as a kind of social ceremony, granting a sense of closure and resolution

---

15 See the discussion of *Footfalls* later in the chapter for a more expansive exploration of this theme

16 'Harrowing', in OED (2017), accessed January 3, 2017, http://www.oed.com.

17 See 'Rehearsal', in OED (2017), accessed January 3, 2017, http://www.oed.com.

18 See 'Hearse', in OED (2017), accessed January 3, 2017, http://www.oed.com.

for a future audience. The theoretical difference between the two terms, hearse and rehearse, is perhaps the difference between last and late: between the last rites and the rites that are always still to come. Where the hearse is a performance intended to enable closure, the rehearsal is a performance that forbids it, promising instead an infinite possible number of future repetitions. Whilst the rehearsal is timed to predate and preempt a specific performance event, it also inevitably exceeds it, since it is always related to an unspecified future point, a 'late' point that exists beyond the limit of a pre-arranged performance.

This idea of rehearsal offers a way to engage with what is traumatic about Beckett's *Not I*. It helps to explain the play's fractured temporality: the way that past, present and future are suspended, even dismantled in the text. Moreover, the notion of rehearsal might be used as a paradigm to understand traumatized subjectivity. (If the human subject is generally considered as an active agent, capable of mastering its surroundings in the present, the concept of rehearsal traumatically unravels its sovereignty.) The voice of the human subject in *Not I* is disembodied, removed from familiar contexts of time, place and identity.

Throughout the play, the notion of rehearsal is synonymous with the role that language plays. For instance, if rehearsal is that which both allows and prohibits memory and experience to be represented in performance, its paradoxical avowal and disavowal is structured by a relation to language. Language is at the centre of LaCapra's assertion that to 'come to terms' with a traumatic event is synonymous with remembrance. It is through language that Mouth is compelled to retrace footsteps into a troubled and disorientating past. Language allows the working-through process to occur. Even acting-out, where physical movements and gestures might attempt to grasp or repeat previous actions, is in some sense a process inaugurated through language. Billie Whitelaw alludes to this in her memoir when describing rehearsal sessions held with Samuel Beckett at her home: 'In *Not I*, as in *Play*, and again later when he directed me in *Footfalls*, what Beckett wanted was not the acting out of an internal thought, but the internal thought itself. He didn't want anything *presented*' (Whitelaw 1995, 120).

The privilege of the 'internal thought', in this case, is akin to a privileging of the text: the text performed without performance, or language without embodiment. Rather than allowing closure or recuperation, acting out emphasizes the distance between the text and the performance, between language and embodiment. Mouth's identity is both undermined and underpinned by its relation to language: 'the whole being … hanging on its words' (89).

On the space of the stage, Mouth appears disembodied, removed from the context of a familiar environment, and exiled from rest of the human body. In the monologue, the protagonist that Mouth describes seems to suffer from a similar sense of disorientation and separation:

> imagine! ... what position she was in! … whether standing … or sitting … but the brain— … what? … kneeling? … yes … whether standing … or sitting … or kneeling … or lying … but the brain—

Experience in the present is undermined and defamiliarized through language. The brain cannot fathom the body's experience without language, but language depends on systems of difference and variation. As a result, reality for Mouth is suspended by a series of possibilities and alternative possibilities, affirmations and negations, confronting the brain with multiple contradictory possibilities. Mouth presents a borderland between the physical world and the realm of language, between the real and the conceptual, the body and the mind. Embodiment implies presence and accountability, whilst language does not belong to any fixed location in time or space. The mouth, in this sense, is a mediating point between two worlds: representing both the immediate present, through its corporeality, and the distant past, in the way it uses a language that necessarily precedes it. In this way, the human mouth can be read as an anachronistic symbol: everything about it that suggests presence or immediacy is counteracted by its dependence on a language that, to some degree, comes both before and after the present. In the passage above, the body attempts to grasp what language is expressing, whilst thought, through language, attempts to comprehend the body: but whatever the approach, language proves insufficient as an accurate descriptor of experience.

Not I can contribute to a wider critique of the human subject's dependence upon language to understand itself, and the role language plays in foundations of being and knowledge. Human consciousness in the play is represented as something always already structured according to a linguistic system of meanings that necessarily precedes and exceeds it. In Mouth's monologue, the phrase 'all the time the buzzing' (87) denotes both an endless stream of words heard by the protagonist, and an inability to stabilize the present; the idea of a buzzing that occurs 'all the time' forbids temporal distinctions; as a result, it is impossible to assert the human subject's supposed presence in the present, without at the same time making reference to an indeterminate past, or an unforeseeable future. Language here is not recognized as language at all, but a deep and resounding noise, a 'dull roar in the skull' (87) that carries no meaningful message. Spontaneous expression is denied by a necessity to rehearse and repeat passages and expressions, reproducing lines according to an infinite and unending demand: 'couldn't make the sound … not any sound … no sound of any kind … no screaming for help for example … should she feel so inclined … all silent but for the buzzing … so-called …' (87). As Mouth's monologue continues, the protagonist begins to identify the buzzing as the repetition of language: 'realised … words were coming … imagine! … words were coming … a voice she did not recognise' (88). We remain unsure what words these might be, or what they might signify, although we might make the assumption that the words referred to are the very ones that constitute the text of the play. If this is the case, then it is worth commenting that the words are not structured sentences as such, but as short phrases punctuated by a series of brief pauses. Mouth's 'acting out' of the narrative continues with the protagonist beginning to recognise the sound of her own voice:

> a voice she did not recognise … then finally had to admit … could be none other … than her own … certain vowel sounds … she

> had never heard … elsewhere … so that people would stare … the rare occasions … once or twice a year… always winter some strange reason … stare at her uncomprehending … and now this stream … steady stream … she who had never … on the contrary … practically speechless … all her days …(88)

Whereas in the conventional understanding of 'working through', representational procedures bring understanding and enlightenment, *Not I* forbids any such comfort. With the protagonist's propulsion into the world of language and individual expression, we might expect to find a renewed and invigorated subject, capable of recalling memories of experiences by recourse to a structured system of signifiers and meanings. But the protagonist's recognition of herself through language is fraught with confusions, ambiguities, and finally outright rejection.

In an essay on the work of Stéphane Mallarmé, Maurice Blanchot suggested that the use of language stages the removal of things in the world with the introduction of ideas, or concepts, that replace them. In Blanchot's words, 'speech has a function that is not only representative but also destructive. It causes to vanish, it renders the object absent, it annihilates it' (Blanchot 1995, 30). This is complicated by the apparitional quality of the signifier, suggestive of 'a more evasive reality, one that presents itself and evaporates, that is understood and vanishes, one made of reminiscences, allusions' (31). The 'evasive reality' of the object is keenly observed in the title of *Not I*, where language becomes both the basis of the protagonist's identity, and its simultaneous disavowal. The memories and history that forge the human subject's identity are constituted in language, and yet language also marks the flickering disappearance of the subject, and its unstable status. The expression 'Not I' implies a speaking subject, but also appreciates the role that language plays in removing that subject: language, after all, is not limited to any one voice or subject position, but is the non-living condition of all voices and all identities. To go one step further, one might suggest 'Not I' as a cheeky refusal of Descartes' famous assertion: 'I think, therefore I am' (Derrida 1999, 25). The phrase 'Not I', in this light, points to the contradiction of language as an unstable foundation for subjectivity, a subjectivity determined by a system of signifiers that both precedes and follows the present moment. In Beckett's play, language is not only a system of signifiers that allows trauma's expression, but the condition of trauma itself:

> … tiny little thing … out before its time … godforsaken hole … no love … spare that … speechless all her days … practically speechless … even to herself … never out loud … but not completely … sometimes sudden urge […] start pouring it out … steady stream … mad stuff … half the vowels wrong … no one could follow … (92)

Language, the means by which the subject structures a relationship between itself and the world, is non-contemporaneous with the subject. The physical self arrives 'before its time', that is to say, before language can be effectively utilised as a communicative tool or signifier of meaning; however, the physical self never catches up with the 'steady stream' of language, the 'mad stuff' that inevitably exceeds it. When Mouth speaks, it is in a language that cannot be fully mastered nor understood, a personal expression that 'no one [can] follow', precisely because it both predates and exceeds the human subject.

Samuel Beckett's texts engage with ideas of trauma in an active and interrogative manner. His 'late' dramatizations for the stage present the problems, fragmentations and slippages of human memory and traumatic testimony. *Not I* operates like a discourse on trauma that forbids all meaningful and coherent gestures, a discourse that does not find a comfortable end in truth and closure but instead rehearses trauma's uncanny themes of loss, absence and disorientation.[19] In *Not I*, memory itself is an acting-out procedure that defines the human subject whilst simultaneously disowning it. All memory is, to some extent, traumatic: the impossible integration of the human and language, of the corporeal body and the articulation that allows it

19 Whitelaw describes the rehearsals for the premiere performance as both physically and mentally traumatizing. In addition to vertigo and nausea, her preparation for the part 'inflamed an already damaged spine and neck'. For an in-depth account of the actress' experiences, see Whitelaw, *Billie Whitelaw… Who He?*, 124-31.

to exist. The language of traumatic experience uttered by Mouth reflects, in part, the trauma of language itself. It is significant that the play begins with the actor performing Mouth 'ad-libbing from text as required leading when curtain finally up' (85) to the first written words of the play; as the play comes to a close, the voice 'continues behind curtain, unintelligible, 10 seconds, ceases as house lights up' (93). The monologue, in this sense, has neither a beginning nor an end: the performance is simply one brief passage from an endlessly recurring series of words, phrases, pauses and exclamations. As traumatic memories continue to haunt and torment the protagonist of *Not I*, the audience are left with only linguistic signifiers, each without a fixed point of origin, conveying no fixed sense of identity, time, or place.

That Time

Time, Trauma and the Self

According to the preface of a 1976 edition of *That Time*, published by Faber and Faber, the play 'was first performed at the Royal Court Theatre in the spring of 1976 during a season mounted to mark the author's seventieth birthday'.[20] Before we have even started reading the play, a pre-text offers to shape certain meanings or interpretations. The ambiguous title can now be grounded by a context, a witness testimony or an historical record. It is a play written and performed to mark a time, the time of a birthday, of an historical anniversary. If nothing else, if the text offers us no clues of its own, audiences and readers alike can satisfy themselves with this simple fact: the empirically stable and historically accurate fact that *That Time* marks an anniversary. But, already, there is a problem. After all, an anniversary is suggestive of cyclical repetition and recurrence. The anniversary is an attempt to acknowledge or commemorate a singular historical event that always occurs at a temporal distance from the event itself. In this sense, the anniversary arrives at a time that is both precise and belated: it is always on time; it is always late. As the text of the play reveals, the assertion 'that time' is an insufficient marker of singularity: *that* time can simultaneously imply a plurality of times.

In the face of this initial problem, we might comfort ourselves with the assumption that at least the original event, Samuel Beckett's birthday, is empirically accurate and historically sound. Whatever the status of the anniversary, there is at least an original event of historical record that can reassure us. But a glance at one of Beckett's biographies makes the problem more complicated still. In *Damned to Fame*, James Knowlson begins with the troubling status of Beckett's birth announcement: while the writer acknowledged his birth date as 13 April 1906, his birth certificate records the date as 13 May. Knowlson

20 Preface note in Samuel Beckett, *That Time* (London: Faber and Faber, 1976), 7.

reads the inscription of 13 May as an error, and uses a birth notice in *The Irish Times* to support his case, but the official document places Beckett's actual birth date a full month earlier (*DF*, 1). In some strange way, one could surmise that Beckett was late for his own birthday. The anniversary performance of *That Time* was also late, with the production opening on 20 May 1976, over a month after Beckett's seventy-fifth birthday had passed. *That Time*, then, is an anniversary marker that hints towards belatedness and indeterminacy.

As I have already discussed, the stage is a paradoxical space. It is a platform where actors rehearse live performances with reference to prepared texts and choreographed gestures. This strange quality, perhaps unique to live drama, enables us to experiment with ideas of trauma in new and interesting ways. As *Not I* demonstrated, the stage adopts transformative potential as a space to enact some kind of recovery, a return or comeback of something buried in the past. The return, however, is never completely coherent, and directs our attention toward the impasses of language and representation. Like *Not I*, *That Time* is also a 'late' play: in its approach to the altered temporality of the stage; in the way it implies the belated return of traumatic memories; and in its presentation of a character who is perhaps no longer alive (an idea I will return to when discussing *Footfalls*). In a 1974 letter to George Reavey, Beckett writes that he has 'written a short piece (theatre): *That Time. Not I* family'.[21] Ackerley and Gontarski point out that Beckett purposefully placed emphasis on listening rather than speaking, but that the play is nonetheless 'cut out of the same texture' as its predecessor.[22]

That Time is also akin to *Not I* in its use of the theatre to articulate a personal history. Applying this approach to the question of trauma, Roger Luckhurst identifies a 'memoir boom' in post-traumatic culture, where the autobiographical work has an ability to 'outstrip the narrative conventionality of fiction in responding to what might be called the pressure of the real' (Luckhurst 2008, 118). Drawing upon

21 Beckett, qtd. in Ackerley and Gontarski, *The Grove Companion*, 568.

22 Beckett, qtd. in Ackerley and Gontarski, *The Grove Companion*, 568.

examples from contemporary art and the work of Hal Foster, Luckhurst discusses a cultural shift toward the real and the traumatic event as 'something that burst through representation and appeared to be its ruination' (118). What arises, then, is a return to certain realist practices and norms, but with an added awareness of their status as representation. To make the point explicit, Luckhurst quotes Michael Rothberg's suggestion that a Traumatic Realism might offer new paths toward reading and representing traumatic narratives: 'a realism in which the scars that mark the relationship of discourse to the real are not fetishistically denied, but exposed; a realism in which the claims of reference live on, but so does the traumatic extremity that disable Realist representation as usual' (Rothberg 2000, 106). Whilst Samuel Beckett's theatrical work does not obey the conventions of the autobiographical form in its most traditional sense, there is perhaps something to be said for the way the texts draw attention to certain realist practices and demands. *Not I* is an autobiography without a concrete author in the same way that *That Time* is a tale without a single teller, but instead a plurality of voices speaking from a plurality of different contexts. Both subvert the expectations of the traditional autobiographical narrative, and cast a wider doubt on the validity or reliability of the narrating subject.

In familiar traumatic memoirs, Luckhurst attests to a formal connection with the genre of autobiography, and so also with the 'deepest Western traditions of self-knowledge and humanism' (Luckhurst 2008, 118). Accordingly, the genre offers 'the unity of identity across time, interpreting life in its totality' (118) via a reliable and coherent narrator. But Luckhurst is careful to stress that the confusion and disorientation of the traumatic event unravel the security of the rational humanist subject position. Beginning with the term 'memoir', he describes the genre as a 'lowlier form' of autobiography, 'an incomplete and fragmentary slice of a life' (118) that is more closely linked to uncertainty and ambiguity than truth or humanist mastery. As he puts it later, 'the trauma memoir recounts a discordance, a circling around a shattering event, from which self-knowledge arrives late, if at all, and with an uncomfortable awareness of the frangibility of the self' (118-9). Both *Not I* and *That Time* obey some of the conventions of the autobiography, but via Luckhurst's description are perhaps closer, in style and content, to the memoir. But neither play displays traditional realist properties, shunning even familiar stage settings to create a stark and disorientating atmosphere. Whereas the 'trauma memoir' continues to rely upon persistent notions of the rational humanist subject position, a guarantor of presence and authority, the plays go further in their examination and deconstruction of these assumptions. What they have in common with Luckhurst's 'memoir', and Rothberg's Traumatic Realism, is their use of personal recollections to examine the limitations of traumatic narrative representation, and the way such narratives confuse and undermine humanist ideas of the rational subject.

Never the Same After That

That Time is structured around three voices, A, B, C, and a Listener who does not speak. The Listener's face is brightly lit, ten feet above the stage platform, while the rest of the theatre remains shrouded in darkness. Listener is described as having an 'Old white face, long flaring white hair as if seen from above outspread' (*TT*, 99). The stage set-up is notably similar to *Not I*: there is the minimalist environment that rejects the familiar surroundings of realist drama, the focus on a specific region of human anatomy (a human head), and the use of a monologue to recall past events. Both plays dispense with the already minimal props of *Waiting for Godot*, *Endgame* and *Krapp's Last Tape* to concentrate on the simplest elements of the human form and its relationship to language. Finally, both plays use a vocabulary that is vague and ambiguous to enact flashbacks to previous historical moments. The first voice heard is that of A:

> that time you went back that last time to look was the ruin still there where you hid as a child when was that [*Eyes close.*] grey day took the eleven to the end of the line and on from there no no trams then all gone long ago that time you went back to look was

> the ruin still there where you hid as a child that last time not a tram left in the place only the old rails when was that (99)

The opening speech sets the tone for the rest of the play, and presents a number of interpretive obstacles. For instance, the first passage contains no punctuation (with the exception of stage directions for Listener). The lack of a formal sentence structure makes it difficult to establish the narrative according to discrete units of thought: we cannot isolate words or segments in the same way, but are compelled to consider passages in their entirety. The voice of A is written without discernable pauses between words, and without any obvious signals of a beginning or an end: we are left, instead, with the impression that we are hearing a narrative *in medias res*, without access to whatever introductory remarks might have preceded it. We are compelled to take in the first passage as an unbroken verbal declaration: a passage that refers to a singular event in the Listener's childhood, a day involving trams and one last return to a derelict ruin. Ironically, while the text itself is composed of words that are read or heard in a strictly linear order, the juxtaposition of images and things pulled together in the same passage confounds temporal expectations and disrupt such a linear understanding. For example, the imperfect repetition 'that time' / 'that last time' is undermined by what is possibly a query, 'when was that'. Because the last three words are cut off by a second voice, we cannot be sure whether it is a complete query, or the incomplete fragment of a longer speech.

What is perhaps most striking about the passage is its direct and indirect references to time. Time is explicitly evoked when the voice of A prompts Listener to remember the past ('that time you went back'), and becomes important once again when evoking a sense of travel and progression ('took the eleven to the end of the line'). But the passage gradually shifts toward references that break down temporal distinctions: 'and on from there no no trams'. It is tempting to read the tram as a symbol of the metropolitan city here, an icon of technology that regulates and is regulated by time; and so, the movement to a space where no trams can reach implies a sense of isolation, or even historical and cultural regression. The presence of the ruin emphasises this idea of historical obsolescence, evoking a space that is not defined by standardized time: it is a space beyond the territory of the modern city, a location beyond the last stop of the trams. Yet, the passage does not suggest a simplistic return to the past, to a time before technology. There is a traumatic element to the opening passage, the fragment of a narrative that speaks of a possible threat and childhood vulnerability ('the ruin still there where you hid as a child'). The word 'ruin' has several meanings and occupies a position of some significance to discussions of time, trauma and return. In the play, it recalls the condition of a building or buildings in a state of collapse: a collection of structures built some time in the past, which now only partially exist in the present. In Brian Dillon's essay collection, *Ruins*, he offers a 'Short History of Decay' which articulates how

> ruins embody a set of temporal and historical paradoxes. The ruined building is a remnant of, and portal into, the past; its decay is a concrete reminder of the passage of time. And yet by definition it survives, after a fashion; there must be a certain (perhaps indeterminate) amount of a built structure still standing for us to refer to it as a ruin and not merely as a heap of rubble. At the same time, the ruin casts us forward in time; it predicts a future in which our present will slump into similar disrepair or fall victim to some unforeseeable calamity. The ruin, despite its state of decay, somehow outlives us. And the cultural gaze that we turn on ruins is a way of loosening ourselves from the grip of punctual chronologies, setting ourselves adrift in time. (Dillon 2011, 11)

The very existence of a ruin is paradoxical, in that it invokes both destruction and remains: the devastation of a thing in a continual and unresolved process of collapse. Ruins do not signal the return of the past, but the potential for a continual and unending process that occurs in the past, present and future. In this way, much like Beckett's representations of trauma, ruins ruin time.

Immediately following the first statement from A comes a second, this time from C, which breaks the expected alphanumerical progression. The distinction is made clear for the reader, but not for the audience. A, B and C are, according to the stage directions, 'one and the same voice', and 'relay one another without solution of continuity—apart from the two 10-second breaks' (97). Beckett notes that the distinction between the three voices 'must be clearly faintly perceptible' to the audience, suggesting either a 'threefold source and context' or 'threefold pitch' using mechanical assistance (97). The second passage contains no trace of the first, and appears to evoke a different memory, an alternative narrative that presents separate times and locations:

> when you went in out of the rain always winter then always raining that time in the Portrait Gallery in off the street out of the cold and rain slipped in when no one was looking and through the rooms shivering and dripping till you found a seat marble slab and sat down to rest and dry off and on to hell out of there when was that (99)

The second passage might continue a thread from the first, where 'when was that' is resolved by 'when you went in out of the rain'. But there is no evidence to confirm this assumption. The voices heard by the Listener appear to lead into one another, weaving narratives together in a way that ruptures chronology and prompts unusual juxtapositions. From the ambiguous memory of a ruin visited during childhood the text suddenly speaks of a Portrait Gallery on a winter's day. The second narrative can be distinguished from the first by its distinct images, and the audience might assume that it takes place some time after the first narrative (since the first relates to the protagonist remembering events from childhood). However, despite the elements that distinguish the second scene—a man taking cover from the rain—there are nonetheless certain echoes from the first. For instance, the action of the man seeking shelter from the winter weather is analogous to the action of the child, finding refuge in the ruin; while the implied threat of the first narrative is not present in the second, the man is still compelled to hide from observers, to enter 'when no one was looking'. In both narratives, the shelter takes similar forms. In both narratives, the spaces are of some historical significance: the ruin is an historical site of decay that has been preserved; the Gallery is an historical site of preservation that is in decay. Both sites enact a conversation with the past, but a past that can only be grasped via fragments, much like the fragments spoken by the voices to the Listener.

When Caruth speaks of the wound and the voice, she suggests a correlation between a traumatic incident that occurred in the past and its belated articulation. To some degree, *Not I* demonstrates the logic of this assumption. In *That Time*, the formula is complicated by the introduction of a second, and then a third voice. Instead of a single traumatic event, unclearly defined by an individual voice, we have three voices presenting three ambiguous narratives. The nature of the trauma remains unclear, but each voice appears to imply or allude to some troubling past incident. Throughout the play, Caruth's model of the wound and the voice becomes a wound (or wounds) with multiple voices. Three varying standpoints define a series of places, times and observations, forging a singular yet divergent stream of referents and associations. By looking at each voice in isolation, it becomes possible to discern recurrent images and verbal repetitions that are unique to them.

Voice A continually references standardised time, along with the timetables that govern modern transport and an industrialised contemporary landscape. For instance, when the character returns to a site of childhood significance, it is framed by the arrivals and departures of ferries and trams:

> A: that time you went back to look was the ruin still there where you hid as a child that last time straight off the ferry and up the rise to the high street to catch the eleven neither right nor left only one thought in your head not a curse for the old scenes the old names just head down press on up the rise to the top and there stood waiting with the nightbag till the truth began to dawn (102)

The character's understanding of his environment in the first narrative is defined against the backdrop of the city and an unspecified surrounding landscape. His understanding of time is, by turns, densely regulated by modern transport, and strangely suspended by zones outside the city limits. It is perhaps significant that what ever traumatic event transpired appears to exist outside conventional notions of time, at an unclear and ambiguous juncture. It is perhaps also significant that the hiding place amid the ruins is beyond the reach of the modern city.

In the narrative of voice C there is the Portrait Gallery as an historical archive, with its repeated references to art, representation, and cultural history. The character is confused and disorientated, seemingly unable to distinguish between himself and others:

> C: when you started not knowing who you were from Adam trying how that would work for a change not knowing who you were from Adam no notion who it was saying what you were saying whose skull you were clapped up in whose moan had you the way you were was that the time or was that another time there alone with the portraits of the dead black with dirt and antiquity and the dates on the frames in case you might get the century wrong not believing it could be you till they put you out in the rain at closing time (102)

Adam, the First Man of Judeo-Christian religion, is used to imply both a confusion of identity and a playful rejection of religious origin stories. Alone with the portraits, the character looks over representations of those now long dead, observing labels and frames that attempt to clarify distinctions between art and reality, or the present and the past. Identity is hinged upon an ability to distinguish such labels, and like the first narrative, the character struggles to differentiate between the present and the past. At an earlier moment, his struggle to make distinctions is crystallized by the appearance of a ghostly form: 'where gradually as you peered trying to make it out gradually of all things a face appeared had you swivel on the slab to see who it was was there at your elbow' (100-1). As Ackerley and Gontarski have suggested, the sudden perception is ambiguous: is it a reflection of his own face, of the guard that has arrived to put him out, or a composite of the two (Ackerley and Gontarski 2004, 569)? The ambiguity surrounding the perception might be read as the ambiguity of perception itself. In the context of contemporary trauma theory, it suggests an inability to tie a representation once and for all to a specific referent. Representation, of the self and of others, is characterized by ghostliness.

The third voice we hear, B, articulates a narrative that seems spectral, conjuring images of fields and fringes, margins, borders and limit spaces:

> B: no sight of the face or any other part never turned to her nor she to you always parallel like on an axle-tree never turned to each other just blurs on the fringes of the field no touching or anything of that nature always space between if only an inch no pawing in the manner of flesh and blood no better than shades no worse if it wasn't for the vows (102)

There is the hint of romance in the third narrative, a companionship described at a moment of separation. The companion exists at a permanent distance from the protagonist: no touching or 'pawing in the manner of flesh and blood'. At best, the passage suggests a relationship that lacked intimacy; at worst, the companion is little more than a figment of imagination. Just as the portraits in the art gallery are 'dead black with dirt', the human figure of the narrator's companion is shrouded in darkness and obscurity: 'no better than shades'. In each of the narratives, the character appears to struggle to make distinctions in the world, whether he is establishing who he is, or the differences between reality and non-reality, present and past.

Three Voices

What are we to make of these strange, competing voices, each emitted from the same unified source? What can it tell us of the Listener, whose facial expressions seem to lend weight and gravity to the pronouncements? It is tempting to read the three-way narrative of the play as a disjoined and unharmonious stream of consciousness, a selection of three separate narratives that are rendered explainable by the existence of a single voice, a human narrator who can secure a fixed and stable origin. Ackerley and Gontarski have suggested that the Listener 'echoes the theater audience's piecing together fragments of a ruined past into a comprehensible narrative, a life' (Ackerley and

Gontarski 2004, 570). In an essay on fragments and form in *Footfalls* and *That Time*, Enoch Brater states that the texts, allow us to 'experience a fragment as an absolute whole', and, moreover, observe that this whole is fully 'materialized and memorialized through a constant return to the same sights and the same sounds' (Brater 1977, 70-81). But does this analysis tell the whole story? Does the text really give us such privileged access? Whilst the notion of a single humanist subject allows the narratives to flow and cohere, the voices and their separate accounts remain strangely unharmonious. Even if all memories and articulations are issued from a single source, how do we account for this plurality of voices, memories, and fragments?

A short essay by Maurice Blanchot, entitled 'Marx's Three Voices', may help to illuminate what is most problematic about *That Time*. In it, Blanchot suggests that a tripartite logic underlies the writing of Karl Marx:

> In Marx, and always coming from Marx, we see three kinds of voices gathering force and taking form, all three of which are necessary, but separated and more than opposed, as if they were juxtaposed. The disparity that holds them together designates a plurality of demands, to which since Marx everyone who speaks or writes cannot fail to feel himself [*sic.*] subjected, unless he is to feel himself failing in everything. (Blanchot 1997, 98)

From this, we might deduce that the voice, as Blanchot defines it, exists both within the writing subject ('In Marx') and beyond it ('always coming from Marx'): we might interpret this any number of ways, but it can be useful at this stage to suggest a distinction between an assumed temporal present ('In Marx'), and, conversely, the implicated reference to the past or the future ('always coming from Marx'). The voice, in this sense, deranges our sense of time, and of the assumed self-presence of the rational subject. This is complicated further by Blanchot's identification of three distinct voices underscoring Marx's texts, three voices that simultaneously evoke clarity and coherence alongside a sense of divergence and plurality. Blanchot, of course, is referring here to a branch of political discourse, but his analysis can have a more general import to our understanding of the voice in drama. There is, after all, a similar principle at play in Beckett's text. The voice in *That Time* occupies multiple subject positions and, in Blanchot's words, 'designates a plurality of demands'. The essay, which goes on to align the three voices of Marx's discourse with the structure of writing itself, might hold implications for our understanding of traumatic narratives.

Returning to Caruth's idea of the wound and the voice, we are faced in *That Time* with a notion of writing and representation that is structured not only according to plurality, but a blend of seemingly opposing traits and signatures. Blanchot writes that his example suggests 'that the voice of writing, a voice of ceaseless contestation, must constantly develop itself and break itself into multiple forms' (Blanchot 1997, 99-100). At its articulation, the voice of the wound is similarly deferred and fragmented, blurring distinctions between subjects and objects, times and places. The problem of representing trauma in Beckett is connected to wider problems surrounding the Western subject: the impossible demands of remembrance, the inadequacies of representation, and the incompleteness of belated fragments. In *That Time*, as in *Not I*, the narrative seems to be the product of a repetition-compulsion, an endless and unceasing story that circles around a traumatic event, but lacks the precise vocabulary with which to signal an approach, or resolve the trauma. Language, the system by which we understand the world and ourselves, also acts as a barrier restricting mastery over past events.

The multiplicity of voices A, B and C are brought together by little more than spectral ambiguities. A connects spectrality to an idea of an obsolete modernity, a modernity defined by ruin and dereliction, while the other voices bring similar ideas to bear on their separate settings. In the B narrative, the individual disappears with the sunset: 'till you could see it no more nothing stirring only the water and the sun going down till it went down and you vanished all vanished' (104). The voice of C is concerned with the way the individual is perceived by others: 'you might as well not have been there at all the eyes passing over you and through you like so much thin air was that the time or was that another time another place another time' (105). Each voice hints towards a divided self, a self split into many fragmented and undifferentiated parts. The protagonist in each narrative is suspended or deferred among their material surroundings, and finds it difficult to establish a clear or precise existence.

Significantly, Blanchot's essay on Marx finds its way into Jacques Derrida's work, *Specters of Marx*, in which Derrida illuminates certain temporal instabilities inherent to writing and the voice. Referring to the three voices of Marx, Derrida suggests that they are defined by a 'necessary *disjunction*', and characterized by a 'non-contemporaneity with themselves' (Derrida 2012, 40). Whilst the humanist subject might appear as a fixed and unified source of meaning, spoken and recorded language exceeds all claims of a temporal present, or metaphysical presence. As Derrida puts it elsewhere, 'the order of the signified is never contemporary', but 'discrepant by the time of a breath' (Derrida 1997, 18). As such, the voice that symbolises claims to harmony or unity in the humanist subject diverges and disperses at the very point of articulation. This, too, is the defining feature of the voices in *That Time*, the voices that forbid even the possibility of 'that time' being clarified, or isolated for closer inspection. The voices are not only separated from the Listener in performance (they are heard from 'both sides and above') (105), but each refers to a different (and largely unspecified) historical moment. If remembering, reenacting or representing trauma depends upon an established correlation between present and past, the three voices disrupt not only our claim to the event, but our grasp and understanding of language itself:

> What one must constantly come back to, here as elsewhere, concerning this text as well as any other (and we still assign here an unlimited scope to this value of text) is an irreducible heterogeneity, an internal untranslatability in some way. (Derrida 2012, 40)

Specters of Marx draws further connections between Blanchot's writing and the concept of a spectral, ghostly voice. The figure of the spectre, in this context, forbids standard binary oppositions of present and past by an appeal to the future; the logic of the spectre obeys a similar logic to the traumatic event, manifesting itself always at a later time according to unspecified and unpredictable criteria. As we shall observe in *Footfalls*, the figure of the ghost signals not only the return of a past traumatic event, but destabilizes Western categories of time, presence and ontology. Derrida describes a voice that 'can never be always present, it *can be, only, if there is any*, it can be only possible, it must remain a *can-be* or *maybe* in order to remain a demand' (39). Traumatic representation in Beckett's texts follows a similar logic, always belatedly manifesting itself via a series of allusions or spectral traces, but never fully present, never graspable. In contrast to the conventions of the 'trauma memoir', treatment of *That Time*'s unspecified traumatic event(s) serve to unsettle and destabilize our understanding of the humanist subject as a coherent and stable identity testifying from a singular and fixed position.

The final passage of the play, which finds the protagonist seeking shelter in a quiet library, is delivered by C. The narrator states that only two sounds can be heard, the character's breathing and the soft sound of 'the leaves turning' (106), a phrase that synchronizes the quiet practice of reading with the shifting of the seasons, and the cold approach of autumn and winter. Reading, then, coincides with some kind of ending or decay. Suddenly, the protagonist is overwhelmed by dust, 'the whole place suddenly full of dust [...] from floor to ceiling' (106). The library, an archive of Western science, philosophy and literature, is crystallized by an image of decay, ruin and collapse. The representation of the archive as a site of instability and has been subsequently explored by writers such as Derrida (*Archive Fever*, 1995) and Blanchot (*The Writing of the Disaster*, 1986), and calls into question the authority of writing and representation in the face of historical crisis and atrocity. In his 2011 work, *Melancholy and the Archive*, Jonathan Boulter draws on both thinkers to explore how the unstable archive subsequently unsettles subjectivity in a traumatizing way:

> It is my argument in what follows that this idea, subjectivity wthout any subject (*subjectivite sans sujet*), is particularly useful for thinking

> about the subject as he [*sic.*] begins to negotiate a relationship to his memory, his history; specifically, as the subject negotiates a relationship to a disastrous history, to a past marked by loss and trauma, the subject becomes more than merely an individual reflecting on a particular kind of economy of tragic loss. The disaster, as I have said, produces some shift in the psyche, in the self, in the interiority of the subject, to the point where the subject finds himself to have become a trace of what he was, a cinder marking the passing of the disaster. (Boulter 2011, 9)

Boulter is interested, here, in a certain kind of post-traumatized subjectivity that we can find in post-1945 and contemporary literature—and, I would suggest, it is a description that finds purchase in the protagonist's traumatized and ambiguous autobiography in *That Time.* Ackerley and Gontarski have already identified a connection between the archival dust of the play and the narrator's distintegration into non-being, drawing specifically on 'God's admonition of Adam, "dust thou art; unto dust shalt thou return" (Genesis 3:19)' (Ackerley and Gontarski 2004, 570). In the play's final moments the dust overwhelmes the library and provokes the last questions of the narration; the text closes with an interrogative tone, unable to distinguish the dust of the library (a repository of language) with the identity of the self, or its place in time: 'only dust and not a sound only what was it it said come and gone was that it something like that come and gone come and gone no one come and gone in no time gone in no time' (106). In what amounts to an allusion to some kind of traumatic event, the play presents a distintegration of language and the archive which coincides with the distintegration of the human subject.

The evocation of events in *That Time* accentuates a distance between the subject and experience. It is precisely language that demarcates this gap: the means by which Beckett's characters identify themselves provides the ultimate source of their undoing. At the close of the play, the Listener and the audience may have a rudimentary understanding of three historical moments, but they are, after all, only moments. They do not constitute a comprehensive grasp of the character's life, nor do they offer a privileged glimpse into the historical origin of his troubled recollections. Instead, the narratives present moments fraught with spectral ambiguities. The multiple voices of *That Time* signal both the anachronistic nature of the theatrical stage, and of speech in a more general sense. Where the face of the Listener implies coherence and unity of the humanist subject, the three voices—issuing from three unknown sources, in three different pitches—pluralize and complicate claims to a singular, rational account. Instead of a voice signaling the coherent return of a traumatic event, we are compelled to resolve three voices that emphasize difference and separation. *That Time* does not satisfy the criteria of a rational, historical account; nor does it fulfill the expectations of an autobiography or memoir. Instead, it is a history of many times, perhaps a sequence of perpetual traumas, that testifies to the difficulties inherent in representing trauma itself.

Footfalls

Not Quite There

We have already established how the traumatic symptom is defined according to a belated logic: a disturbance or perversion of conventional chronology, and, as such, of orthodox empirical values. The traumatic symptom signals a return, or recurrence, of that which was not fully understood or comprehended at the moment of its first occurrence. As such, it presents certain questions about the validity of subsequent attempts to capture it via representation. How, for example, can you re-present that which was not recognized as fully present to begin with? By this account, trauma is that which resists the *logos*; it resists attempts by the rational humanist subject to accommodate it within a clear and unified system of meanings and differences. Trauma resists narrative closure.

In Cathy Caruth's reading of the traumatic symptom, the inaugural event takes ultimate precedence. The way we approach the symptom, by implication, is always already an attempt to ascertain its cause, the historical moment that founds it. This methodology takes after Sigmund Freud, who analysed the symptoms of his patients as the manifestations of a previous traumatic encounter. This method utilizes the assumption that ambiguities and confusions inherent to symptoms can be resolved by recourse to a causal, historical explanation, restoring order through a coherent narrative. It was Freud's belief that the traumatic symptom, compulsively repeated in a patient's case history, could be resolved at the moment an explanation was found, and the original traumatizing event finally confronted by the rational mind.[23]

23 Freud's essay, 'Remembering, Repeating and Working Through' offers an interesting outline of the theory and practical challenges of such an approach. See Freud, *Beyond the Pleasure Principle and Other Writings*, trans. John Reddick (London: Penguin, 2003), 31-42.

We might observe, at this stage, a strange kinship between Caruth's reading of traumatic events, and the event of an individual's death. For example, we might begin by observing that the concept of death serves two important symbolic functions. Firstly, death is an event that imposes an absolute limit point on experience and understanding, a threshold that no human subject can cross. And, secondly, it provides a static point of reference: if death is an absolute limit point, then it is necessarily a point that is fixed, that cannot change. In this way, death becomes an empirical stabilizer free from the chaotic flux of life, which is defined in contrast according to constant and unpredictable change. And, as a stabilizer, death becomes, at first glance, a useful foundation for Western knowledge. As David Houston Jones observes, 'it is hard to find any theoretical account of testimony which does not appeal to the notion of presence, whatever the vicissitudes of the witness's passage through language' (Houston Jones 2011, 27).

In contemporary trauma theory, I would suggest there is a temptation to apply a similar standard. Here, the traumatic event becomes a replacement for the event of a person's death—an event that is similar in the way it presents a limit to empirical understanding. Like death, trauma is that which perpetually resists comprehension or mastery. And, like death, the event becomes the focus of hermeneutic investigation: in this sense, it is assumed to be a cornerstone for reference and reflection. In addition, both the event of death and the traumatic experience become the focus of humanist narratives of knowledge and progress. For instance, the ever-changing circumstances of a person's life can only be fully explained and rationalized in a narrative at the point of that person's death: a stable point from which a person's life might be considered as a unified whole. Similarly, traumatic symptoms and side-effects present a chaos of change and flux existing between two distinct historical moments: the moment when the trauma occurs, and the moment when the trauma is resolved. In both cases, ambiguities and uncertainties are understood in an historical narrative with reference to temporal and empirical certainties. The traumatic event, as event, provides a referent, or source, by which all ambiguity can be circumvented and explained. Where traumatic symptoms provoke empirical crises or temporal derangement, reference to a causal event restores at least some semblance of harmony and order.

Beckett's late theatre manages to preserve this empirical crisis, retaining a sense of concepts such as death and trauma as something that cannot be assigned as discrete, historically circumscribed events. They remain foreign, unassimilated and strange. Rather than offer stable observation points on which to reflect, or challenges for humanist rationality to overcome, traumatic experience in Beckett's writing confronts that which cannot be assimilated into human identity, that which fragments or undermines what is generally constituted as a unified and unproblematic whole, revealing the paradoxical nature of a Western humanist subject defined through language.

Shades

At this point, the curtain opens on *Footfalls*, perhaps the most enigmatic of Beckett's 'late' plays. First performed at the Royal Court Theatre in London in 1976, the production starred Billie Whitelaw under the writer's own direction. Begun in 1975, the play was written to accompany *That Time*, with Whitelaw in mind for the lead role. Notably, much like *That Time* before it, *Footfalls* was written to celebrate the author's seventieth birthday: once again, the concept of an anniversary precedes the production of a text. James Knowlson and John Pilling noted that after its premiere, 'many critics confessed themselves intellectually baffled' (Knowlson and Pilling 1979, 221) by it. Academics have suggested that *Footfalls* is Beckett's 'most delicate play' (Ackerley and Gontarski 2004, 202), a work where the costume design and stage setting appear strangely insubstantial, even unearthly. It is in *Footfalls* that we find what is possibly Beckett's most intricate representation of the traumatic symptom, with all of its spectral ambiguities. The text is 'late' in all sorts of ways: like *Not I* and *That Time* before it, *Footfalls* belongs to a sequence of texts that were written late in Beckett's writing career; much like the other texts, there are allusions to past events that belatedly return to haunt the present; and, perhaps more than in any other case, the audience is left to wonder whether its lead protagonist is 'late' in that third sense. Like the ghost of Hamlet's father stalking the battlements, the protagonist of Beckett's play treads a nocturnal path, and is, quite possibly, a ghostly apparition.

In her autobiography, Billie Whitelaw recalls rehearsals for the first production, when on several occasions the strange status of the lead character became a source of debate. She begins by describing the setting, and the action:

> The play is about a woman of indeterminate middle age, dusty and old before her time, pacing up and down a strip of carpet. She is caged in by this one little strip. She's not even pacing around the room, she's confined to *one specific area* of the room, and there she has been pacing up and down, or so it seemed to me, for 999 years, unable to break out of her compulsive, narrow rut—the strip of carpet is now bare. She's having a conversation (which may be going on in her head) with her mother, obviously an invalid, who can't be seen but is heard to speak in the next room. The woman, May, or Amy as she's later called, has the appearance of a spectre. She is looking after this invisible but audible mother, who may be real or not. (Whitelaw 1995, 142)

The invisible but audible mother recalls the voices heard by the Listener in *That Time*, a human form that is neither present on the stage nor absent, but which seems to hover indeterminately between the two states. However, whereas in *That Time* the figure of the Listener offers the audience a stable, corporeal focus, May/Amy is less reliable. As Whitelaw puts it, 'May seems to be in the process of disappearing like smoke' (142). Was the character Whitelaw played living or dead? When the actress approached Beckett with this question, he responded, after a moment: 'Well, let's just say *you're not quite there*' (143). He suggested to Whitelaw during rehearsals that she was 'too earthbound', stressing that he was hoping for 'a voice from beyond the grave' (143). Beckett noted elsewhere that May appears in 'the costume of a ghost',[24] a remark realized in the astonishing garment designed for the production by Jocelyn Herbert. As Whitelaw understood it, 'The woman existed in that ghostly spiritual half-way house between living and not living' (Whitelaw 1995, 143). The figure has something in common with Dante's depiction of Virgil as a 'shade' in the *Commedia*, a text that exerted a strong influence on Beckett's work; at the opening of the *Inferno*, the protagonist, Dante, tries to establish whether Virgil 'is a shade or a living soul [...] he looks as though he is alive, and yet somehow not'.[25] This is precisely the enigma of the spectre in *Footfalls*: that which hovers between the corporeal and the spiritual, between presence and absence, and so between categories of life and death. May's ambiguous state destabilizes central empirical foundations of ontology and epistemology, confusing the hierarchical distinctions that structure Western knowledge and subjectivity.

Ackerley and Gontarski have written about *Footfalls* in terms of the theatrical challenge that it presented to Beckett; in other words, how the writer might seek 'to represent in language and stage iconography the incomplete being, the *être manqué*. *Footfalls* may be his most thorough realization of the theme' (Ackerley and Gontarski 2004, 202). Beckett noticed that, in the final section of the play, presenting May's absence from the stage could result in audience members prematurely exiting the performance, thinking it had ended. He writes: 'How to avoid end of play audience reaction after 3rd fade-out before last chime, fade up & final fade out?'[26] The solution was to shorten 'the two previous fade-outs [and] adding a vertical strip of light visible in the background, to give the impression that the light was falling

---

24 Textual notes on *Footfalls* in *The Theatrical Notebooks of Samuel Beckett: The Shorter Plays,* Vol. IV, ed. Stanley Gontarski (London: Faber and Faber, 1999), 283.

25 Robert Hollander's observations on Virgil in Dante Alighieri, *Inferno*, trans. Robert Hollander and Jean Hollander, intr. Robert Hollander (New York: Anchor Books, 2002), 18-9n65-66.

26 Samuel Beckett, *The Theatrical Notebooks of Samuel Beckett: The Shorter Plays* (London: Faber and Faber, 1999), 297.

through the crack of a door, and that light slowly fading' (Ackerley and Gontarski 2004, 297). This production decision presents absence through the image of a door, a threshold, or boundary, demarcating an opposition between contrasting states: binary oppositions of life and death, being and non-being, presence and absence. The figure of the spectre in *Footfalls* does not strictly belong on either side of this threshold, but seems to occupy both spaces simultaneously.

The significance of the spectre in *Footfalls* could hold several possible implications. The first question we might ask is whether May is, in fact, really there at all. Her name, 'May', suggests a moment of conjecture or uncertainty: may, or may not. Is she the product of the voice's imagination? If this is the case, we might read May as a fictional construction, emblematic of the spectral qualities of language itself. There are a number of cues that might lead us to such a conclusion. The voice responds to May's call, before adding 'I heard you in my deep sleep [...] there is no sleep so deep I would not hear you there' (*F*, 109). From this, it might be tempting to surmise that May is the product of voice's imagination, a mother conjuring the presence of an absent daughter. The characters do not occupy the same space, and all allusions to physical interaction have either taken place in the past, or are scheduled to take place sometime in the future. Voice reports the motions of May upon the stage, as the figure walks from left to right and right to left: this gesture forms the basis of a narration, which describes May's movement and, in doing so, affirms her existence—at least in some limited sense. The second part of the play, signalled by the sound of a second chime, narrates the life of May from the mother's perspective. The passage suggests some interruption of natural development, as a younger May is narrated indoors when 'the other girls of her age were out' (*F*, 111). The house where May is confined, either by individual will, the will of an authority figure, or simply circumstance, is rendered as an *unheimlich* domestic space, a house that evokes images of the womb:

> She has not been out since girlhood. [*Pause.*] Not out since girlhood. [*Pause.*] Where is she, it may be asked. [*Pause.*] Why, in the

> old home, the same where she—[*Pause.*] The same where she began. [*Pause.*] Where it began. [*Pause.*] It all began. [*Pause.*] But this, when did this begin? (111)

What are we to suppose 'it' refers to in this context? Is it, perhaps, May's birth? Possibly. But it also suggests an unclear historical trauma from May's childhood, the reason for her confinement and the origin of her repetitive gestures. In his biography of the author, James Knowlson charts one of the sources of *Footfalls* in 'Beckett's long-standing interest in abnormal psychology' (*DF*, 615). When directing Billie Whitelaw in the role, the playwright made reference to a public lecture by the psychoanalyst Carl Jung that he had once attended. The actress recalls that 'Jung was talking about the case of a young woman. He used the expression that this woman had never been properly born' (Whitelaw 1995, 142). The instance is referred to on more than one occasion in Beckett's work, and is even quoted in his 1957 radio play *All That Fall* (see Chapter Three of this study). But what is most significant to us, in the case of May, is the confusion of beginnings and endings. Perhaps birth, in this sense, can be read as analogous to the traumatic event: an empirical and epistemological blind spot to which the individual subject cannot have full access.[27] Where the human subject is bereft of a secure origin, it can only appear to us as a partial presence, a ghostly form: May is both born and not born, both present and absent. Her existence confuses traditional categories.

While May could be a fictional construct of Voice's imagination, the same might inversely also be said of Voice herself. The mother, after all, is never visually represented in the play, but exists—if she exists at all—off-stage and out of reach. Could the mother be a mere fantasy of May's? When addressing her mother, May asks whether she can straighten her pillows, change her sores or administer injections (*F*, 110). May's exposition sheds light on the mother's infirm

27 Freud suggests that the act of birth holds a traumatic resonance in his lecture on 'anxiety' in Freud, *Introductory Lectures on Psychoanalysis*, ed. James Strachey and Angela Richards, trans. James Strachey (London: Penguin, 1973), 444-5.

and immobile condition, but also suggests a fixation on repetitive actions and procedures; we might be led to assume that the mother has already passed away, and that May continues to follow routine processes in a form of denial. Knowlson and Pilling lend credibility to this possibility, confirming that in manuscript annotations Beckett refers to the parental figure as May's 'dying mother' (Knowlson and Pilling 1979, 224). Perhaps the 'deep sleep' of the mother is the deep sleep of death itself: 'There is no sleep so deep I would not hear you there' (*F*, 109). Might it be that the mother's voice is calling out from beyond the grave? Knowlson and Pilling go further still, suggesting that 'even the mother's voice may simply be a voice in the mind of a ghost, everything may be regarded as illusion in this little play' (Knowlson and Pilling 1979, 227). This, of course, is all conjecture, but *Footfalls* is rich with such mysterious and unresolved questions. The spectre gives us a glimpse at the dark and muddied environs of the dramatic text: a series of actions described through language, and so offering only partial and ghostly clues to its characters and settings.

The spectral figure of May might have another significance in the play, symbolizing the uncanny repetition of a trauma. May has an uncanny double in the form of Amy (notice the re-ordering of the letters in May's name), who seems to replace her towards the end of the text. Can we be sure it is May who walks to and fro on the stage, or might we assume that it is Amy? The text refers to the figure who walks as May, and none other. But names in *Footfalls*, like language itself, can be deceptive. When May describes the woman figure who walks around the 'little church' (112), it is difficult not to imagine that she is, in fact, describing herself:

> The semblance. Faint, though by no means invisible, in a certain light. [*Pause.*] Given the right light. [*Pause.*] Grey rather than white, a pale shade of grey. [*Pause.*] Tattered. [*Pause.*] A tangle of tatters. [*Pause.*] Watch it pass—[*Pause.*]—watch her pass before the candelabrum, how its flames, their light...like moon through passing rack. [*Pause.*] Soon then after she was gone, as though never there, began to walk, up and down, up and down, that poor arm. (112-3)

May's narrative leads to the description of an exchange between Amy and Old Mrs Winter, 'whom the reader will remember' (113). Old Mrs Winter has not been mentioned before, but we might assume she is either the mother, Voice, at some previous moment, or a double. *Footfalls*, a play about remembrance and repetition, demands that we remember something that has not been referred to or represented previously, and so cannot be remembered: this test of the reader draws attention to the act of remembrance as impossible demand. Mrs Winter asks her daughter, Amy, a series of questions about a strange incident at the church: in all likelihood, she is referring to the ghostly figure that walks the grounds. The daughter reports that she saw nothing, and asks 'what exactly, Mother, did you perhaps fancy this…strange thing was you observed?' (113). The mother of May's narrative becomes confused by her daughter's inability to remember or recall any strange occurrence. Amy states: 'I saw nothing, heard nothing, of any kind. I was not there' (113). This confuses the situation further, prompting the mother to ask Amy to repeat herself. Once again, Amy states that she was not there. 'But I heard you respond', says Mrs Winter, '[h]ow could you have responded if you were not there? [*Pause.*] How could you possible have said Amen if, as you claim, you were not there?' (113). This mysterious contradiction is not resolved by the play, and Amy becomes yet another spectral figure who defies categories of presence and absence, present and past.

Voice asks May, repeatedly: 'Will you never have done revolving it all?' (110). Steven Connor describes the figure's movement in terms of a 'compulsion to repeat', but points out that 'her walking up and down can never complete itself, an never succeed in producing that full sense of being which she seems to seek' (Connor 2007, 178). It seems that both the dialogue and movements of the play belong to an organized system of repetition, which, in turn, seems to refer to an obscure traumatic event buried in the past. If we pursue this idea further, then both the steps and the repeated narratives become symptoms of traumatic repetition, signals of a working-through process enacted by May/Amy, or imagined by the off-stage voice of the mother. No causal explanation for these uncanny returns is recounted.

Knowlson and Pilling have asserted that the play has been 'shaped to evoke feelings of distress, strangeness and mystery, a sense of inexplicable seeking, and yet the distillation of absence and loss' (Knowlson and Pilling 1979, 223). We are left, then, with what might be read as traumatic symptoms without any apparent historical cause.

The spectre in *Footfalls* appears to signal the belated return of something that was never fully present to begin with. It represents both return and non-return, something that was always already spectral, ghostly and indefinite. The spectre is akin, perhaps, to Maurice Blanchot's evocation of the 'mark' and the 'trace' in *The Step Not Beyond*. Firstly, the spectral May can be read in terms of the mark, which 'is to be absent from the present and to make the present be absent' (Blanchot 1992, 54). Like the 'mark', May appears on the stage as a presentation of absence, and simultaneously as the absence of full presence. This is best compared to the role that the signifier can play in the process of representation: with the signifier, language attempts to make present those things which are absent, whilst simultaneously revealing the absence that lingers behind the presence of all signifiers. The strange quality of the trace, for Derrida, 'affects the totality of the sign', insofar as 'the signified is originarily and essentially (and not only for a finite and created spirit) trace, that it is *always already in the position of the signifier* [italics in original]' (Derrida 1997, 73). Blanchot goes on to describe the 'trace' as that which lacks originary presence: 'the trace, being always traces, does not refer to any initial presence that would still be present, as remainder or vestige, there where it has disappeared' (Blanchot 1992, 54). The trace is different from the mark, in that it cannot be connected to a specific event, symbol or inaugurating moment: it is without a source. It is worth remembering, at this point, the final description of May in *Footfalls*, which is a stage direction denoting her absence: '*No trace of May*' (*F*, 114). The audience and the reader alike are left wondering two things: firstly, the manner in which May drifted from presence into absence (recalling Blanchot's description of the 'mark'); and secondly (recalling Blanchot's second description), whether there was any trace of May to begin with.

Describing one of Blanchot's short stories, 'The Return', Leslie Hill has suggested that 'the figure of return is not a figure at all, but more an evanescent trace always already effaced' (Hill 1997, 194). In his book, *Blanchot: Extreme Contemporary*, we might begin to draw thematic connections between Blanchot's fictional writing and Beckett's enigmatic play:

> At any event, and in either case, the term [return] provides some clue as to how, in its suspension of narrative, Blanchot's *récit* may be approached; it also gives an indication of the nature of the book's reliance on a series of events that constantly resist designation as events, and which, if one concedes the term, are in fact more like absent events, events without event, in which case they demand most plausibly to be read as a form of all-pervasive metatextual commentary on the event without event that is the *récit* itself. (192)

Samuel Beckett's work for the theatre addresses similar concerns to Blanchot's work in prose. Even the notion of 'events without event' has been alluded to, as we have seen, in critic Vivian Mercier's review of *Waiting for Godot*: 'The Uneventful Event', the play in which 'nothing happens, *twice*'.[28] *Footfalls* is occupied with the problems of identity and its representation: of the subject and its manifestation through language. The play both suspends and enacts several competing narratives, each leading readers and audience members along ambiguous paths. Where the stage appears to guarantee presence, as a confined spatial and temporal platform for the performance of texts, *Footfalls* undermines the possibility of a stable temporality, or of presence as such. The result is a suspension of identity, the inability to confirm, once and for all, the presence or agency of the human subject. The traumatic event at the heart of Beckett's play is perhaps a repetition without origin: the narratives that allude not to one stable referent, but several unclear possible sources. The traumatized subject,

---

28 Vivian Mercier, 'The Uneventful Event' in *The Irish Times*, 18 February 1956.

in this case, is not the sum of historical influences per se, but the sum of language: its differences, its deferrals, and its uncanny temporality.

Pas

Beckett confided to Billie Whitelaw that, perhaps not surprisingly, footfalls were the key to the performance of *Footfalls*. As she relates in her memoir: 'He was primarily concerned with my character's *movements*, not the words. I felt that *Footfalls* was going to be different for him: he was interested in something other than his text' (Whitelaw 1995, 141). It is, of course, in the text, that the pacing of the play is first defined: 'starting with right foot (r), from right (R), to left (L), with left foot (l) from L to R' (110).[29] But it was during Beckett's rehearsals for the Royal Court Theatre production that precise details of May's movements were most meticulously plotted. Stanley Gontarski writes that the production notebooks 'suggest Beckett's […] obsessional attention to […] pacing and May's position along her path when she speaks particular lines'.[30] What is the significance of pacing to the meaning of the play? We might begin by suggesting that the walking to and fro is a traumatic symptom, a compulsive repetition that offers May's character a vestige of control and mastery. Pacing, for May, might be a way to assert agency, the result of a conscious and deliberate decision. But we have reason to believe that May is compelled to make her steps for reasons outside her immediate control.

The mother's voice, counting in synchrony with the steps May takes, suggests that control might lay more with the mother figure, the woman whose illness necessitates that May keep a rigidly fixed routine. In this sense, the act of counting narrates May's progress toward the left or right of the stage, and also sets the tempo[31] for her action and

29 A diagram accompanies this stage direction.

30 Editorial notes on the Royal Court manuscript of *Footfalls* in *The Theatrical Notebooks of Samuel Beckett: The Shorter Plays* (London: Faber and Faber, 1999), 311.

31 Or 'pace', etymologically linked with 'pas'. The latter shall be explored in more depth below.

inaction. The steps mark a progression through time and space in a regulated and predictable manner: May's steps keep time in a similar fashion to a metronome for a practising musician, or the chiming of the bell that repeats four times during the performance: 'Faint single chime. Pause as echoes die' (109).[32] The stage directions draw explicit attention to this, describing the 'clearly audible rhythmic tread' (109) of May's steps across the stage. The production of *Footfalls*, then, is a carefully organized collaboration of text and choreography, arranged the way one might orchestrate a musical work. It is precise, exacting and regular.

However, whilst drawing the audience's attention towards the orderly progression of time, Beckett's text also does much to bend and distort it. All is not as it should be, and a closer attention to the details reveals a number of ambiguities. The decision to name the play 'Footfalls' rather than 'Footsteps', for instance, might be a straightforward aesthetic choice on the part of the author, but each word suggests a certain kind of temporality. The word 'falls' is empirically unstable, a foot that is neither raised, nor on the ground, but occupying an in-between space: the word designates a kinetic state, neither here nor there, but in continuous motion. The word 'step', in its conventional sense, would have been a more stable choice: it finds the foot on firm ground, and can be linked more strongly to ideas of presence. If 'footsteps' suggests a discreet series of moments that combine to make a journey or period of time, then 'footfalls' unsettles this journey, this time period, as we are always waiting for each step to land. The word 'footfalls' also holds a strong aural resonance, recalling the echo of a footstep that has already been made: we are thus held at a belated temporal distance from the step itself.

When Beckett translated *Footfalls* into French, his selected title made reference to the French translation of *Not I*. The earlier play was translated as *Pas moi* (literally 'not me'—with 'moi' also suggestive of

32 Notice that a bell is used to mark time in both *Footfalls* and the narrative spoken by Mouth in *Not I*.

the 'self' or 'ego') and premiered in Paris in 1975 under Beckett's direction. *Footfalls* was translated as *Pas*, and premiered in Paris in 1978, also directed by the writer. *Pas* is a French word meaning both 'step' and 'not': a strange contradiction that denotes both action and inertia. The simultaneous progression and negation of footsteps in *Footfalls* suggests a tension between the present and the non-present, the movement and inertia that characterizes the spectral figure of the play. Whilst the pacing to and fro appears to signal the acting out of a traumatic compulsion, each step is flawed by a paradox, and the progression of time becomes deregulated and disorderly. Just as the term 'stage' might describe both a stable point of reference or a discreet part of a larger sequence, spanning past, present and future, the step also affirms and confounds conventional temporality. With this in mind, we might surmise why Beckett told Whitelaw that 'pacing was a most important aspect of *Footfalls*' (Whitelaw 1995, 141). The play not only draws attention to the uncanny temporal space of the theatrical stage (a space of rehearsal and traumatic return), but also our ability to represent the past in a secure and orderly present.

Maurice Blanchot utilizes the tension of *pas* in the fragmentary work, *The Step Not Beyond* (*Le Pas Au-Delà*).[33] Lycette Nelson, translator of the English edition, introduces the text as a representative of '[t]he essential feature of the neuter in Blanchot's overall critique of the idea of presence as all'; this essential feature being 'its displacement of the subject in writing, which ultimately displaces the whole notion of the subject as the locus of self-presence' (Nelson 1992, ix). For Blanchot, writing 'alienates presence' (Blanchot 1992, 32):

> Writing, the demand to write, does not struggle *against* presence in favor of absence, nor *for* it in pretending to preserve it or communicate it. Writing is not accomplished in the present, nor does it present, nor does it present itself: still less does it represent, except

[33] For a detailed discussion of *pas* in relation to Maurice Blanchot's written output, seek out Jacques Derrida's 'P*ace Not*(s)' in *Parages*, ed. John P. Leavey, trans. Tom Conley, James Hulbert, John P. Leavey, Avital Ronnell (Stanford: Stanford University Press, 2011), 11-101.

> to play with the repetitive that introduces into the game the temporally ungraspable anteriority of the beginning again in relation to any power to begin (32)

Writing, then, far from acting as a locus of presence, is registered by Blanchot as an activity that permanently unsettles and undermines such a notion; conversely, re-presentation does not make present an originary time, place or state of being, but only duplicates or supplements a writing without presence. In one of the many first person fragments that comprise *The Step Not Beyond*, Blanchot writes '*I am not master of language. I listen to it only in its effacement, effacing myself in it* [italics in original]' (30). Blanchot's work, in Nelson's account, 'displaces first the subject, then identity in general, and finally the present itself' (Nelson 1992, ix).

In *Footfalls*, the steps are important to May as signifiers of her existence in a stable present. As Voice narrates, her daughter states that she 'must hear the feet, however faint they fall' (*F*, 111), a phrase that is repeated for emphasis. But her circuitous movements, affirmed and negated by the concept of the step that is not a step, cannot grant her control over past events. The spectre appears to allude to a traumatic event that, somewhat paradoxically, does not guarantee a stable promise of existence, it is perhaps the signifier of an event that never was; the spectre is akin, in this sense, to what Blanchot designates as 'traces [that] do not refer to the moment of the mark, they are without origin, but not without end' (Blanchot 1992, 54). And, just as the spectre suggests a trauma that perhaps never was, each step is the repetition of a step that can never fully be. As May travels through time and space, the steps both accumulate and dissolve away. In *The Step Not Beyond*, Blanchot uses the Nietzschean model of the Eternal Return as a basis for his ruminations on time, presence and subjectivity:

> The Eternal Return of the Same: the same, that is to say, myself, in as much as it sums up the rule of identity, that is, the present self. But the demand of the return, excluding any present mode from time, would never release a now in which the same would come back to the same, to myself. (11)

The demand of the return is thus problematic. The notion that the sameness of the present (and the present self of identity) is divided between a sameness of the past or the future, creates an irreconcilable conflict of temporal unity. From Blanchot, we might suggest that the demand of the return forbids the possibility of a meaningful present self, and instead order our understanding of individual identity as a kind of non-present trace, or spectre. A trace that, like Nietzsche's Eternal Return, repeats without limit, while obeying a strictly circular logic; it is, in some ways, akin to the turns and wheels of May as she moves from right to left, from left to right, a cycle without beginning, middle or end: 'One two three four five six seven eight nine wheel one two three four five six seven eight nine wheel' (*F*, 110). Whereas conventional notions of the 'return' imply a promise of exchange between the present and the past, an opportunity to grasp or comprehend what is out of reach, Blanchot's allusions to the Eternal Return offer no such consolation. For example, if we apply Blanchot's notion to contemporary understandings of trauma, or indeed, if we read *Footfalls* as a traumatic text, we are driven to conclude that the traumatic symptoms are without a certain referential cause. In Nelson's reading, 'the circulation [repetition] brings about is never circulation of the same—of a full present—but only repetition without origin' (Nelson 1992, x). The acting out of traumatic events, or the working through of a traumatic symptom, is not so much an act of remembrance as one of forgetfulness; Nelson connects this idea to Blanchot's description of the trace, which 'is at once tracing and effacement, [while] the *pas* [is] at once prohibition and transgression' (xv).

Trauma, in Beckett's late plays, focuses on the problems of language, meaning and representation, rather than on historical excavation or personal realization. Where the literary space allows for a discourse that both welcomes and suspends disbelief, the dramatic stage invites us to imagine rehearsed presentations as live and spontaneous. The theatre depends on this complicity to elicit our interest and our understanding. The assumed presence of the theatrical stage allows actors and dramatists to present scenes of cultural or historical importance, and grants audience members an opportunity to seize their representations, in order to re-visit and perhaps understand them better. Samuel Beckett's work for the theatre makes different demands of the audience. In place of realistic representations that can immerse us in the past, we have unreliable voices emanating from unclear sources. Instead of illumination, the curtain opens on darkness and obscurity. The protagonists of these shady texts are unreliable, both in their appearance and in what they relate to us: some are mere fragments, a disembodied mouth or an isolated head; others are perhaps without a body altogether. Their narratives are partial and unclear, circling around distressing events and traumatic blackouts. But the repetition of these narratives, the acting out of neurotic symptoms, does not bring closure on Beckett's stage. Instead of returning us to a moment in the past, repetition, like rehearsal, only projects us toward a later unforeseeable future. These gestures of repetition, whether they are spoken or acted out, do not bring the past within grasp in the present, but break down our grip on what we think the present to be.

The issue of trauma, whether it is manifested in a sudden and unpredictable event, an unspecified absence, or a terrible unknown loss, is intrinsically linked to the question of language in Samuel Beckett's work. His late plays, from *Not I* to *That Time* to *Footfalls* and beyond, each approximate, in their own way, issues of subjectivity, identity and representation. The texts are preoccupied with the lateness of language, the belatedness of representation, and its effects on the assumed mastery of humanist subjectivity and Western categories of knowledge.

Imagining Later

As the curtain falls on Beckett's plays, and we occupy that strange space between performances, it is worth making a few points in summary. The playwright's late dramatic works, of which we have glimpsed just a small selection, often address themselves to particular traumatic events and a single protagonist's attempt to work through them, or act them out. The belatedness, or 'afterwardsness', that defines traumatic returns is analogous in many ways to the staged performance: the performance that is always already a rehearsal, an event from the past, acted out in an unstable and disorientating present that might be repeated again in an indeterminable future. The theatrical stage is both a guarantor of presence, of conventional temporality, and a space that deregulates or suspends such presence. The traumatized subject in Beckett's late works is contextualized by a space that belongs neither to the present nor the past, but hovers indeterminately as a rehearsed repetition, endlessly repeating itself without closure or resolution.

In *Not I* we have what is perhaps the most straightforward representation (or non-representation) of the traumatic event. Mouth hovers on-stage recounting a narrative that is fragmented and, at times, incoherent. The audience is deprived of conventional exposition or the familiarity of a realist stage-set, and witnesses a theatrical performance that is accelerated and disorientating. If understanding is possible, it is a belated understanding, as an audience member or reader attempts to reorder and reconstruct the text to cohere within a more concise narrative. But the text ultimately resists such gestures. Allusions and partial descriptions of a harrowing or distressing event proliferate possibilities, and the true cause of the protagonist's distress remains obscure. If there is any clue to the cause or origin of the trauma of *Not I*, it is only the language that represents it: a language that both reveals and conceals, that speaks for and against the protagonist, both enabling and disabling a relationship between the subject and the surrounding culture. *Not I* makes a connection between the belated and fragmented traumatic symptom and the nature of language. The language of expression is also the language of rehearsal and repetition, belonging neither to the past nor the present, deferring and delaying the humanist subject's claim to presence or mastery.

Belatedness is also a prominent theme in *That Time*, where a Listener is besieged from several directions by one voice articulating three separate historical narratives. Once again, the narratives are fragmented and unclear, but allude to a distressing, half-forgotten event from the protagonist's childhood. The text refers to the standardized time of ferries and trams, contrasting an accelerated urban modernity with the strange timelessness of ruins. Cultural archives that preserve or restore historical consciousness are simultaneously rendered as spaces of decay and ambiguity. One voice narrates via three voices, assenting and dissenting with complementary and competing narratives, three separate stories from one life, presented to the audience as a non-contemporaneous stream. Once again, it is language that defines the protagonist's relationship to trauma, and his inability to secure a fixed identity. The Western humanist subject's ability to re-present the past, to cohere a stable narrative, is traumatized by language itself: voices non-contemporaneous with themselves unravel and undermine the protagonist's grip on both the past and the present. *That Time* reveals the impossibility of recalling or representing any single, specific historical moment in its completeness. The cultural archives and institutions of language, history and expression become a spectacle of decay and disintegration in *That Time*, finally overwhelming the subject at the close of the play.

But it is *Footfalls* that offers perhaps the most nuanced dramatization of the traumatized subject, forever blurring the distinction between past memories and present reality through its pacing spectral figure. The figure's progression through time becomes a point of confusion as she repeats her course from left to right of the stage, and back to left from right. A distant voice, perhaps from beyond the grave, narrates her course to and fro and draws our attention further back to some disquieting past event. While the events alluded to in the text are tempered by traumatic resonance, they are events without conclusive foundations: there is an unsure beginning, where 'it all' began, but we are never sure what 'it' might refer to. We only know that 'it' revolves unceasingly, repeated time and again through speech and gesture. The encounter with the ghostly figure, half-seen by Mrs Winter, is the uncertain centre of the play: a human form that is neither present nor absent, an event that is not, strictly-speaking, an event at all. The ghost at the ambiguous centre of the narrative is nothing more than a partial repetition of an inaccessible past. Even what is on-stage (and thus observable) concedes to a similar logic; May (or is it Amy?) steps across the stage as a ghostly double, a repetition without an origin.

In *Footfalls*, as in *Not I* and *That Time* before it, trauma, language and the problem of representation are inseparable. The repetition that signals traumatic return becomes the repetition of an event that has no fixed source, an event that was never properly born. The problem of presenting trauma on the stage, or indeed of manifesting any empirical presence, is beset by the intrinsic belatedness of the stage, of the performance that is always already a textual rehearsal, referring to the past whilst simultaneously deferring to the future. *Footfalls*, *That Time*, and *Not I* each present an traumatic impasse in language and meaning. Language exists before events are conceived or understood as such, but its representations are always formed belatedly, at an insurmountable temporal distance from the event. Beckett's work for the stage, and indeed much of his other creative output, focuses on the tension between the self and language, the formulation and dissolution of Western humanist subjectivity. Narratives of trauma become a useful way to explore these ideas, as their representation draws questions of memory, identity and knowledge into sharp focus. Language is the means by which the humanist subject guarantees presence and mastery over his or her surrounding environment, but in Beckett's texts it belongs neither to the present or the past: it is spectral, hovering between states, always already too early and too late. Accordingly, stage manifestations do not guarantee full presence, but are like belated textual rehearsals that can never entirely manifest. They, too, belong neither in the present nor the past, but are always late, always to come.

3. Radio: The Voice Breaks

Haunted Media

Radio

Samuel Beckett's relationship with the BBC was not only productive in an artistic sense, but promoted the widespread dissemination of his work throughout the UK and parts of Europe. Beckett's use of radio also allowed for the 'exploitation' of an alternate dramatic medium to the theatre. Through a reading of such works, with a particular emphasis on *All That Fall*, I am going to suggest that Beckett's radio drama draws upon qualities that are unique to the medium, and which bring concepts of traumatic experience and modernity into close communication. Of course, to contextualise the importance of radio to such a discussion, it would be useful first to understand the way it was understood in the late nineteenth and early twentieth centuries. By reading radio as an emblem of social, cultural and technological advancement, we might begin to analyse some of its ideological significance, and assess how Beckett's plays for the medium engage with themes of trauma and modernity in a number of subtle and evocative ways.[1]

Telecommunications is widely understood as one of the most significant modern developments of the last two hundred years. Since the introduction of the electromagnetic telegraph in 1831, communications technology has profoundly changed the social and economic landscape. The first half of the twentieth century witnessed a rapid

1 For a detailed exposition of the role that radio and radio theory played in Samuel Beckett's life and work, see Brynhildur Boyce's 'The Radio Life and Work of Samuel Beckett', *Nordic Irish Studies*, 8:1 (2009), 47-65. Interestingly, Boyce begins by pointing out that Beckett's life 'precisely spanned the age of analogue radio' (47), and begins with a brief history that coincides with the writer's lifespan.

evolution in telephone and radio devices, objects mass-produced for companies, organizations and affluent family homes. It afforded the possibility to increase productivity and efficiency within Western capitalist markets, and appeared to alter traditional limitations of time and space. But the benefits were not simply of a practical or commercial nature: the growth of radio coincided with its recognition as an entertainment device. In 1933, as a young Samuel Beckett lodged in London, the BBC began an international programme of public broadcasting. In addition to daily news bulletins, their schedule offered a range of aspirational dispatches, focusing on culture, history and the arts. Throughout the 1930s, radio technology fast became a cultural wellspring of news and information. It featured 'vigorous debates on the most current social, moral and philosophical issues', offered 'traditional and avant-garde music with world-renowned musical virtuosi' and dramatized 'an unparalleled range of old and new plays, [...] performed by the best actors in the English-speaking world' (Gordon 1996, 94). Radio was perceived as a beacon of modern progress, with early broadcasts carrying the idealistic, even utopian, remit of enlightening and educating its audience.

In the 1940s, through the advance and recession of the Second World War, the radio became a vital component of daily life. It was via radio broadcasts that war was first announced to the public, and from radio that civilians were kept informed of political and historical changes, both home and abroad. In the wake of the Second World War, radio broadcasting provided reports of the devastation, and aspired to play a part in the recuperative process. Public broadcasters considered radio as 'the prime re-educative agency of the post-war world' (Carpenter 1997, 6), a device that reaffirmed traditional societal values, and attempted to consolidate conventional understandings of gender, class and national identity.

As early as 1930, the Head of the BBC's Education Department, J. C. Stobart, suggested a radio station 'that would offer continuous serious listening'; Stobart fondly suggested calling it the Minerva Programme, 'after the Roman Goddess of the arts' (Carpenter 1997,

3). In 1946, the BBC Third Programme was launched, a network aiming to circulate an awareness and appreciation of culture and the arts. The network accumulated a strong following from artistic and academic communities for its promotional support of noted writers and dramatists, including Philip Larkin, Harold Pinter and Dylan Thomas. But there were accusations that the Third Programme promoted an elitist cultural agenda. The audience was presumed to be 'persons of taste, of intelligence, and of education' (3), eager to preserve a high cultural and artistic standard. Humphrey Carpenter, in his account of the Programme's history, has applauded its ambitious intentions, allowing 'the young and the not well educated [to] be introduced to good music and speech'. Carpenter goes on to align the Third Programme with the wider goals of post-war radio broadcasting, asserting that 'the prime function of public service broadcasting' is to aid and maintain the 'cultural health of the country' (xiii).

Historically, Samuel Beckett's plays for radio might be considered as an extension of this narrative. *All That Fall*, his first work for the medium, was written on commission from the Third Programme—a decision made on the strength of the writer's growing popularity in Europe. First broadcast on 13 January 1957, and again on 19 January, it was welcomed with a positive critical response. One reviewer noted that it was 'produced with great skill', 'something new, and fitted' for the medium. The play was praised for its realism, an evocative and familiar portrait of rural Irish life, complete with recognizable characters and everyday tribulations: the same reviewer celebrated how 'in seconds Beckett established a world complete'.[2] Many of the play's elements were ideally suited for radio: the use of sound effects, for instance, of rural animals at the opening, of small vehicles coming and going, were each used to enhance the realism of its Irish landscape (but more on that later). The composition of characters' names often playfully implied their qualities: aural puns such as

---

2 Christopher Logue, 'For those still standing', *New Statesman*, 14 September 1957.

Maddy, Mr Slocum, or Miss Fit become an important part of the performance. We might consider Beckett's *All That Fall* as a kind of exemplary radio text, an artistic work that satisfies dramatic convention, and something that can be placed without difficulty within the Third Programme's cultural repertoire. It is a work that appears to express some truth about the world, while continuing public perceptions of radio as an emblem of regeneration and modern progress. Or is it?

All That Fall is stranger than it sounds.[3] In a letter to Nancy Cunard, dated 4 July 1956, Beckett reflected on an early idea for the play: 'Never thought about radio play technique but in dead of t'other night got a nice gruesome idea full of cartwheels and dragging of feet and puffing and panting which may or may not lead to something.'[4] The idea was developed throughout the autumn and winter months, and reflected on ideas of death, decay and deterioration. Punctuated with moments of black humour, the text comprised a series of observations on old age and premature death. At its conclusion, few of the narrative strands are resolved and the audience are denied traditional closure. Yet, while Beckett's text is accepted by the wider culture as a valid and meaningful work of art, the play troubles our expectations of radio as a public symbol of progress and regeneration. Instead, *All*

---

3 In some sense, Beckett's *All That Fall* can be read as a radio play that both evokes and revolts against the standards set by other contemporary works broadcast by the BBC's Third Programme, chief among them being Dylan Thomas' *Under Milk Wood*, first broadcast in 1954. On 19 November 1958, Beckett expressed his distaste for Thomas' work to Barbara Bray, BBC script editor for the Third Programme: 'I listened to Dylan Thomas reading his fat poems and being witty on poetry, poets and himself and didn't like any of it, the pulpit voice and hyperarticulation and sibilation, but I'm lousy public'. Excerpted from *The Letters of Samuel Beckett, Volume III: 1957-1965*, eds. George Craig, Martha Dow Fehsenfeld, Dan Gunn, Lois More Overbeck (Cambridge: Cambridge University Press, 2014), 184.

4 Samuel Beckett to Nancy Cunard, 4 July 1956, in *The Letters of Samuel Beckett, Volume II: 1941-1956*, eds. George Craig, Martha Dow Fehsenfeld, Dan Gunn, Lois More Overbeck (Cambridge: Cambridge University Press, 2011), 631.

That Fall becomes a locus of struggle and ambiguity. Instead of knowledge and enlightenment, the broadcast ends with a tone of sadness and uncertainty. As Ackerley and Gontarski have noted, 'There are black secrets in the lives of the moribund Rooneys, about which they brood and which we glimpse only darkly' (Ackerley and Gontarski 2004, 12). The production of Beckett's works for radio trouble the medium.

Readers and critics have often sought thematic connections between *All That Fall* and Beckett's other work, and it is not difficult to see why. The play might appear to correspond quite clearly with any number of the writer's dark and troubling texts. But where the prose might address the problems of language, and the stage-plays might complicate our notion of action and agency, *All That Fall* revolves around the technical problems of its medium. That is to say, it is a radio play very much concerned with the medium of radio itself. In a 1974 letter to director Alan Schneider, Beckett suggested that

> *All That Fall* is really for radio only. It has been tried in some out of the way theatres, in the dark & with faces only lit on [word illegible], but not much point in that [...] I think better leave it where it belongs.[5]

Beckett's letter most obviously refers to the radio-specific production values of the play, which would make productions in another medium unsuitable. Notably, some years later, Beckett was sent a proposition by Swedish filmmaker Ingmar Bergman, who hoped to visually stage both *All That Fall* and *Embers*. James Knowlson reports that 'the answer was a firm "No"' (*DF*, 505), the implication being that the texts were simply not compatible. But Beckett's notion that *All That Fall* 'belongs' in radio is curious, and should perhaps be explored further. Jeffrey Sconce has suggested that radio is one of several electronic technologies that disrupt our understanding of place, presence and

5 Samuel Beckett to Alan Schneider, 1 September 1974, qtd. in *No Author Better Served: The Correspondence of Samuel Beckett and Alan Schneider*, ed. Maurice Harmon (Cambridge: Harvard University Press, 1998), 319.

origin, defining them in his study as 'haunted media' (Sconce 2000). Sconce begins his investigation with the 'social and historical circumstances [that led] electronic media [...] to be seen as "living" and "alive"', a study that unfolds as 'a cultural history of electronic presence, an interpretive examination of the fields of electronic fiction socially generated around telecommunications technologies' (6). How strange it is, then, to consider Beckett's remarks alongside those of Sconce. *All That Fall* itself is, to some degree, a performance concerned with presence, or, more specifically, with notions of the ghostly. Beckett's dramatic work for the medium disturbs traditional categories of place and belonging.

Drawing on the work of Jeffrey Sconce, we can begin to unravel what is so strangely disconcerting about radio technology, and discover that the peculiar, superstitious origins of radio bears strong thematic ties to the content of Beckett's plays. Sconce's work is ambitious, a project that attempts to reveal why we continue to associate various telecommunications devices with 'mystical powers' (6) and ghostly emanations. If we are to be equally ambitious, perhaps we can ascribe some of Sconce's observations and suggestions to Beckett's work, and ascertain whether there are any obvious correlations. In Sconce's study, the developments of modern communications, or 'haunted media', are understood in relation to changing definitions of human consciousness and identity. Whilst there is no doubt that Beckett's radio plays often explore issues surrounding personal identity and subjective consciousness, it is worth exploring just how deep these kinds of questions run.

Since the introduction of the electric telegraph, modern ideas about presence and consciousness have been mediated at an intersection between technology, language and subjectivity. In Sconce's words, the telegraph prompted a proliferation of new technologies that evoked 'a new way of conceptualizing communications and consciousness' (7). Traditional concepts of human consciousness and presence underwent a series of new evaluations, as notions of time, space and presence were redefined by modern globalizing technologies. The telegram and the birth of wireless broadcasting were two major elements in this new modern era. Throughout the nineteenth century, the idea of electricity became endowed with a paranormal significance, conceived by many as 'a mystical and even divine substance that animated body and soul' (7):

> Telegraph lines carried human messages from city to city and from continent to continent, but more important, they appeared to carry the animating 'spark' of consciousness itself beyond the confines of the physical body. (7)

The assumed dissemination of human consciousness across such a broad range of technological platforms inevitably led to new and 'increasingly disassociative relationships among body, mind, space, and time' (7). Radio was seen as just one device capable of conveying a semblance of human consciousness across an electrical current. Sconce points out that the very idea of an electric current grew in popularity alongside William James' appointment of the 'stream of consciousness': two very similar metaphors that imply a strong confluence between modern technology and the human mind (Sconce 2000, 8). The assumed independence of mind over body culminated in a powerful cultural mythology, and, in the nineteenth century, new media were perceived as a platform that allowed the subject to 'leave the body and transport his or her consciousness to a distant destination' (8-9).

While we reflect on the problems of origin and identity, it is worth saying a few words about arrivals and destinations, the movement of broadcast content from one discrete location to another. In essence, audiences bear witness to an impossible moment: a singular, 'live' event that is always-already delayed by spatial and temporal distances. A recorded wireless broadcast can be transmitted to any number of unspecified and undifferentiated spaces, and can be played at any time in any number of different contexts: a broadcast has no origin, in the strictest sense, and no final destination. And so, paradoxically, if *All That Fall* is a play that truly belongs to radio, it does not, or cannot, finally belong anywhere. I would suggest that it is this strange quality of electronic broadcasting that is appropriate to a 'gruesome' play like *All That Fall*, along with Beckett's other radio work. The broadcast signal is akin, in some ways, to the traumatic memory that resurfaces as if from nowhere, disrupting the subject's coherent experience of the world. While the play itself adopts and dramatizes a number of traumatic themes or events, it simultaneously suggests something traumatic at the heart of the medium itself, and, indeed, of modernity.

Spectral Radio

In the last twenty years, there has been a proliferation in studies that invoke spectrality as a theoretical paradigm. Roger Luckhurst has described the phenomenon, as it applies to critical and cultural studies, in an article for *Textual Practice*, labelling it as a current trend in academic scholarship:

> A certain strand of cultural theory in France, Britain and America embraced a language of ghosts and the uncanny—or rather of anachronic spectrality and hauntology—following the publication of Jacques Derrida's *Specters of Marx* in 1993 (translated into English in 1994). This text has proved extremely influential, prompting something of a 'spectral turn' in contemporary criticism. (Luckhurst 2002, 527)

The influence of this 'turn' has had a striking effect across a broad range of Humanities disciplines; and it has taken a strong and convincing hold in contemporary Beckett scholarship. In 1996, Jean-Michel Rabaté published 'Beckett and the Ghosts of Departed Quantities' as part of a larger work, *The Ghosts of Modernity*.[6] Nicholas Royle also dedicated a chapter to Beckett in his 2003 study, *The Uncanny*, suggesting that his writing calls 'for another thinking of mourning and spectrality, in short the impossible experience of posthumous culture' (Royle

---

6 See Jean-Michel Rabaté, 'Beckett and the Ghosts of Departed Quantities' in *The Ghosts of Modernity* (Florida: University Press of Florida, 1996), 148-170. See also 'Shades of the Color Gray', 171-187.

2003, 224). Jonathan Boulter's recent *Beckett: A Guide for the Perplexed* (2008) features similar thematic concerns, addressing the uncanny, trauma and issues of mourning in the writer's theatre and prose. Possible intersections between spectrality and modernity, or modern technology, have also been explored. Ulrika Maude's *Beckett, Technology and the Body* included a chapter entitled 'Seeing ghosts' (Maude 2009, 113-34), and several major scholars have explored the spectral 'shades' of the television plays. More recently still, the Autumn 2010 issue of academic journal *Limit(e) Beckett* was entitled 'Spectral Beckett', a collection of articles debating the role that Derridean spectrality, or the Freudian uncanny, plays in Beckett's oeuvre.[7]

The presence of spectres in Beckett's radio plays has also been touched upon as an area worthy of deeper investigation.[8] In fact, Ruby Cohn, in her essay 'Ghosting Through Beckett', draws attention to the first appearance of the word 'Ghost' in Beckett's radio play, *All That Fall*,

> when Maddy Dunne Rooney accuses the Station-Master Mr. Barrell: 'You look as if you had seen a ghost.' But on radio, a blind medium, neither Mr. Barrell, nor Maddy, nor we can see anything, much less a ghost.[9]

The appearance of the word 'ghost' coincides with Maddy's impression of the Station Master, whom she describes as someone who has seen, or witnessed, something that has not, or cannot, be fully seen or witnessed. In this way, the appearance of the word 'ghost' occurs simultaneously with its non-appearance, since it fails to materialise. This

---

7 *Limit(e) Beckett* 1 (2010) <http://www.limitebeckett.parissorbonne.fr/one.html> [Accessed: 15 March 2011].

8 Notably, Sarah West's chapter on *Embers*, entitled 'Talking Ghosts', in *Say It: The Performative Voice in the Dramatic Works of Samuel Beckett* (Amsterdam and New York: Editions Rodopi B.V., 2010), 64-87.

9 Ruby Cohn, 'Ghosting Through Beckett' in *Beckett in the 1990s: Selected Papers from the Second International Beckett Symposium, Held in The Hague, 8-12 April, 1992*, eds. Marius Buning and Lois Oppenheim (Amsterdam: Rodopi, 1993), 2.

happening, which holds some ominous significance in the play, draws attention not only to our own inability to witness or apprehend events, as listeners, but to the strange affinity that appears to exist between spectrality and the medium of radio.

In an article discussing the influence of Rudolf Arnheim on Beckett's radio work, Gaby Hartel is resolutely tuned-in to the medium's strange possibilities. Hartel identifies a number of parallels between radio technology and popular nineteenth-century superstition, where the *zeitgeist* entailed an obsession with spirits from other times:

> The uncannily immaterial presence of sounds severed from a traceable source, of disembodied voices reaching the listener from a non-defined, vast space, and the power they exercised on the human mind, permeated nineteenth-century thought. There was talk of voices from the grave and of mysterious messages, emanating from the mesmerising electric field of parallel worlds. These ideas surfaced after the invention and public introduction of telephony, of the phonograph cylinder and the gramophone. In 1878 Edison presented his invention of the phonograph in tune with the *zeitgeist* as a machine, capable of producing acousting deathmasks in that they could record the 'last words of the dying'. (Hartel 2010, 221)

Possible connections between Beckett's aesthetic and the spectral capabilities of radio broadcasting are touched upon in Jeffrey Sconce's chapter, 'The Voice from the Void' (Sconce 2000, 59-91). Describing the transmissions of the Latvian psychologist Konstantin Raudive, who had utilised a radio device 'to hear the voices of the dead' (87), Sconce states a possible thematic affinity with Beckett's post-war prose, suggesting that 'it is difficult to read the transcripts of Raudive's radio conversations with the dead without thinking of the formless narrator of Samuel Beckett's *The Unnamable*' (88). These 'formless narrator[s]' do indeed seem to emanate from an indeterminable source, as voices from an elsewhere, an unknown exterior space. Raudive, who was a disciple of Carl Jung, published the results of his experiments in the United States in 1971, but the original title of his study, published in German, is significant: *Unhoerbares Wird Hoerbar* (*The Inaudible Made Audible*). There is, it would seem, a correlation that exists between the epistemological concerns of Raudive's project, and the aesthetic preoccupations of Samuel Beckett's work. Both devoted themselves to projects concerned with the possibility of representing, or making present, something that ordinarily defies empirical means of assessment. In Beckett's case, a letter written to Axel Kaun on 9 July 1937,[10] appears to reveal something close to a personal aesthetic project:

> As we cannot eliminate language all at once, we should at least leave nothing undone that might contribute to its falling into disrepute. To bore one hole after another in it, until what lurks behind it—be it something or nothing—begins to seep through; I cannot imagine a higher goal for the writer today.[11]

Where Raudive attempts to make the inaudible audible, Beckett's writing attempts to represent unrepresentability. Through the latter's work in radio drama, this attempt is constructed as a kind of examination, or deconstruction, of the everyday appearances of the real world, followed by presentations of the function of individual agency within that world. If Sconce's observation about Beckett's affinity with Raudive has value, it is in their shared approach to the cultural fascination that surrounds radio, and its perceived powers to signal something spectral, deferred or othered. In Beckett's texts for radio, this becomes a means to explore human relationships with technology, and the effect that processes of modernity might have upon constructions of Western humanist subjectivity.

Beckett's navigation of the assumed naturalness of culture takes form in the radiophonic world of *All That Fall*, a nostalgic evocation of rural Ireland. John Pilling has observed that elements of the play's setting are 'deliberately exaggerated to remind us of [their] fictional status', giving rise to the impression its characters, too, could be

---

10 Often referred to in Beckett Studies as the *German Letter of 1937*.

11 Samuel Beckett to Axel Kaun ('German Letter of 1937'), 9 July 1937, trans. Ruby Cohn in Samuel Beckett, *Disjecta: Miscellaneous Writing and a Dramatic Fragment*, ed. Ruby Cohn (London: John Calder, 1983), 172.

aware of their status as 'mere fictional constructs' (Pilling 1976, 94-5). This attention to both verisimilitude and its inevitable artifice blurs the boundaries between what is real and what is not. As Pilling describes it:

> The human voice and the sound induced by radiophonic devices thus interact to create a world constantly aware of its own artifice, powerfully engaging because of our habitual suspension of disbelief, but disturbingly transient and insubstantial when we try to examine it, constantly tending to fragment itself into individual, disconnected sounds. (94-5)

Throughout Beckett's writing for radio, the medium itself breeds all manner of defamiliarising associations: it stands not only as a beacon of modern technological progress, but a site of dissolution, fragmentation and paranormal superstition. This undoubtedly has an impact on the way we perceive the world of the play, but, more significantly, these qualities impact on the way we consider Beckett's construction of character. There is in *All That Fall*, and indeed in much of Beckett's writing, the notion of human identity as little more than representation, an uneasy fabrication of language, culture and technology.

Wireless Subjects

Throughout the late 1950s, Samuel Beckett continued to experiment with dramatic narratives for wireless broadcast. His radio works vary in length, from rough twenty-minute sketches to full-length dramas, and Beckett was often unhappy with the final results. Of *Embers*, he wrote to a friend that it was 'not very satisfactory, but I think just worth doing… I think it just gets by for radio'.[12] Biographer James Knowlson notes that 'in spite of Beckett's own view that it was a "rather ragged" text, [*Embers*] still won the RAI prize in the 1959 Prix Italia contest' (*DF*, 446). Whether the play is a masterpiece or a failed experiment is perhaps beside the point: what is interesting to us is the

---

12 Samuel Beckett qtd. in Ackerley and Gontarski, *The Grove Companion*, 169.

way *Embers* utilizes the medium. The development of modern technology has often been closely interwoven with developing ideas about the Western humanist subject: the Cartesian notion of a mind-body split, a binary opposition that privileges human consciousness as transcendent. These ideas are persistent throughout the radio's history, and find a ghostly manifestation in Samuel Beckett's play. Much like *Endgame*, written during the same period, critics have suggested that *Embers* takes place within a human skull;[13] in both plays, the audience is presented with confined spaces, with two windows that open out onto the world. Rather than remain confined to the physical, corporeal skull, thoughts and voices are transmitted beyond. In Sconce's account, the invention of wireless communications led, in some instances, to reports of telepathic communication: the possibility of a transcendent communication from one mind to another, breaking down distinctions between private and public spheres. The notion of 'mental radio' (Sconce 2000, 76), suggesting a confluence between the human and the machine, prompted 'a flurry of theorization and experimentation in the first years of the [twentieth] century', and created lasting associations for the possibilities of telepathy and radio. In its treatment of concepts of identity, isolation, and communication, *Embers* might be said to invoke the cultural history of radio itself.

The ambitious promise of transmitting human consciousness, unproblematically, from one time and place to another has become the defining appeal of many contemporary technologies. But historically, such modern evolution has raised several complex questions about what constitutes human consciousness, and the reality of wireless' early utopian promise. Sconce's cultural history of 'haunted media' reveals a technologically-altered vision of humanity as fundamentally uncanny and estranged. Sconce observes that the invention of 'the telegraph and early wireless held the tantalizing promises of contacting the dead in the afterlife and aliens of other planets' (Sconce

---

13 Ackerley and Gontarski, *The Grove Companion*, 170: 'Written shortly after *Endgame*, the radio drama could be a monodrama, the action taking place in a skull'

2000, 10-11). It is an account that bears strong correlations with Nicholas Royle's observations in his collection of essays on the uncanny, specifically, what we might consider to be uncanny about modern radio devices:

> The most striking example of the uncanny has to do with ghosts and haunting, and Freud might have started with that but apparently didn't, didn't want to, forgot to, or couldn't. The passage in question suggests that the reason for not starting there has to do with 'what is purely gruesome', with the strange reality of death, with dead bodies and the frightening persistence across the centuries of belief in the 'return of the dead', including modern-day 'spiritualism' with its proclamations about being able telepathically 'to get in touch with the souls of the departed'. (Royle 2003, 51)

In Beckett's *Embers*, we are confronted by a series of strange, in-between spaces, and the uncanny return of the protagonist's dead father. The original title of the play, 'Water's Edge' (Ackerley and Gontarski 2004, 169), articulates the divide between an empirical, territorialized land and a vast, de-territorialized unknown: between the rational and the irrational, the land of the living, and the sea of the dead: 'It's only on the surface, you know. Underneath all is as quiet as the grave' (*E*, 44). The drama unfolds 'on the margins of land and sea' (Ackerley and Gontarski 2004, 169), where the protagonist, Henry, is haunted by memories of his drowned father: 'I thought I might try and get as far as the water's edge. [*Pause. With a sigh.*] And back. [*Pause.*] Stretch my old bones' (*E*, 42). The sea is 'scarcely audible' (35) in *Embers*, but used to punctuate the father's absence at every dramatic pause:

> *Slither of shingle as he sits. Sea, still faint, audible throughout what follows whenever pause indicated.*

Ackerley and Gontarski point out that 'Henry is haunted by the sound of the sea' (Ackerley and Gontarski 2004, 170), the water acting as a symbol of death and uncanny return. The water also evokes the metaphors of 'stream of consciousness', and 'electric current', a blend of the human and the technological. To the audience, the sound of the sea is evocative of static interference, noise that interrupts the signal:

this interference also marks the space of a tragedy that troubles Henry's peace of mind. The sound of the sea, then, demarcates a haunted space of inarticulate human consciousness, disembodied voices and traumatic returns.

Embers

Jeffrey Sconce has described how soon after the first public demonstration of the electromagnetic telegraph, America became occupied by a 'tremendously popular social and religious movement that would come to be known as "Modern Spiritualism"' (Sconce 2000, 12). A belief that it was possible to contact with the dead was reinforced by the recent developments in communications technology. Séances were held by mourning friends and families hoping to communicate with loved ones, and a new terminology was coined around existing technological vocabulary (the 'spiritual telegraph', for instance): 'More than a metaphor, the spiritual telegraph was for many an actual technology of the afterlife, one invented by scientific geniuses in the world of the dead for the explicit purpose of instructing the land of the living in the principles of utopian reform' (12). In Beckett's *Embers*, the radio appears to enable some form of ghostly reunion between dead father and mourning son, bringing both generations into contact in the same ambiguously defined space:

> Who is beside me now? [*Pause.*] An old man, blind and foolish. [*Pause.*] My father, back from the dead, to be with me. [*Pause.*] As if he hadn't died. [*Pause.*] No, simply back from the dead, to be with me, in this strange place. [*Pause.*] Can he hear me? [*Pause.*] Yes, he must hear me. [*Pause.*] To answer me? [*Pause.*] No, he doesn't answer me. (*E*, 35)

Beckett has commented on the oddness of this encounter in his correspondence, suggesting that *Embers* rests 'sur une ambiguité: le personage a-t-il une hallucination ou est-il en presence de la réalité?' [My translation: 'on an ambiguity: is the character having an hallucination, or in the presence of reality?']ʼ[14] Throughout *Embers*, the medium destabilizes a number of empirical certainties: the audience cannot see or discern action or locations, the play is closed to smell, touch, or taste - even hearing is at least partially disabled through the dramatic use of silence, or the presence of misleading sounds. The only empirical dimension that seems viable is time, which governs the narrative along a straight course from beginning to end. But dramatic time is no exception, continually fractured and deranged within the plays, or seemingly altogether absent. In *Embers*, we have Ada's character calling out from twenty years before the narrative is set, an ambiguous stage direction rather than an explicit cue for the audience:

> ADA: [*Twenty years earlier, imploring.*] Don't! Don't ! (42)

Radio technology in Beckett's work appears to place sound into a kind of suspended animation. Such temporal disorientation was used with great dramatic success in *Krapp's Last Tape*, where a tension perpetually exists between the live Krapp we observe on the stage, and the old Krapp (in fact, the younger Krapp) we hear on a recording. Sounds become 'old sound' in *Embers*, where, as the 'remote' (39) voice of Ada reflects, the events of the present seem to resemble 'another time, in the same place' (40).

Jacques Derrida notes the derangement of time in his outline of hauntology in *Specters of Marx*. In an analysis of Shakespeare's *Hamlet*, Derrida draws attention to the Prince's midnight encounter with his dead father as an encounter with spectrality, a non-embodied embodiment of rational and empirical uncertainty that undermines traditional logic and order. The appearance of the spectre marks the destabilization of Western categories of knowledge, each founded, in some way, on the modern classifications of presence and time. If we consider presence to be mediated by time, that is, the presence of the living within a given context at a particular moment, the spectre troubles our recognition of both the present and the past.

---

14 Samuel Beckett qtd. in Ackerley and Gontarski, *The Grove Companion*, 169.

In *Embers*, we have already observed the uneasy border territory between land and sea, but other memories are evoked at a time 'past midnight' (37). It is a 'strange place' (35) of twilight and temporal uncertainty, where events of the past emerge and coexist with events of the present. Memories are ambiguously brought to the fore, appearing to the protagonist as though they were live events. All appears in recession, all appears to be dying, but there remains some trace of old presences, old realities, which continue to haunt the present. In place of the metaphor of 'The Water's Edge', we have 'Embers', the dying embers of a fire that refuses to fade:

> HENRY: Dead silence then, not a sound, only the fire, all coal, burning down now [...] Bolton at the window his back to the hangings, holding them a little apart with his hand looking out, white world, even the spire, white to the vane, most unusual, silence in the house, not a sound, only the fire, no flames now, embers. [...] not a sound, only the embers, sound of dying, dying glow (*E*, 37)

The 'dead silence' is supplanted by the fire burning down, but never quite extinguished. The sound of the fire, and the sound of the embers, is 'not a sound' as such, since the sound would suggest full presence; instead, the embers present a dying of sound and light, a state of continuing diminishment that remains stalled between full presence and complete absence. Temporal distortions throughout *Embers* suggest an encounter with spectrality, of what Derrida calls 'the going of the gone' (Derrida 2012, 28) that is somehow resistant to telos, conclusion or resolution. It is a moment of transition between two states of presence, or between two temporal moments, that disrupts traditional concepts of knowledge and understanding. It is a 'disjointure in the very presence of the present, this sort of non-contemporaneity of present time with itself' (29) that troubles our classifications of origin, of destination, of Western empirical certainty and rational thought. In Beckett's play, the temporal and spatial borderlands could be said to mark 'a transitory moment, but whose transition comes, if one can say that, from the future' (28). There is a lack of closure in the play, reflected through the minds and attitudes of Beckett's characters. As Henry remarks in *Embers*:

> HENRY: I never finished it, I never finished any of them, I never finished anything, everything always went on for ever. (36)

The disorientation of time and memory in Beckett's play refuses to be gone: the traditional narrative marking beginning to end is little more than a beginning to an end—an end that never stops, never concludes, but instead exists in a kind of 'radical untimeliness' (29).

Diminishing in Tone

Samuel Beckett's original title for the radio play *Cascando* was 'Calando', a musical term meaning 'diminishing in tone'. RTF[15] officials informed Beckett of its similarity to another word, 'calendos', a slang term for 'cheese', which somewhat deterred the playwright (Ackerley and Gontarski 2004, 83). Throughout his radio plays, there is a close consideration of the way sound regulates or breaks time within the narrative, and the way sound is used to represent characters or landscapes. In some sense, 'calando' is a useful way of considering the more ghostly, or spectral, elements of Beckett's radio characters: they are, in some sense, only partly present. As electronic representations, they are, in another sense, not really there at all:

> ADA: Is there anyone about?
>
> HENRY: Not a living soul. (43)

Beckett's use of radio appears to be concerned with the nature of the form itself: its ambiguities, its shifting deferrals, and its silences. There are, for example, strong parallels between Beckett's texts and Sconce's cultural history of broadcasting technologies. In the second chapter of *Haunted Media*, Sconce explores perceptions of a 'more melancholy

15 Radiodiffusion-Télévision Française.

and alienating sense of presence, examining both its general emergence in the vast social transformations of modernity and in specific moments that inextricably linked wireless technology with death' (Sconce 2000, 15). Sconce tightens his focus on 'the more alienating aspects of modernity's social and technological transformations' (62).

Sconce begins to identify historical trends in wireless broadcasting with the isolating and even alienating effects of modern technology. But there is more to this account than philosophical ennui, or a reactionary response to historical events. In Sconce's study, and perhaps also in Beckett's plays, we might begin to observe that modern technology holds some kind of traumatic potential for its users, a traumatic side-effect that is not easily classified. This is an issue that will be explored in much greater detail later in the chapter, but for now we can begin to imagine a connection between the spectral figures of Beckett's radio plays, and the troubling, alienating perceptions many began to perceive in the medium itself. For instance, Sconce points out that many popular cultural evocations of wireless broadcasting offered a 'terrifying vision of absolute isolation' for its users:

> Tales of wireless in the first three decades of the [twentieth] century frequently centred on lovers separated by death but reunited through wireless, paranormal romances that were bittersweet meditations on the radio subject's electronic inscription and mediation. [...] these stories portrayed wireless, not only as a medium of mass communication, but as a marker of personal isolation where the loss of the wire allowed for extraordinary yet potentially terrifying forms of electrical disembodiment. (15)

Samuel Beckett's radio characters are subjects cast into a stream, or current, or sea, that renders them little more than ghostly emanations, partial and fragmentary spectres. Are the characters even akin to the listeners at home, sitting in dark and enclosed domestic spaces, hearing strange voices coming out of the dark? Catherine Covert has researched the disconcerting effects that radio appeared to have upon early generations of listeners, noting a sense of 'individual alienation from social and personal involvement, an alienation which appeared to be encouraged by peculiar aspects of the process, content and form of the new technology'.[16] As Sconce so succinctly puts it, 'citizens of the early century were astonished by wireless and yet remained apprehensive about the often terrifying world it seemed to bring into the home' (62-3).

In a 1960 review of Beckett's *Embers*, published in the *Times Literary Supplement,* an anonymous contributor made a general observation about the playwright's artistic preoccupations: '[The plays are], in so far as that distinction can ever be properly made about Mr. Beckett's work, realistic rather than allegorical, or perhaps it would be better to say psychological rather than philosophical in their interest'.[17] And there is certainly an argument to be made for the way Beckett represents complex psychological ideas to an audience. But, with the present discussion in mind, I would argue that Beckett's writing combines psychological interests within a broader philosophical context—neither realistic nor allegorical, but rather theoretical in its basis. Beckett's radio plays provoke discussion, rather than imply an empirical reality governed by specific rules and values. Beckett's work evokes the problem of representation, more than perhaps any other singular theme, interrogating conventional assumptions about the mediums we use to communicate. For example, *All That Fall* does not dramatise the event at the centre of the text, but evokes it retrospectively, after the fact; *Embers* shifts between an ambiguous present and memories of a distant past. There is a suggestion of some traumatic event or experience in both plays, but it is subject to a pervasive mood of ambivalence and ambiguity—of that which will not, or cannot, be adequately represented.

Sconce has broadly articulated the sense of alienation and melancholy of radio and television throughout *Haunted Media*, and accounts for the social and religious movements that brought uncanny associations to mind. At the centre of his argument appears a convic-

---

16 Catherine Covert, qtd. in Sconce, *Haunted Media*, 62.

17 Anon., 'The dying of the light', *Times Literary Supplement*, 8 January 1960.

tion that modern communication technologies somehow threaten traditional social-economic orders. The introduction of wireless technology forged a new landscape whereby classical boundaries of

> time, space, nation, and body no longer seemed to apply, and although this provided a giddy sense of liberation for some, it also threatened the security and stability of an older social order in which body and mind had been for the most part coterminus [*sic.*] (63)

Sconce evokes an image of Western society caught in a stifling technological limbo:

> In a world now supernaturally blanketed by human consciousness afloat in the air, stories of paranormal radio as the 'voice from the void' pondered the fate of the still corporeal yet increasingly isolated individuals who found themselves bathing, often reluctantly, in the waves of the wireless sea. (64)

According to this view, the Western world is suddenly aligned with a kind of pre-modern Dantean image: despairing lost souls and disembodied mortals. Beckett's radio dramas may not explicitly call attention to the alienation Sconce refers to, but many portray troubling states of mind. As we shall begin to see in the next section of this chapter, Samuel Beckett's radio characters are all, in their way, struggling with some kind of personal subjective crisis, most often of a traumatic nature. What is most significant about these characters is not the supposed insight or enlightenment they bring to our understanding of a supposed human condition, nor is it the assumption that Beckett's work diagnoses and reflects upon some common misfortune. Rather, Beckett's works for radio, in ways we shall soon explore, offer a comment on our ideas about trauma, and the way we understand traumatic constructions of human subjectivity.

Trauma and the Subject

Unspeakably Excruciating

Trauma affects many of the protagonists in Beckett's radio plays, whether directly or indirectly. There are often hints of a terrible event in characters' pasts, or veiled references to some broader historical catastrophe. But whatever the origin of the trauma, Beckett's work seems most concerned with the problem of representing it. As previously stated, Cathy Caruth defines trauma as an impasse to representation: that which cannot be grasped conventionally precisely because of its disruption of known chronologies, or rational systems of understandings. Traumatic representations are thus concerned with 'a central problem of listening, of knowing, and of representing that [which] emerges from the actual experience of the crisis' (Caruth 1996, 5).

Caruth's comments here are significant to our understanding of traumatic representation in Beckett's texts for radio. It is convenient that Caruth uses references to transmission and listening, which have such clear parallels with the way the radio dramas convey trauma to an audience. We have already glimpsed the problems radio representations offer to listeners, and the strange aura they give to supposedly realistic scenes: radio creates a distance between the witness and the event itself. There is the absence of vision, the inability to interact with events as they occur, alongside temporal and spatial distances that deny an audience the ability to understand the traumatic event coherently.

Luckhurst has described trauma as a term 'stalled somewhere between the physical and the psychical' (Luckhurst 2008, 3), a suspension that Beckett's radio plays strikingly evoke. Trauma operates in a kind of subjective hinterland; it is neither strictly physical nor psychological, but occupies a space between the two. The status of trauma in this context is difficult to establish with any certainty. It is more than anything a crisis concerning what can be known: a suspension of empirical values and moral or ethical certitudes. Luckhurst summarizes

Caruth's account of trauma as a 'crisis of representation, of history and truth, and of narrative time'. He goes on to suggest that 'there is the claim that psychoanalysis and literature are particularly privileged forms of writing that can attend to these perplexing paradoxes of trauma' (5).

In *Embers*, Ada seems unconsciously attuned to these paradoxes. Her memory evokes the simultaneous existence of contrary states:

> ADA: It is like an old sound I used to hear. [*Pause.*] It is like another time, in the same place. [*Pause.*] It was rough, the spray came flying over us. [*Pause.*] Strange it should have been rough then. [*Pause.*] And calm now. [*Pause.*] (40)

There is something unhinged about this sense of calm in *Embers*, much like the contrived rural peace that opens *All That Fall.* Jonathan Kalb has singled out *All That Fall* for its contrast to Beckett's 'later plays', as a 'quaint aural picture of provincial Ireland around the turn of the century' (Kalb 1994, 126). But there is undoubtedly more to the subject matter of the play than its idyllic landscape first suggests. As David Pattie has written, 'the semi-rural Ireland imagined in the play is a land where decay, inertia and death are shown to be the norm' (Pattie 2000, 78). These normatives range from bleak observations on life and death, to quasi-comical exchanges:

> CHRISTY: I suppose you wouldn't be in need of a small load of dung?
>
> MRS ROONEY: Dung? What class of dung?
>
> CHRISTY: Stydung.
>
> MRS ROONEY: Stydung… I like your frankness, Christy. [*Pause.*] I'll ask the master. [*Pause.*] (*AF*, 4)

Mrs Rooney ends the exchange on a slightly melancholic note: 'Dung? What would we want with dung, at our time of life? [*Pause.*]' (4). Dung, in this context, signals both waste and new growth, but its promises of rejuvenation seem insufficient to the ageing Mrs Rooney.

In previous studies of the play, analysis has remained concerned with Beckett's own personal encounters with death and mourning. For Pattie, *All That Fall*'s representation of Ireland, the Ireland of Beckett's childhood, 'is haunted by the deaths of his father, his brother and his mother' (Pattie 2000, 36-7). Biographer Anthony Cronin makes a similar point, linking events of the play with the author's private psychological difficulties:

> There is no doubt that [Beckett] thought that the diagnosis was a profoundly suggestive illumination of his own case, his sense of alienation from the world and of not being ready or fitted to cope with it, to join in its activities as others did, or even to understand the reasons for them. (Cronin 1999, 221-2)

Connections between Beckett's play and the circumstances of his life can have a highly suggestive resonance. *All That Fall* was written at around the same time that his brother, Frank, had died of cancer, while the author was still coming to terms with the death of his parents. But while Pattie and Cronin might help us begin to establish trauma as a theoretical starting point, the dependence on biographical accounts takes us too far from the texts themselves. *All That Fall* does not have to be read as autobiography in order to be relevant here, and I suggest that such efforts cannot adequately account for the traumatic manifestations that occur in the play. *All That Fall* is a text about trauma, yes, but it is also a text about traumatic representation, and the difficulty of connecting psychological neuroses to a specific originary moment.

(Character) Studies of Trauma

Mrs Rooney, the first female protagonist in a Beckett work, begins something of a tradition in the writer's dramatic texts, where characters embody some form of latent trauma or neurosis, while struggling to communicate adequately with the outside world; it is a motif that persists in plays such as *Not I* (1973), *Footfalls* (1977) and *Rockaby* (1982):

> MRS ROONEY: Do you find anything… bizarre about my way of speaking? [*Pause.*] I do not mean the voice. [*Pause.*] No, I mean the words. [*Pause. More to herself.*] I use none but the simplest words, I hope, and yet I sometimes find my way of speaking very… bizarre. [*Pause.*] Mercy! What was that? (4)

Mrs Rooney exemplifies this difficulty, suggesting that the language she uses is not her own, inadequately accounting for her thoughts and experiences.

On the subject of representation and female identity, Kalb has made some fascinating points on the 'sound-world' of *All That Fall.* He identifies the 'flagrantly artificial' rural sounds that open the play, which in 1956 were already familiar radio devices, that remind us of the play's artificiality: 'animals and objects greet Maddy's mention of them with absurd efficiency and dispatch. […] In any case, Beckett also clearly intends to suggest that the entire action may take place in Maddy's mind' (Kalb 1994, 127). Whilst Beckett's final intention is unavailable to us, Kalb's point remains an interesting one. Radio, as we have seen, originates from the utopian promise of a transmission of consciousness, the transcendence of the human mind to distant locations. Perhaps we might consider *All That Fall* as an ironic interpretation of that possibility: instead of the truth of human consciousness, we have an unreliable, 'flagrantly artificial' substitution.

Everett Frost has written that *All That Fall* is a kind of precursor to Beckett's later attempts to 'locate the drama inside the head of the protagonist'. Throughout the play, it would seem, we are invited to 'hear the world inside the mind of Maddy Rooney, not as if we were "there", but as it might be experienced by a woman "in a state of abortive explosiveness", as Beckett once described Maddy to Billie Whitelaw' (Frost 2009, ix). The narrative, then, is necessarily fragmentary, not so much a realist portrayal as a subjective one. Objectively incomplete, it is characterized by private thoughts and inner torments.

We can further observe the interiority of *All That Fall* in its use of personal memories and reflections, in addition to the subjective nature of the audience's encounter (we are alone with Maddy at several points in the play, and the only witnesses to her most private reflections or asides). But the play does not claim to represent subjectivity itself, or anything as complete and cohesive as a human identity. What we are left with, in the end, is a broadcast text that hints towards presence, towards truth, towards closure, but simultaneously resists it. It is an effect not only of Beckett's text, but the medium of radio.

Trauma and female identity are symbolically unified by a Franz Schubert string quartet repeated at key moments in the play: 'Death and the Maiden.' For Kalb, the music is 'associated with memories of "little Minnie" (apparently her dead daughter), the chronic cause of which is much more general and profound' (Kalb 1994, 128). In Beckett's text, the sound of Schubert's music coincides with a slowing down of Maddy's footsteps, followed by an eventual halt:

> *Music faint from house by way. "Death and the Maiden."*
>
> *The steps slow down, stop.* (*AF*, 3)

The disruptive memory of a traumatic event troubles the onward progress of the narrative; it is not only a painful site of return, but an uncanny hinterland where time appears to stop. At one moment, recalling memories too difficult to share, Maddy talks about returning home, impeding the progress of her journey and cancelling the rendezvous with her husband. The passage is significant for two reasons: it reinforces the notion that trauma runs contrary to conventional progress, whilst simultaneously illustrating the way memory cannot be adequately expressed through conventional representation. Maddy, overcome with grief, is temporarily unable to form complete sentences, and ellipses mark the trauma that cannot be expressed:

> If you see my poor blind Dan tell him I was on my way to meet him when it all came over me again, like a flood. Say to him, Your poor wife, She told me to tell you it all came flooding over her

> again and… [*The voice breaks.*] …she simply went back home … straight back home…. (7)

Once again, her speech is punctuated by gaps and telling omissions. Her voice breaks as she is overcome emotionally. This break is repeated throughout the play, and signals a broader fragmentation of the unity and cohesion of the human voice. After all, the voice is the only evidence we have that suggests that Maddy exists—but its power as a stable marker of presence is becoming more difficult to maintain. The text's reference to sensory perception is also notable for its focus on vision, something that her husband, Mr Rooney, and we, the listening audience, decidedly lack. If vision unlocks some hidden access to Maddy's misery, then the radio ensures that all paths remain obscure and out of reach:

> MRS ROONEY: Do not flatter yourselves for one moment because I hold aloof, that my sufferings have ceased […] oh if you had my eyes…you would understand…the things they have seen…and not looked away…this is nothing…nothing…what did I do with that handkerchief?' (17)

The proclamation is quickly dissolved by an everyday distraction, and the seriousness of Maddy's situation comes into the perspective of everyday trials and tribulations. But the trauma of her past never completely abates:

> [*Dragging feet.*] So long ago… No! No! […] [*The dragging steps resume.*] Oh I am just a hysterical old hag I know, destroyed with sorrow and pining and gentility and church-going and fat and rheumatism and childlessness. [*Pause. Brokenly.*] Minnie! Little Minnie! (5)

Maddy's trauma creates a point of reflection where two separate and contradictory chronologies co-exist in her mind. There is the way things are, a reality punctuated by loss and absence, and the way things could have been. Maddy poignantly reflects, with humour, on what her daughter might have become: 'In her forties now she'd be, I don't know, fifty, girding up her lovely little loins, getting ready for the change....' (6). Trauma in this case operates as an agent of human disruption; Maddy's words reflect not just a personal and emotional loss, but the way trauma unravels our understanding of natural human progress and development. A gap forever exists between the human notion of what should have been, and the way things are. Trauma is a name we give to this gap.

Psychoanalytic thought,[18] and indeed the Jung anecdote recounted in Chapter Two of this work, is vitally significant to an exchange in *All That Fall.* This time, it is the troubled Mrs Rooney who remembers 'attending a lecture by one of these new mind doctors. I forget what you call them' (27). For a time, Maddy struggles to describe the man, and never remembers the profession itself. She dismisses her husband's suggestions of 'lunatic specialist' and 'neurologist' as inaccurate, and we are given the sense that psychiatry holds an alternative view of the human body, and of the mind as a history of trauma, past and present. She responds to Mr Rooney: 'No no, just the troubled mind [...] mental distress, the name will come back to me' (28):

> MRS ROONEY: I remember his telling us the story of a little girl, very strange and unhappy in her ways, and how he treated her unsuccessfully over a period of years and was finally obliged to give up the case. He could find nothing wrong with her, he said. The only thing wrong with her as far as he could see was that she was dying. And she did in fact die, shortly after he had washed his hands of her.
>
> MR ROONEY: Well? What is there so wonderful about that?
>
> MRS ROONEY : No, it was just something he said, and the way he said it, that have haunted me ever since.

---

18 Psychoanalytic treatment is also hinted at *en passant* in *Embers*, when Ada remarks: 'There's something wrong with your brain, you ought to see Holloway, he's alive still isn't he?', *Embers*, 43.

> MR ROONEY: You lie awake at night, tossing to and fro and brooding on it.
>
> MRS ROONEY: On it and other...wretchedness. [*Pause.*] When he had done with the little girl he stood there motionless for some time, quite two minutes I should say, looking down at his table. Then he suddenly raised his head and exclaimed, as if he had had a revelation, The trouble with her was she had never really been born! (28)

The case study itself might refer to any number of psychoanalytic problems or events, whether objective or speculative. Otto Rank's notion of birth trauma has often been evoked by Beckett scholars as a rich avenue for exploration (see Moorjani 2004, 173). But the anecdote is central to the play for the way that it shapes the representation of Maddy Rooney. Images of fertility, or its loss, recur throughout *All That Fall*, and seem to conspire in Maddy's mind as grim reminders of her lost child. There is Mr Tyler, for instance, who reflects on the health of his daughter and her recent medical procedure: 'They removed everything, you know, the whole... er... bag of tricks. Now I am grandchildless. [*Dragging feet.*]' (5). The sound of the dragging feet poignantly links the inability to conceive with Mrs Rooney's ageing body. At a lighter moment, Mr Tyler admits to cursing under his breath: 'I was merely cursing [...] God and man, under my breath, and the wet Saturday afternoon of my conception' (6).

Time is a central representative motif in Beckett's traumatic radio plays, and is of great importance to each of the characters' accounts. In *Gramophone, Film, Typewriter*, Friedrich A. Kittler notes the capacity of the phonograph and cinematograph to store and re-present time:

> Time as a mixture of audio frequencies in the acoustic realm and as the movement of single-image sequences in the optic. Time determines the limit of all art, which first has to arrest the daily data flow in order to turn it into images or signs. What is called style in art is merely the switchboard of these scannings and selections. (Kittler 1999, 3)

While Kittler is concerned here with audio-visual technologies, radio could be said to fall under a similar prescription. According to this evaluation, technological media 'arrest' time, breaking or fracturing it as it occurs before re-presenting via images and signs for the purposes of performance, broadcast or display.[19] Kittler's outline of art and artistic style is analogous, in some sense, to the role that time plays in our understanding of trauma: a tension exists between unresolved events arrested in the past and their conversion into altered forms in present manifestations. Beckett's work for the medium of radio appears to play with this notion of time arrested or suspended through its construction of a strange temporality. For instance, Mr Rooney's reflection on his birthday, which links a lack of sensory cognition with a confusion of chronology:

> MR ROONEY: If I could go deaf and dumb I think I might pant on to be a hundred. Or have I done so? [*Pause.*] Was I a hundred today? [*Pause.*] Am I a hundred, Maddy? [*Pause.*] (24)

Throughout *All That Fall*, Maddy is under siege from memories of premature death, specifically that of her daughter. This is perhaps the heart of her traumatic crisis, punctuated throughout the play with images of reproduction, fertilization and ageing. In the light of said traumatic event, the realistic gloss of the play begins to resemble an uncanny symbolic landscape, a system of dark reminders and mnemonic triggers that keep Maddy's thoughts rooted in the past, whilst she lumbers on in the present. But whatever is being repressed cannot be entirely grasped by the audience: we can only be sure that it returns, in its various guises, throughout the play, with varying degrees of intensity and effect. It is the traumatic element that prevents a possibility of happiness.

---

19 For a more detailed engagement with Friedrich A. Kittler and Beckett's work in relation to the 'discourse network of 1900', see Yoshiki Tajiri's essay 'Samuel Beckett et la Mécanisation d'Echo' in *Samuel Beckett Today / Aujourd'hui*: *Présence de Samuel Beckett / Presence of Samuel Beckett: Colloque de Cerisy*, Vol. 17 (2006), 435-448.

Time is also represented dramatically in *All That Fall*, using music and sound effects to mark arrivals and departures, or the way Maddy's footfalls mark temporal and spatial distances. And yet, whilst each footstep suggests a progression, its repetitive sound implies a kind of stasis. Repetition not only destabilizes our idea of a progressive and ordered chronology, but is central to ideas about contemporary trauma. Freud has spoken at length about patients who 'regularly repeat the traumatic situation in their dreams' (Freud 1991, 315):

> Thus in traumatic neuroses, and particularly in those brought about by the horrors of war, we are unmistakably presented with a self-interested motive on the part of the ego, seeking for protection and advantage—a motive which cannot, perhaps, create the illness by itself but which assents to it and maintains it when once it has come about. The motive tries to preserve the ego from the dangers the threat of which was the precipitating cause of the illness and it will not allow recovery to occur until a repetition of these dangers seems no longer possible or until compensation has been received for the danger that has been endured. (429)

We might begin to think of *All That Fall*, and *Embers* too, as akin to the perceptions and thought processes of a traumatized subject. In *Embers*, there is the return of the sea, repeatedly heard at every dramatic pause, presenting a memory of a drowned father. In *All That Fall*, the return is rather neatly encapsulated by Schubert's 'Death and the Maiden', heard towards the beginning and the end of the play. Trauma is not represented as such in either case, but hinted at through abstract substitutions. The music, for instance, has an added association with an unknown, unseen woman in a ruinous old house—a classic uncanny symbol of the repressive domestic space, or an ageing female body. Ruin and decay:

> MRS ROONEY: Poor woman. All alone in that ruinous old house. [*Music louder. Silence but for music playing. The steps resume. Music dies.* MRS ROONEY *murmurs, melody. Her murmur dies.*] (3)

Mr Rooney reinforces our idea of the house as a repressive domestic space with his own reflections on daily life. His assumption of a narrative tone subtly enforces authority, but he seems to hold some sympathy for what he considers the inevitable character of domestic existence:

> MR ROONEY: [*Narrative tone.*] On the other hand, I said, there are the horrors of home life, the dusting, sweeping, airing, scrubbing, waxing, waning, washing, mangling, drying, mowing, clipping, raking, rolling, scuffling, shoveling, grinding, tearing, pounding, banging and slamming. And the brats, the happy little healthy little howling neighbours' brats. Of all this and much more the weekend, the Saturday intermission and then the day of rest, have given you some idea. (25-6)

While the lady in the ruinous old house is the first character to suggest domesticity and traumatic repetition, we can begin to trace similar themes in the lives of the Rooneys. The horrors of home life are defined as a seemingly endless series of chores and responsibilities that gradually transition into a series of violent actions. The actions themselves are repetitious in a way that recalls repetition-compulsion, an act or series of acts that are felt to be essential to the individual conducting them. The gradual movement from dusting and sweeping toward grinding, tearing and banging implies that domestic routine is indistinguishable from some kind of traumatic action or repetition. The everyday is interrupted and undermined by the intrusion of latent traumatic content. The 'happy little healthy little' children next-door become reminders of the child the Rooneys have lost, and traumatic losses of the past persistently haunt and trouble the present.

Spectrality

In *All That Fall*, the suffering protagonist, Maddy, makes a number of remarks alluding to her unfit mental state. But they hold a strange significance, acting as reminders of Maddy's textual make-up. To return to Billie Whitelaw's performance of *Footfalls*, it is almost as though Mrs Rooney is 'not quite there' at all. At one moment, Maddy confides to another character: 'You have piercing sight, Miss Fitt, if you only knew it, literally piercing' (14). At another moment, Mrs Rooney ironically remarks: 'Don't mind me. Don't take any notice of me. I do not exist. The fact is well known' (11). And, at another moment: 'Am I then invisible, Miss Fitt? Is this cretonne so becoming to me that I merge into the masonry?' (13). There are, of course, several ways of interpreting these exchanges. Firstly, they may constitute a comment on cultural perceptions of age and female identity; they may suggest the personal reflections of Mrs Rooney's troubled mind; or they may act as useful reminders of Maddy's representational status. We are engaging with a radio text, after all, where our own 'piercing sight' reveals the dissolution of the corporeal and the material into thin air. Spectrality is a condition that affects other characters in varying degrees, and adds to the ethereal, almost dreamlike (or nightmarish) quality of the text:

> MISS FITT: I suppose the truth is I am not there, Mrs Rooney, just not really there at all. I see, hear, smell, and so on, I go through the usual motions, but my heart is not in it, Mrs Rooney, my heart is in none of it. Left to myself, with no one to check me, I would soon be flown…home. [*Pause.*] So if you think I cut you just now, Mrs Rooney, you do me an injustice. All I saw was a big pale blur, just another big pale blur. (14)

Looking at a young child in the play, Maddy makes several remarks about his apparent state of malnutrition. But her colloquial phrases now have an added significance: 'Heavens, child, you're just a bag of bones, you need building up' (15). The same play many critics considered a realistic evocation of rural Ireland seems more akin to a literal ghost-town—populated by partially constituted characters, ill-seen and ill-heard. Maddy's innocuous description of the child as a bag of bones sets a macabre tone, inevitably connecting to the death of little Minnie whilst simultaneously foreshadowing the death of the child on the railway tracks. As each traumatic image is encapsulated by the image of a boy, a gruesome *memento mori*, we are confronted once again with the spectre: alive, but not alive, only partially corporeal. In the radio landscape the empirical mastery offered by sight is absent, and one's sense of hearing cannot necessarily be trusted: it is a landscape where 'All is still. No living soul in sight. [...] We are alone. There is no one to ask' (24).

In compliance with much contemporary thought on trauma, there are certainly hints in each characters' past of some terrible event. But they are never fully explained. Contemporary trauma theories' reliance on the originary, founding traumatic moment cannot really apply to the Beckettian model, where standard, progressive chronology is a luxury the characters can ill afford. In some sense, there is no distinction between past, present and future in Beckett's writing: time is uncannily suspended between moments, and the empirical certainty of historical events is similarly confused and troubled. As Mr Rooney succinctly puts it: 'I have never known anything to happen' (23). We might consider this as the fundamental characteristic of trauma, for its focus on rational suspension and chronological fragmentation. Perhaps we might consider Beckett's radio plays as unparalleled representations of trauma itself: of its unwelcome symptoms and its uncanny effects. But in denying the representation of the traumatic event, whether it is the death of the father in *Embers*, or of the two children in *All That Fall*, the texts escape any possibility of rational comprehension. The audience is, in some sense, traumatized: an apprehension of the facts is forever denied, and we are left only with the symptoms. The event, if such an event can be said to have existed, becomes analogous to the landscape of the plays, or the texts, themselves. Everything becomes coloured by it, and, to some degree, each character or happening within the play becomes a substitution for the trauma itself, becomes a part of its representation. With this in mind, I would suggest that in Beckett's work there simply is no clearly rooted, originary event at all. Perhaps there is no single, inaugurating moment, but many. Trauma confers a condition of belatedness that relates more to the future than the present or the past; a state of afterwardness that is always coming, and never resolved. And, like Hamlet's ghostly father stalking the battlements of Elsinore, Beckett's characters embody a strange anachrony:

> MRS ROONEY: Are we very late, Mr Tyler? I have not the courage to look at my watch. (6)

Lateness has an added significance when considered alongside metaphors of fertility and childbearing in the play. In this case, being late can be a sign of medical difficulties in the birth of a child. But lateness also impacts on our understanding of trauma, in its representation of an event that has not yet happened, but is nonetheless anticipated. The word 'late' suggests a deferred event that can only occur in the present or the future. It is also a term that, as previously discussed, could signify death. Everything is running late in *All That Fall.* The play is constantly being disrupted by events and interruptions, and, as Jonathan Kalb has pointed out, '"derailed", by quasi-philosophical discourses that ultimately have to do with Maddy's fears, and the greatest of her fears is, apparently, of disappearance' (Kalb 1994, 128). The train that Maddy anticipates at the station is late, as a result of a child's death, we discover. 'We drew out on the tick of time', Mr Rooney says, 'I can vouch for that' (*AF*, 24). The time is out of joint, and the temporal linearity of the narrative is continually disrupted and undermined. But I would suggest that disappearance is not necessarily a psychological fear of Maddy's, but more a 'quasi-philosophical' observation. Maddy, and indeed the entire text, is traumatized, uncanny, and spectral. As Kalb notes:

> Beckett's primary focus in this uncharacteristically populous play, in other words, is a strange condition of precarious suspension between existence and non-existence, which radio is ideally suited to explore, "Only the present speaker's presence is certain [in radio]." Writes Zilliacus: "the primary condition of existence for a radio character is that he [*sic.*] talk." Hence the author's famous objection to the idea of presenting *All That Fall* on stage: "Whatever quality it may have [...] depends on the whole thing's *coming out of the dark*", he wrote in a 1957 letter to his American publisher. Artistic constructions based on the solipsistic notion of people and things jumping willy-nilly in and out of existence simply cannot function in fleshy, concrete media. (Kalb 1994, 129)

The spectral quality of the characters is reflected time and again in their exchanges. And Mrs Rooney's protestations to the contrary seem to do little but accentuate this condition:

> MRS ROONEY: Alive?
>
> MR TYLER: Well half alive shall we say?
>
> MRS ROONEY: Speak for yourself, Mr Tyler. I am not half alive nor anything approaching it. [*Pause.*] What are we standing here for? The dust will not settle in our time. And when it does some great roaring machine will come and whirl it all skyhigh again. (*AF*, 7)

Much of Beckett's post-war writing denies the closure and resolution of conventional narrative fiction and drama. In much of his work, we can speculate that trauma plays a significant part: whether in the psychological make-up of the characters, or events alluded to within the texts. But, in each case, Beckett's texts experiment with the role that the medium plays in accurately conveying (or, rather, failing to convey) the full picture to an audience. Through his prose, we begin to see the way that language constructs human subjectivity, and our understanding of the world around us: trauma makes us aware of this mediation via its interruptions, fragmentations and ellipses. In Beckett's work for the stage, trauma undermines our expectations of presence, and so our control and understanding of a subject's negotiation of space and time. In the radio plays, technology becomes the principle mediator of the message, and we can begin to discern uneasy connections between humanist subjectivity, traumatic experience, and Western modernity.

Traumatic Modernity

Trauma, Modernity, Radio

Whilst *All That Fall* is the first full-length dramatic work Samuel Beckett wrote for radio, it was not his first experience of the format. He had previously composed a brief report intended for public broadcast. In the immediate aftermath of the Second World War, the writer volunteered with the Irish Red Cross on the European continent. With a strong grasp of a number of languages, including French, German, Spanish and Italian, Beckett was assigned to an aid group in the devastated Normandy city of Saint-Lô: working as a driver and translator, Beckett transported medical supplies and mediated conversations between the city's locals and volunteers. In 1945, while still stationed in the city, Beckett was requested to submit a record of his experiences, to be transmitted by Ireland's national broadcaster, Radio Telefis Éireann (RTÉ). Although the report was never aired, Everett Frost suggests we might read Beckett's transcript as one of the 'prologues to the radio plays' (Frost 2009, vii), as the founding introduction to wireless broadcasting that inspired and informed some of his later work. While Beckett's factual report for RTÉ is by no means comprehensive, Frost makes an interesting connection. The radio report can offer a useful historical context for discussion, providing a timely analysis of the trauma and devastation of a specific post-war moment. The report, entitled 'The Capital of the Ruins', is also a kind of philosophical meditation, attempting to account for the human cost of modern warfare:

> Saint-Lô was bombed out of existence in one night. German prisoners of war, and casual labourers attracted by the relative food-plenty, but soon discouraged by housing conditions, continue, two years after the liberation, to clear away the debris, literally by hand […] And having done so I may perhaps venture to mention another, more remote but perhaps of greater import in certain quarters, I mean the possibility that some of those who were in Saint-Lô will come home realizing that they got at least as good as they gave, that they got indeed what they could hardly give, a vision and sense of a time-honoured conception of humanity in ruins, and perhaps even an inkling of the terms in which our condition is to be thought again. (*CR*, 75-6)

Lois Gordon has researched similar reports about the region in national newspapers and periodicals, including *The London Times*' harrowing descriptions of the city where Beckett was consigned, which 'treated with equal thoroughness the transformation of the once beautiful Saint-Lô into a city of death and rubble and frequently published images of inexpressible human despair' (Gordon 1996, 190). With this in mind, it is difficult not to observe parallels between first-hand reports of Saint-Lô and Beckett's post-war theatre and prose. The Normandy landscape of wounded civilians and devastated homes offers tempting comparisons with Beckett's uprooted characters and traumatic, psychological spaces.

'The Capital of the Ruins' is useful to our reading of the radio dramas, not as biographical explanation, but as the clue to a crisis. It articulates a moment of post-war uncertainty and reflection: a conception of 'humanity in ruins' that begins to interrogate dominant Western values and beliefs. If the report can be considered a 'prologue' or precursor to Beckett's post-war writing, it is for its discussion of the after-effects of trauma and catastrophe. But the trauma is not expressed psychologically, but rather philosophically, as a disruption of the values and beliefs underlying Western modernity.

Beckett's dramatic works for radio respond to a traumatic crisis in human subjectivity: a disruption of moral and ethical values created by historical atrocity and modern Western trauma. But the published texts rarely explicitly refer to the events of the Second World War, and indeed their settings sometimes seem to predate the period altogether. The trauma that characterizes the plays cannot, under these circumstances, be straightforwardly ascribed. If the texts represent a traumatic condition, it transcends their immediate historical surroundings to form part of a broader critique: a critique of modernity itself, of its traditional narratives of historical progress, and faithful investment in the values of the Cartesian humanist subject. The texts acknowledge the modern landscape as a technological one, not only by virtue of their format (radio), via reference to modern recording devices, communication and transport. Modernity disrupts the characters' ability to understand the world around them, and often sparks the repetitive traumatic motifs in the text. In the final section of this chapter, I argue that modernity forms the basis of the traumatic episodes in Beckett's radio plays, and that notions of modern progress, or modern technology, lead to a dissociation in the minds of the characters. Familiar ideals of rationalism and progress are undermined in the texts, even reversed into points of uncertainty and regression. It some sense, it is not the characters that are traumatized, but the texts themselves, and I would like to suggest modernity as a possible cause.

The Birth of Modern Trauma

Whilst the notion of trauma has existed since Greek antiquity, as physical 'wound', its contemporary psychological dimension originates in nineteenth-century industrialization, and is inextricably linked with the development of modernity:

> The global network of telegraphy and telephony, the "nerves of empire", [were] haunted by the spectral voices of the dead that travelled along the wire at the same speed as the electrical spark. It should come as no surprise, then, that the general scholarly consensus is that the origin of the idea of trauma was inextricably linked to the expansion of the railways in the 1860s. (Luckhurst 2008, 21)

Writing about traumatic neurosis during the First World War, a condition 'produced with special frequency precisely at the present time', Sigmund Freud notes a precedent for the condition in the birth of the railway: 'Similar cases, of course, appeared before the war as well, after railway collisions and other alarming accidents involving fatal risks' (Freud 1991, 314). Luckhurst notes that from the first departure of Stephenson's Rocket in 1830, a Member of Parliament was struck dead on the tracks. And as accidents began to be officially recorded in 1871, in the thirty years that followed 'there were never less than 200 passenger deaths a year, with the peak in 1874 of 758 deaths' (Luckhurst 2008, 21). Yet, in spite of this, the railway remained 'the icon of British modernity', an emblem of 'engineering genius' that led to a nationwide standardization of British clock-time (21). In addition to the traumatic reports of violent deaths that attends the history of train travel, the new compressions of space and time were met with another set of separate anxieties. In mastering vast distances in short periods, train travel became traumatic in another sense, disrupting passengers' ability to apprehend the present, leading to feelings of disorientation, confusion and even fear. It is interesting that Beckett's work returns to the theme of the railway on a number of occasions, notably ending the published edition of *Watt*, written during the Second World War. In *All That Fall*, the train destabilizes time, and the course the play takes:

> MISS FITT: But the time is now getting on for-
>
> MR TYLER: [*Patiently.*] We all know, Miss Fitt, we all know only too well what the time is now getting on for, and yet the cruel fact remains that the twelve thirty has not yet arrived.
>
> MISS FITT: Not an accident, I trust! [*Pause.*] Do not tell me she has left the track! [*Pause.*] Oh darling mother! With the fresh sole for lunch!
>
> [*Loud titter from* TOMMY, *checked as before by* MR BARRELL.]
>
> MR BARRELL: That's enough old guff out of you. Nip up to the box now and see has Mr Case anything for me.
>
> [TOMMY *goes.*]
>
> MRS ROONEY: Poor Dan!
>
> MISS FITT: [*In anguish.*] What terrible thing has happened?
>
> MR TYLER: Now now, Miss Fitt, do not give way…to despair, all will come right…in the end. [*Aside to* MR BARRELL.] What *is* the situation, Mr Barrell? Not a collision surely?
>
> MRS ROONEY: [*Enthusiastically.*] A collision! Oh that would be wonderful ! (18)

As the train is confirmed late, its delay is presumed to signify a terrible accident. Distressingly, as the birth of the railway signals a standardization of time, conversely temporal regularity is dependent on the prompt arrival and departure of the train. Upon its eventual arrival in the station, a narrative is required to establish what caused the train's delay. Time, it seems, has been lost, and can only be regained via a rational narrative. Mrs Rooney asks her blind husband, as he walks on the station platform, to account for the train's belated arrival, but he can offer no satisfactory explanation:

> MRS ROONEY: But you must know! You were on it! Was it at the terminus? Did you leave on time? Or was it on the line? [*Pause.*] Did something happen on the line? (23)

The train might be understood as a spectral object of modernity. It is empirically present at each station at a specifically regulated time, but occupies a temporal and spatial non-space during journeys. Between departure and arrival, origin and terminus, the train in *All That Fall* cannot be accounted for in any true sense of the word. It occupies a space that lies outside traditional territories, somewhere unspecified 'on the line'. What delayed the train's arrival is never fully represented in the text, and the lost minutes are never satisfactorily restored. At the close of the play, an accident is revealed to be the cause of the delay, specifically the death of a child. A young boy informs the Rooneys that 'It was a little child fell out of the carriage, Ma'am. [*Pause*] On to the line, Ma'am. [*Pause.*] Under the wheels, Ma'am' (32). The traumatic revelation signals an uncanny return of Maddy's own personal grief. Maddy groans as she is told the details by the boy, whose abbreviated use of the word 'Madam' as 'Ma'am' (Mam) interpellates her as a mother figure. As the boy departs, so the play ends in wind and rain. The Rooneys attempt to continue their journey home, but are kept from arriving at their destination, stalled by the news:

> [*Silence.* JERRY *runs off. His steps die away. Tempest of wind and rain. It abates. They move on. Dragging steps, etc. They halt. Tempest of wind and rain.*] (*AF*, 32)

Ruth Leys has argued that our contemporary understanding of trauma originates in the work of John Erichson, a physician who first identified the condition during the 1860s. Erichson's patients were commonly 'suffering from the fright of railway accidents and attributed the distress to shock or concussion of the spine' (Leys 2000, 3). Later, the psychological nature of their distress was attributed, and 'hypnotic catharsis thus emerged as a technique for solving a "memory crisis" that disturbed the integrity of the individual under the stresses of modernity' (4). Micale and Lerner have suggested that trauma, in its essence, is 'response to and constitutive of "modernity"' (Micale and Lerner 2001, 10). New forms of transport accelerated and fragmented an individual's ordinary experience of time and space, closing-off or rupturing one's familiar negotiation of space, or landscape. Michel de Certeau makes an apposite point in his essay 'Railway Navigation and Incarceration' when he describes the process of a train ride as a 'travelling incarceration', a condition whereby one stands or sits 'immobile inside the train, seeing immobile things slip by' (de Certeau 1984, 111). For Freud, the concept of 'dying is replaced in dreams by departure' (Freud 1991, 186), with the modern train journey cited as a key example. With this in mind, it is perhaps not surprising that Selzer argues that 'the modern subject has become inseparable from the categories of shock and trauma' (Luckhurst 2008, 20).

In *All That Fall*, traumatic modernity finds expression via a number of temporal distortions. The empirical standard set by Mrs Rooney's watch is only ever approximate, and even when announced, is undermined by dramatic pauses that allow the announced moment to slip by. Mrs Rooney exists in a suspended position, pondering whether her position in the present has 'sped by' to the future, while she is simultaneously held back by a moment from her past:

> MRS ROONEY: But according to my watch which is more or less right-or was-by the eight o'clock news the time is now coming up to twelve…[*Pause as she consults her watch.*]…thirty-six. [*Pause.*] And yet upon the other hand the up mail has not gone through. [*Pause.*] Or has it sped by unbeknown to me? [*Pause.*] For there was a moment there, I remember now, I was so plunged in sorrow I wouldn't have heard a steam roller go over me. (13)

Modernity and trauma 'collide' in a moment at the train station, as Mrs Rooney witnesses the arrival of the train and the mysterious non-arrival of her husband. As the station empties, she summons Mr Barrell the station master, a staff member aware that something terrible has occurred:

> MRS ROONEY: Where is he?...Dan!...Did you see my husband?...Dan!...[*Noise of station emptying. Guard's whistle. Train departing, receding. Silence.*] He isn't on it! The misery I have endured to get here, and he isn't on it!... Mr Barrell! ... Was he not on it? [*Pause.*] Is anything the matter, you look as if you had seen a ghost. (19)

For the audience, Maddy's lines create a sense of dramatic tension. There is the anticipation of her lost husband, and the pale look of the distressed station master. But at that moment in the text, we remain ignorant of the tragedy that will close the play, and are left to ruminate on Mr Barrell's expression. There is also something ghostly about the train itself, about its untimely arrival and its sudden departure. The train, of course, can only be heard on the radio, and so draws attention to the instability of the medium: immaterial broadcasts that are continually arriving, departing, receding. It is one of several ghostly mechanical devices in Beckett's work, suspending the texts' respective grips on time, space and reality.

The Mechanism Jams

Kittler observed that 'the media age proceeds in jerks' (Kittler 1999, 18). Modern devices in *All That Fall* symbolize a temporal tension between progression and recession. The railway has typified this relation, not so much a modern beacon of progress as an emblem of belatedness and confusion. When the station master is asked why the train is late, he helplessly replies 'I know nothing. All I know is there has been a hitch. All traffic is retarded' (19). The train, in this case, is not only the precipitant of the traumatic event in *All That Fall*, but is defined according to a kind of traumatic logic: neither present, nor absent, its arrival is perpetually anticipated. When it finally does draw into the station, the platform is a site of only partially successful reunions:

> MR TYLER: You have lost your mother, Miss Fitt?
>
> MISS FITT: She said she would be on the last train. (17)

Miss Fitt[20] searches for her mother, as Mrs Rooney searches for her husband. Even upon arrival, these characters have not, in one sense, arrived at their destination. The train becomes an embodiment of traumatic belatedness, what Laplanche playfully labeled 'afterwardness', keeping people apart, divided, separate. The death of the child revealed at the end of the play testifies to this strange condition, lost under the wheels of a train caught between two locations: a place between origin and terminus, between the two empirical times of departure and arrival. This child, in this way, is suspended outside rational limits by the spectral locomotive.

Progress is frustrated throughout *All That Fall.* Just minutes into the opening, Mrs Rooney witnesses Christy's cart horse, which stubbornly refuses to move forward:

> MRS ROONEY: She does not move a muscle. [*Pause.*] I too should be getting along, if I do not wish to arrive late at the station. [*Pause.*] But a moment ago she neighed and pawed the ground. And now she refuses to advance. Give her a good welt on the rump. [*Sound of welt. Pause.*] Harder! [*Sound of welt. Pause.*] Well! If someone were to do that for me I should not dally. (4)

---

20 A number of critics have discussed the aural significance of Beckett's punning name choices, and their aptness for radio and oral performance. For example, Ruby Cohn notes that alongside a change of title, from 'Lovely Day for the Races' to *All That Fall,* Beckett changes the protagonist's name 'from Emma Kennedy to Maddy Dunne Rooney (mad done ruin)' in Ruby Cohn, *A Beckett Canon* (Ann Arbor: The University of Michigan Press, 2011), 233. Additionally, we might read the choice of Miss Fitt as a comment on the character's social standing or mental stability.

After this event, other vehicles are similarly halted, stalled and delayed. But from this point onward (if onward is the word) the vehicles are all of mechanical, technological construction. Maddy encounters Mr Tyler cursing 'God and man, under [his] breath, and the wet Saturday afternoon of [his] conception' (6). The motif of fertility recurs once again through his depressed (and humorous) lament, but the reason for his downtrodden attitude is technological. He complains: 'My back tyre has gone down again. I pumped it hard as iron before I set out. And now I am on the rim' (6). Without the car, Mr Tyler is perpetually stalled, stuck on the circumference, denied the centre.

Images of death and violence hover on the margins of the conversation, as Mr Slocum attempts to reassert his control over a failed engine:

> MR SLOCUM: [*Dreamily.*] All morning she went like a dream and now she is dead. That is what you get for a good deed. [*Pause. Hopefully.*] Perhaps if I were to choke her. (10)

It is a moment of foreboding and foreshadowing. At another point, Mr Barrell enquires: 'Who's that crucifying his gearbox, Tommy?' (11)—the image of modern technology becomes entwined with subtle religious connotations of persecution and death. There are two traumatic deaths in *All That Fall.* There is the loss of the child under the wheels of the train, and there is a hen, killed by Slocum's car on its way to the station (observe Slocum's belated response to the death, as he blows the car horn too late to be of any consequence):

> MRS ROONEY: [*In anguish.*] Mind the hen! [*Scream of brakes. Squawk of hen.*] Oh, mother, you have squashed her, drive on, drive on! [*The car accelerates. Pause.*] What a death! One minute picking happy at the dung, on the road, in the sun, with now and then a dust bath, and then –bang!-all her troubles over. [*Pause.*] All the laying and the hatching. [*Pause.*] Just one great squark and then…peace. [*Pause.*] They would have slit her weasand in any case. [*Pause.*] Here we are, let me down. [*The car slows down, stops, engine running.* mr slocum *blows his horn. Pause. Louder. Pause.*] What are you up to now, Mr Slocum? We are at a standstill, all danger is past and you blow your horn.

> Now if instead of blowing it now you had blown it at that unfortunate- (10)

Modernity becomes indistinguishable from the lingering threat of some traumatic event. This pattern can also be identified in Beckett's radio play adaptation of Robert Pinget's *La Manivelle* (as *The Old Tune*). Once again, the theme of an ageing woman, stalled towards the end of her life, is juxtaposed with the idealistic progress of scientific technology (tellingly, Gorman's remarks are drowned out at one point by the sound of a car engine):

> GORMAN: When I think of my poor old mother, only sixty and couldn't move a muscle. [*Roar of engine.*] Rheumatism they never found the remedy for it yet, atom rockets is all they care about (*TOT*, 161)

The motor car is a constant source of distraction and disruption to the ageing characters of *The Old Tune*. And while the play cannot be credited to Beckett in its entirety, it is worth noting the thematic concerns common to his other works. Two leading characters, Gorman and Cream, continually return to the threat of the motor car as a representation of younger generations, and physical dismemberment:

> GORMAN: Ah dear oh dear, Mr Cream, dear oh dear. [*Pause.*] Ah yes that's children that's the way it is. [*Roar of motor engine.*] They'd tear you to flitters with their flaming machines.
>
> CREAM: Shocking crossing, sudden death.
>
> GORMAN: As soon as look at you, tear you to flitters.
>
> CREAM: Ah in our time Gorman this was the outskirts, you remember, peace and quiet. (156)

The elderly Gorman and Cream reminisce nostalgically about a simpler time, far in the past, before the advent of mass production: 'it wasn't the likes of nowadays, their flaming machines they'd tear you to shreds' (157).

Vehicles signal modernity like no other symbol in Beckett's radio plays. They are rapid, troublesome machines, dangerous and unpredictable. Their relationship to time is disruptive and confusing, completely at odds with the 'regular' time-keeping of characters' ordinary footsteps. One can observe the change in tempo of Maddy's footsteps as each vehicle arrives and departs, altering perceptions of time as she draws to a complete stop. Incidentally, Maddy's encounter with each vehicle follows an approximate historical progression, as her journey from the country to the station similarly demarcates a transition from agricultural landscape to early-twentieth-century industrialization. There is Christy's horse cart, to begin, evoking a pre-industrial, agricultural age; then, a bicycle appears alongside Mrs Rooney, a popular mode of transportation from the late nineteenth century onwards; and then, as she nears the station, trucks and motor cars begin to populate the roads. Through the course of the play, Maddy appears to have moved through a number of historical periods, in spite of the fact that she has barely moved at all. There is the sound of 'approaching cartwheels' (*AF*, 3), then the 'Sound of bicycle-bell' (5), followed by the 'Sound of motor-van. It approaches, passes with thunderous rattles, recedes' (6). In each case, Maddy halts, as though her encounters with each vehicle are an active impediment to progress. The car arrives at Maddy's side at an emotional culmination of frustration and despair:

> MRS ROONEY: What's wrong with me, what's wrong with me, never tranquil, seething out of my dirty old pelt, out of my skull, oh to be in atoms, in atoms! [*Frenziedly.*] ATOMS! [*Silence. Cooing. Faintly.*] Jesus! [*Pause.*] Jesus! [*Sound of car coming up behind her. It slows down and draws up beside her, engine running. It is* MR SLOCUM, *the clerk of the racecourse.* (8)

The play is concerned throughout with the modern acceleration of arrivals and departures, manipulating our expectations of time, space and presence. Mr Cream in *The Old Tune* appears very sceptical of such developments, and makes a subtle remark that might now be interpreted as the impact of global pollution:

> My dear Gorman do you know what it is I'm going to tell you, all this speed do you know what it is has the whole place ruinated, even the weather. [*Roar of engine.*] (*TOT*, 157)

Cream and Gorman begin a discourse on the subject, likening the scientific enlightenment of humankind to an era of darkness and insanity:

> GORMAN: So you're against progress are you.
>
> CREAM: Progress, progress, progress is all very fine and grand, there's such a thing I grant you, but it's scientific, progress, scientific, the moon's not progress, lunacy, lunacy.
>
> GORMAN: Ah there I'm with you progress is scientific and the moon, the moon, that's the way it is.
>
> CREAM: The wisdom of the ancients that's the trouble they don't give a rap or a snap for it any more, and the world going to rack and ruin, wouldn't it be better now to go back to the old maxims and not be gallivanting off killing one another in China over the moon, ah when I think of my poor father. (165)

The motor car forms the backdrop of their conversation as it moves onto the subject of war, explicitly referencing the First World War beginning in 1914. Gorman remarks of someone he knew: 'He died in 14. Wounds' (167). The information is conveyed with telegrammatic succinctness, and with little attempt at describing or representing. Language is unreliable shorthand for history, leaving many details unrevealed. Trauma, once again, seems to exist beyond language in Beckett's work. Another war casualty is mentioned in the same manner, an almost identical description, this time set to the background of a passing motor car:

CREAM: Hadn't she a brother.

GORMAN: The Lootnant yes, died in 14. Wounds.

[*Deafening roar of engine.*] (168)

The First World War was the first conflict to make major use of technologies developed in an industrial age. The presence of the unseen motor car acts as a reminder of these technologies, breaking up their conversation, if only for a moment or two.

The Rooneys are disorientated by the apparatus of modernity, their sense of time and space both uprooted and fragmented. After a long day, their journey home is fraught with empirical confusions, and in place of progress or egress there is simply gress, movement without meaning:

MR ROONEY: Shall we go on backwards now a little?

MRS ROONEY: Backwards?

MR ROONEY: Yes, or you forwards and I backwards. The perfect pair. Like Dante's damned, with their faces arsy-versy. (*AF*, 24)[21]

The blind Mr Rooney remarks: 'I have forgotten which way I am facing' (28). There is, in each example, a destabilization of time and space, of the certainty of human presence and the reliability of Western rationality. Modernity in the radio plays, whether it is represented through the medium of radio, recording devices, or modern transport, all, to some degree accentuate the disruptions between progress and egress, and the relative sanity of the leading characters.

Dirk Van Hulle has illustrated certain connections between Maddy's personal trauma in *All That Fall* and her stressful encounter at the train station. He suggests that the themes of maternity, fertility

21 See also the discussion of Watt's inverted walking in Chapter 2 of this study.

and birth that recur throughout the text culminate in a kind of symbolic birth at the belated arrival of the train:

> Birth is a prominent theme in *All That Fall.* There is a short interval between the train's arrival and the moment Dan Rooney "suddenly appears". When he appears, Maddy explains why she has come: she wanted to surprise him, for his birthday. Birth is being staged both on the way to the station and on the way back. Like a midwife, Tommy has to help Maddy out of Mr Slocum's car: "Crouch down, Mrs Rooney, crouch down, and get your head in the open. (...) Now! She's coming! Straighten up, Ma'am! There!" To which Maddy replies with the astonishment of a newborn baby: "Am I out?". On the way back she remembers the lecture by "one of these new mind doctors" and the phrase "never really been born" (196), a variation on the theme from Jung's Tavistock lecture. (Van Hulle 2010b, 123-36)

Maddy's trauma also coincides with the musical repetition of Schubert's Death and the Maiden quartet, mentioned briefly earlier in this chapter. In a sense, the piece bookends the play, and hints towards a traumatic repetition that is endlessly looping. In both cases, trauma and subjectivity in the text are mediated via the endless repetitions of modern technology. Once again, we might draw parallels with another of Beckett's radio plays. For example, a similar instance occurs in the aforementioned *The Old Tune*, which opens and closes with an instrument from a previous time, playing an old tune that is recognised by the characters, but also somehow haunting and unfamiliar. In symptomatic fashion, the instrument begins to break down, and we are denied a sense of closure that the melody's resolution might offer:

> *Background of street noises. In the foreground a barrel-organ playing an old tune. 20 seconds. The mechanism jams. Thumps on the box to set it off again. No result.* (*TOT*, 155)

In another text, it is the gramophone that performs an uncanny, traumatic function. In *Embers*, Henry describes how he walks about with the device to remind himself, via a recording, of his dead father. Ada remarks:

> I suppose you have worn him out. [*Pause.*] You wore him out living and now you are wearing him out dead. [*Pause.*] The time comes when one cannot speak to you any more. [*Pause.*] The time will come when no one will speak to you at all, not even complete strangers. [*Pause.*] You will be quite alone with your voice, there will be no other voice in the world but yours. [*Pause.*] Do you hear me? (*E*, 44)

The technology offers a ghostly, uncanny connection to a lost past. But characters occupy a strange in-between space, unable to fully connect with their memories, yet similarly unable to engage meaningfully with the present. The woman in the ruinous old house exemplifies this tragic, traumatized condition:

> [*They move on. Wind and rain. Dragging feet, etc. Faintly same music as before. They halt. Music clearer. Silence but for music playing. Music dies.*] All day the same old record. All alone in that great empty house. She must be a very old woman now.
>
> MR ROONEY: [*Indistinctly.*] Death and the Maiden. (*AF*, 30)

During their journey home, the Rooneys happen to speculate about the sinking of the *Lusitania* and *Titanic* ocean liners:

> MRS ROONEY: Wasn't it that they sung on the *Lusitania*? Or Rock of Ages? Most touching it must have been. Or was it the *Titanic*? (16)

It is mentioned only in the briefest of moments, as they try to ascertain a piece of music that was sung on board one of the ships as they sank in the Irish Channel and the Atlantic, respectively. In some ways, the *Titanic* offers a perfect emblem of the ideal of modern progress alongside a sense of the traumatic. Sconce suggests that the sinking of the *Titanic*

> concretized the potentially agonizing paradoxes of wireless like no other event, a disaster that seemed to confirm the most sinister suspicions of the new worlds created and accessed by radio. [...] Promoted as the fastest, sturdiest, and most technologically advanced of all the world's ocean vessels, the *Titanic* was quickly laid low

> by a simple iceberg, a supreme human achievement utterly destroyed by the elemental forces of nature. As such, the vessel became a potent symbol of technological hubris and human vulnerability, a reminder that humanity's most impressive achievements were still subject to a higher law and judgment. (Sconce 2000, 72)

All That Fall does not dwell on the *Titanic*'s tragic sinking; in fact it is a fleeting moment of indecision, but its brief invocation is nonetheless a powerful one. The *Titanic's* fated course marks a powerful intersection between trauma and modernity, whether we consider modernity as the culmination of technological enterprise, or Western humanist ideology. The importance of radio technology to the tragedy is also significant, as further evidenced in Sconce's book:

> Interestingly, accounts of the *Titanic* concentrated on the role of wireless in the aftermath of the catastrophe as much as on the disaster itself. [...] Through such mass coverage, the concept of wireless found its largest audience ever, as a technology that had existed primarily in the abstract suddenly became inextricably and vividly bound to the public's imagination of a tangible disaster. In this context, wireless forged an even stronger relationship with separation, death, and absence. (72-3)

Beckett's *All That Fall* discusses and explores the unsettling resonances of modern radio broadcasting, and indeed of modernity in a more general sense. It is a text that revolves around the personal traumatic symptoms of its protagonist, whose position in the modern world becomes increasingly destabilized and confusing. In the final analysis, the connection between Mrs Rooney's trauma and the acceleration of modern technology is best summarized using an example from the text.

The protagonist's loss of a child is effectively repeated at the end of the play when news breaks that a child has fallen under the tracks of a train. It is unclear whether this is the uncanny repetition of the original traumatic event (Minnie's death, which is only ever alluded to), or whether it is a separate and unique event. But, as the news is revealed at the play's close, the incident no doubt carries a strong and pervasive influence. One might even say that the child's tragic end on the railway is, in some sense, an echo of Minnie's early death.

We have begun to trace an understanding of modern trauma with the introduction of the railways in the nineteenth century. The railways have become established as ambiguous spaces where time is accelerated and space is divided into a binary of departure and destination, origin and telos. The place where the child is killed on the tracks is a non-space, or no-man's land that exists between the two. This is, of course, similar to the *Titanic*, which also disappeared between two terminal points of a journey—the sea marking a kind of abstract deterritorialized zone outside human understanding and mastery.

In *All That Fall*, trauma becomes indistinguishable from the processes and characteristics of modernity. The traumatic event, as a specific and originary moment, is lost to conjecture and uncertainty. Its representation is manifested through a system of symbols and substitutions, all modern and technological. The traumatic episode is subsequently staged and restaged in Beckett's play, in the mind of the protagonist and in the fabric of the text itself. Like the endlessly repeatable performance of a radio play, technological recording devices and mechanical operations hold ghostly, ethereal and traumatic qualities. It is modernity itself that disrupts the text of Beckett's play, which undermines the Western rational subject, and ultimately representation itself. Modernity stages a series of suspensions and troubling returns, disrupting empirical distinctions of past and present, here and there, life and death.

Conclusion: *As the Story Was Told*

As the Story was Told

When Günther Eich, a poet and writer who was personally known to Beckett (Nixon 2010, xix), committed suicide at the age of sixty-six, the German publisher Siegfried Unseld decided to publish a volume of works in his memory. Unseld contacted Beckett as a possible contributor, and the request was accepted. Between 4 August 1973 and 13 August (Ackerley and Gontarski 2004, 26), a short prose text entitled 'As the Story Was Told' was completed, a story read by Ruby Cohn as 'astonishing in its surface simplicity' (Cohn 2001, 324).[1] As Mark Nixon notes in a recent Faber reissue of the text:

> The story revolves around notions of guilt and punishment as a speaker endeavours to comprehend his part in the interrogation and torture of a man who is being held in a tent nearby. Although the piece is written with ostensible simplicity, it withholds the precise nature of the crime of the first-person narrator, or of the person under scrutiny. (Nixon 2010, xix-xx)

The text offers perhaps one of Beckett's most explicitly realised accounts of a possible wartime setting, and alongside texts such as *Rough for Radio II* and *What Where* demonstrates a recurrent correspondence between language, testimony and torture:

> As the story was told me I never went near the place during sessions. I asked what place and a tent was described at length, a small tent the colour of its surroundings. Wearying of this description I asked what sessions and these in their turn were described, their object, duration, frequency and harrowing nature. (*AST*, 159)

1 Considering this book's preoccupation with timeliness and untimeliness, it might be worth noting that the manuscript of 'As the Story Was Told' was completed on Beckett scholar Ruby Cohn's 51st birthday, 13 August 1973.

As Cohn states, 'the narrator does not reveal the accounts he is given. The events in the tent (where the sessions take place) are so harrowing that the narrator raises his hand—presumably to cut the report short' (Cohn 2001, 324-5). Whether consciously or unconsciously, through choice or necessity, the narrator concludes the 'story' with a refusal to learn the final fate of the torture victim:

> It must have been shortly after six, the sessions closing punctually at that hour, for as I watched a hand appeared in the doorway and held out to me a sheet of writing. I took it and read it, then tore it in four and put the pieces in the waiting hand to take away. (*AST*, 159-60)

While the narrative clearly appears to outline and relate a traumatic event (or series of events) to the reader, their precise nature remains withheld by the form of the narrative itself. 'As the Story Was Told' seems to articulate a series of limit points, borders of understanding that prohibit any full understanding: 'heard or read, the story can only circle around the pain at its core' (Cohn 2001, 325). The sessions are said to end punctually at a specific time, six o'clock, but the time that the hand appears is less clear: little more than an approximation. The doorway demarcates a threshold between the known and the unknown, revealing a hand that is disembodied, belonging to no one specific or identifiable. The significance of the piece of paper is similarly ambiguous. Is it an official document? A report, perhaps? A confession or revelation of some kind? Its significance remains unclear, as violence is acted upon it—the paper is torn, divided and fragmented, before disappearing once again into an unseen and unknown space.

The ambiguity that lies at the heart of Beckett's text has since come to be understood as one of the key characteristics of literary representations of torture. Michael Richardson's *Gestures of Testimony*, which explores the representation of traumatic acts of torture in modern and contemporary literature. Richardson writes that 'there might be something inherent to torture itself, a denial, or resistance of representation in language' (Richardson 2016, 8), and so 'to bear witness to torture is to confront the failure of representation and language' (8).

But what is significant, for Richardson, is that the account which remains somehow ambiguous can offer a fidelity to the trauma of the event that more conventional realist accounts cannot reach: 'a straightforward, blow-by-blow description of torture might describe its external actions exactly—and yet fail to account for its fundamental violence' (8). The potential of literary representations lies in their paradoxical status, as events which convey fidelity to a trauma indirectly, whilst appearing to veil or hide its outward appearance from view.

The closing sentences of the narrative are the most enigmatic of all, and have prompted a number of Beckett scholars to draw connections to the work of Czech writer Franz Kafka.[2] As the story ends, 'at the Kafkaesque last' (Cohn 2001, 325), we learn that the old man being questioned 'succumbed in the end to his ill-treatment' (*AST*, 60), but might have been saved:

> But finally I asked if I knew exactly what the man—I would like to give his name but cannot—what exactly was required of the man, what it was he would not or could not say. No, was the answer, after some little hesitation no, I did not know what the poor man was required to say, in order to be pardoned, but would have recognized it at once, yes, at a glance, if I had seen it. (60)

The final moments of the text are formulated by the tension between knowing and not knowing, an ambiguity that forges an opening up of possibility that is simultaneously available and absent from the text. The narrator cannot identify the word that is required for a pardon, but has, nonetheless, paradoxically identified and retained the unspoken word in advance of the event itself. In addition, the expression 'if I had seen it' not only emphasises the narrator's distance from the traumatic sessions, but destabilises the possibility of an adequate resolution or conclusion. The page that is delivered to the narrator does not deliver the right word, but the right word cannot be known until it is finally witnessed, at some unspecified point in the future. In

2 Ackerley and Gontarski write that 'the import is enigmatic, Kafkaesque' in *The Grove Companion*, 26.

this sense, the promise of recognition is continually deferred, and words are presented in the text as those which manifest themselves, and yet do not make themselves present at the appropriate time and place, in the appropriate context.

When now?

Throughout Samuel Beckett's prose and theatre, trauma is a common thread, frayed at the places it begins and ends. In his written work, we are able to discern the operation of language as a system of deferrals and dispersals, approximating an idea of presence without its delivery. Similarly, Beckett's stage does not guarantee presence to the audience, but questions and unravels the means by which presence is thought; the plays recall vague and unclear events from their protagonists' pasts, while rehearsing traumatic themes that resist closure or resolution. The radio plays find trauma in the mechanisms of modernity, the looped repetition of gramophone records and histories of railway and maritime disaster. In each case, trauma raises questions regarding the status of language and the humanist subject and their respective relation to time, presence and deferral.

And yet, while trauma appears to dismantle the systems of organisation that traditionally define the Western humanist self, in Beckett's work it also offers new ways to conceive or consider time, place and the subject. In this sense, trauma becomes a productive space of discussion and debate, a space not just of destruction and decay, but of continuance and possibility. As Peter Boxall has suggested, 'Beckett's writing is determined by an uncanny collaboration between persistence and termination' (Boxall 2009, 2). He writes:

> Samuel Beckett's writing is at once a poetics of exhaustion, and a poetics of persistence. It is a writing which stages the end of an entire range of cultural and literary possibilities, but it is also a body of work which extends these possibilities, inventing new and richly productive ways to 'stir', as 'Beckett' puts it in one of his dialogues with Georges Duthuit, 'From the field of the possible'. (1)

Adopting the term 'late', we might begin to re-imagine Beckett's work in relation to a kind of traumatic belatedness: a kind of lateness that suggests not only traumatic disintegration, but a form of persistence that opens up into the future. The partial recognitions that puncture readers' acceptance of his plays, poems, novels and short stories do not settle, but perpetually drift and scatter; cultural or historical references do not have a final resting place, but demonstrate a spectral status that hovers between presence and absence. This dis-engagement with history is attuned with the symptoms of the traumatic event itself, throwing familiar conceptions of time, place and identity into a state of perpetual crisis. Trauma and traumatic experience in Beckett's writing articulate a point of ambiguity: a vague and often contradictory condition whereby the familiar values of time, place and self are called radically into question. Trauma, in Beckett, is a condition of Western modernity that disobeys, deconstructs, and challenges the way we perceive ourselves in the present, our continuing ethical responsibilities to the past, and constructive possibilities for the future.

Bibliography

General Bibliography

Ackerley, C. J., and S. E. Gontarski, eds. *The Grove Companion to Samuel Beckett: A Reader's Guide to His Works, Life, and Thought.* New York: Grove Press, 2004.

Adorno, Theodor W. 'Trying to Understand *Endgame*' in *Can One Live After Auschwitz?: A Philosophical Reader,* ed. Rolf Tiedemann, trans. Rodney Livingstone and Others, 259-94. Stanford, California: Stanford University Press, 2003.

Anderton, Joseph. *Beckett's Creatures: Art of Failure After the Holocaust.* London: Bloomsbury, 2016.

Anon., 'The dying of the light', *Times Literary Supplement,* 8 January 1960.

Anon., 'Prince of Darkness', *Times Literary Supplement,* 17 June 1960.

Attridge, Derek. 'Taking Beckett at His Word: The Event of *The Unnamable*', *Journal of Beckett Studies,* 26:1 (2017), 10-23.

Bailey, Iain. *Samuel Beckett and the Bible.* London: Bloomsbury, 2014.

Bair, Deidre. *Samuel Beckett: A Biography.* New York: Summit Books, 1990.

Ballard, J. G. *The Complete Short Stories: Volume II.* London, New York, Toronto, Sydney: Harper Perennial, 2006.

Ballard, J. G. *Crash.* London: Vintage, 1995.

Ballard, J. G. *Miracles of Life: Shanghai to Shepperton.* London: Harper Perennial, 2008.

Banville, John. 'Beckett's Last Words' in *Samuel Beckett: 100 years,* ed. Christopher Murray, 122-131. Dublin: RTÉ, 2006.

Barfield, Steven, Matthew Feldman, and Philip Tew, eds. *Beckett and Death* London: Continuum, 2009.

Barry, Elizabeth. 'Samuel Beckett and the Contingencies of Old Age', *Samuel Beckett Today/Aujourd'Hui,* 28:2 (2016), 205-17.

Beckett, Samuel. *All That Fall and Other Plays for Radio and Screen*. Preface and Notes by Everett Frost. London: Faber and Faber, 2009.

Beckett, Samuel. 'The Capital of the Ruins.' In *As No Other Dare Fail: For Samuel Beckett on His 80th Birthday by His Friends and Admirers*, edited by John Calder, 75-6. London: John Calder, 1986.

Beckett, Samuel. *Company, Ill Seen Ill Said, Worstward Ho, Stirrings Still*, edited by Dirk Van Hulle. London: Faber and Faber, 2009.

Beckett, Samuel. *Disjecta: Miscellaneous Writing and a Dramatic Fragment*, edited by Ruby Cohn. London: John Calder, 1983.

Beckett, Samuel. *Endgame*, edited by Rónán McDonald. London: Faber and Faber, 2009.

Beckett, Samuel. *The Expelled, The Calmative, The End with First Love*, edited by Christopher Ricks. London: Faber and Faber, 2009.

Beckett, Samuel. *Happy Days*. London: Faber and Faber, 2010.

Beckett, Samuel. *How It Is*, edited by Édouard Magessa O'Reilly (London: Faber and Faber, 2009).

Beckett, Samuel, *Krapp's Last Tape and Other Shorter Plays*, edited by S.E. Gontarski (London: Faber and Faber, 2009).

Beckett, Samuel. *The Letters of Samuel Beckett, Volume I: 1929-1940*, edited by Martha Dow Fehsenfeld, Lois More Overbeck, George Craig, Dan Gunn. Cambridge: Cambridge University Press, 2009.

Beckett, Samuel. *The Letters of Samuel Beckett, Volume II: 1941-1956*, edited by George Craig, Martha Dow Fehsenfeld, Dan Gunn, Lois More Overbeck. Cambridge: Cambridge University Press, 2011.

Beckett, Samuel. *The Letters of Samuel Beckett, Volume III: 1957-1965*, edited by George Craig, Martha Dow Fehsenfeld, Dan Gunn, Lois More Overbeck. Cambridge: Cambridge University Press, 2011.

Beckett, Samuel. *The Letters of Samuel Beckett, Volume IV: 1966-1989*, edited by George Craig, Martha Dow Fehsenfeld, Dan Gunn, Lois More Overbeck. Cambridge: Cambridge University Press, 2011.

Beckett, Samuel. *Malone Dies*, edited by Peter Boxall. London: Faber and Faber, 2010.

Beckett, Samuel. *Mercier and Camier*, edited by Seán Kennedy. London: Faber and Faber, 2010.

Beckett, Samuel. *Molloy*, edited by Shane Weller. London: Faber and Faber, 2009.

Beckett, Samuel. *More Pricks Than Kicks*, edited by Cassandra Nelson. London: Faber and Faber, 2010.

Beckett, Samuel. *Murphy*, edited by J. C. C. Mays. London: Faber and Faber, 2009.

Beckett, Samuel. *Texts for Nothing and Other Shorter Prose, 1950-1976*, edited by Mark Nixon. London: Faber and Faber, 2010.

Beckett, Samuel. *That Time*. London: Faber and Faber, 1976.

Beckett, Samuel. *The Theatrical Notebooks of Samuel Beckett: The Shorter Plays*, Vol. IV, edited by Stanley Gontarski. London: Faber and Faber, 1999.

Beckett, Samuel. *The Unnamable*, edited by Steven Connor. London: Faber and Faber, 2010.

Beckett, Samuel. *Waiting for Godot*, edited by Mary Bryden. London: Faber and Faber, 2010.

Beckett, Samuel. *Watt*, edited by C. J. Ackerley. London: Faber and Faber, 2009.

Bernstein, Jay. 'Philosophy's Refuge: Adorno in Beckett' in *Philosophers' Poets*, ed. David Wood, 177-91. London and New York: Routledge, 1990.

Blanchot, Maurice. *Friendship*, trans. Elizabeth Rottenberg. Stanford: Stanford University Press, 1997.

Blanchot, Maurice. *The Infinite Conversation*, trans. Susan Hanson. Minneapolis and London: University of Minnesota Press, 1993.

Blanchot, Maurice. *The Step Not Beyond*, trans. Lycette Nelson. New York: State University of New York Press, 1992.

Blanchot, Maurice. 'Literature and the Right to Death' in *The Work of Fire*, eds. Werner Hamacher & David E. Wellbery, trans. Charlotte Mandell, 300-44. Stanford, California: Stanford University Press, 1995.

Blanchot, Maurice. 'Marx's Three Voices' in *Friendship*, trans. Elizabeth Rottenberg, 98-100. Stanford: Stanford University Press, 1997.

Blanchot, Maurice. *The Work of Fire*, trans. Charlotte Mandell. Stanford: Stanford University Press, 1995.

Blanchot, Maurice. *The Writing of the Disaster*, trans. Ann Smock. Lincoln and London: University of Nebraska Press, 1995.

Blanchot, Maurice. 'Where Now? Who Now?', trans. Richard Howard in *Critical Essays on Samuel Beckett,* ed. Lance St John Butler, 86-92. Aldershot: Scolar Press, 1993b.

Boulter, Jonathan. *Beckett: A Guide for the Perplexed.* London: Continuum, 2008.

Boulter, Jonathan, 'Does Mourning Require a Subject? Samuel Beckett's *Texts for Nothing*', *MFS Modern Fiction Studies*, 50:2, Summer 2004, 332-350.

Boulter, Jonathan. *Melancholy and the Archive.* London: Continuum, 2011.

Boxall, Peter. *Since Beckett: Contemporary Writing in the Wake of Modernism.* London: Continuum, 2009.

Boxall, Peter. '"Stirring from the field of the possible": Beckett, DeLillo, and the Possibility of Fiction' in *Beckett's Literary Legacies*, eds. Matthew Feldman, Matthew and Mark Nixon, 207-226. Newcastle: Cambridge Scholars Publishing, 2007.

Boyce, Brynhildur. 'The Radio Life and Work of Samuel Beckett', *Nordic Irish Studies*, 8:1 (2009), 47-65.

Brater, Enoch. 'Fragment and Beckett's form in *That time* and *Footfalls*', *Journal of Beckett Studies*, 2 (1977), 70-81.

Bryden, Mary. *Samuel Beckett and the Idea of God.* London: Macmillan Press, 1998.

Buning, Marius, and Lois Oppenheim, eds. *Beckett in the 1990s: Selected Papers from the Second International Beckett Symposium, Held in The Hague, 8-12 April, 1992.* Amsterdam: Rodopi, 1993.

Butler, Lance St John, ed. *Critical Essays on Samuel Beckett*, trans. Richard Howard. Aldershot: Scolar Press, 1993.

Byron, Mark S., ed. *Samuel Beckett's Endgame.* Amsterdam and New York: Rodopi, 2007.

Carpenter, Humphrey. *The Envy of the World: Fifty Years of the Third Programme and Radio Three.* London: Phoenix, 1997.

Caruth, Cathy, ed. *Trauma: Explorations in Memory.* Baltimore and London: The Johns Hopkins University Press, 1995.

Caruth, Cathy. *Unclaimed Experience: Trauma, Narrative, and History.* Baltimore and London: The Johns Hopkins University Press, 1996.

Caselli, Daniela. *Beckett's Dantes: Intertextuality in the fiction and criticism.* Manchester: Manchester University Press, 2006.

Clifton, Glenn. 'Pain without Incarnation: *The Unnamable*, Derrida, and the Book of Job', *Journal of Beckett Studies*, 20:2 (2011), 149-71.

Cohn, Ruby. *A Beckett Canon.* Ann Arbor: The University of Michigan Press, 2011.

Connor, Steven. 'Auf schwankendem Boden', *Samuel Beckett, Bruce Nauman*, 80-7. Vienna: Kunsthalle Wien, 2000.

Connor, Steven. 'Beckett and Bion', *Journal of Beckett Studies*, 17:1-2 (2009), 9-34.

Connor, Steven. 'Preface' to Samuel Beckett, *The Unnamable*, vii-xxv. London: Faber and Faber, 2010.

Connor, Steven. *Samuel Beckett: Repetition, Theory, and Text.* Aurora, Colorado: The Davies Group, 2007.

Connor, Steven. '"Traduttore, traditore": Samuel Beckett's Translation of *Mercier and Camier*' in the *Journal of Beckett Studies*, 11/12 (1989), 27-46.

Cronin, Anthony. *Samuel Beckett: The Last Modernist.* New York: Da Capo Press, 1999.

Cunningham, David. 'Trying (Not) to Understand: Adorno and the Work of Beckett' in *Beckett and Philosophy*, ed. Richard Lane, 125-39. Basingstoke: Palgrave Macmillan, 2002.

Dante Alighieri. *Inferno*, trans. Robert Hollander and Jean Hollander, intr. Robert Hollander. New York: Anchor Books, 2002.

de Certeau, Michel. *The Practice of Everyday Life*, trans. Steven Rendall. Berkeley: University of California Press, 1984.

Deane, Seamus. 'Introduction' to James Joyce, *A Portrait of the Artist as a Young Man*, ed. Seamus Deane, vii-xliii. London: Penguin, 1992.

Derrida, Jacques. *Acts of Literature*, edited by Derek Attridge. London and New York: Routledge, 1992.

Derrida, Jacques. *Of Grammatology*, trans. Gayatri Chakravorty Spivak. Corrected edition. Baltimore and London: The Johns Hopkins University Press, 1997.

Derrida, Jacques. 'Pa*ce Not*(s)' in *Parages*, ed. John P. Leavey, trans. Tom Conley, James Hulbert, John P. Leavey, Avital Ronnell, 11-101. Stanford: Stanford University Press, 2011.

Derrida, Jacques. *Parages*, edited by John P. Leavey, trans. Tom Conley, James Hulbert, John P. Leavey, Avital Ronnell. Stanford: Stanford University Press, 2011.

Derrida, Jacques. *Specters of Marx: The State of the Debt, the Work of Mourning and the New International*, trans. Peggy Kamuf, intr. Bernd Magnus and Stephen Cullenberg. New York and London: Routledge, 2012.

Derrida, Jacques. 'The End of the Book and the Beginning of Writing' in *Of Grammatology*, trans. Gayatri Chakravorty Spivak, 6-26. Baltimore and London: The Johns Hopkins University Press, 1997.

Derrida, Jacques. 'The Other's Language: Jacques Derrida Interviews Ornette Coleman, 23 June 1997', trans. Timothy S. Murphy, *Genre,* 37:2 (Summer 2004), 319-329.

Derrida, Jacques. '"This strange institution called literature": An Interview with Jacques Derrida', in *Acts of Literature*, ed. Derek Attridge (London and New York: Routledge, 1992), 33-75.

Descartes, René. *Discourse on Method and Related Writings*, trans. Desmond M. Clarke. London: Penguin, 1999.

Dillon, Brian, ed. *Ruins*. London: Whitechapel Gallery, 2011.

Dillon, Brian. 'Introduction: A Short History of Decay' in *Ruins*, ed. Brian Dillon, 10-4. London: Whitechapel Gallery, 2011.

Feldman, Matthew, and Mark Nixon, eds. *Beckett's Literary Legacies*. Newcastle: Cambridge Scholars Publishing, 2007.

Fischer, Eileen. 'The Discourse of the Other in *Not I*: A Confluence of Beckett and Lacan', *Theatre*, 10:3 (Summer 1979), 101-3.

Fletcher, John. *The Novels of Samuel Beckett*. London: Chatto and Windus, 1964.

Freud, Sigmund. *Beyond the Pleasure Principle*, trans. John Reddick. London: Penguin, 2003.

Freud, Sigmund. 'Remembering, Repeating, and Working Through' in *Beyond the Pleasure Principle and Other Writings*, trans. John Reddick, 31-42. London: Penguin, 2003.

Freud, Sigmund. *Introductory Lectures on Psychoanalysis*, trans. James Strachey, eds. James Strachey and Angela Richards. Penguin Freud Library, Vol.1. London: Penguin, 1991.

Frost, Everett. 'Preface' to Samuel Beckett, *All That Fall and Other Plays for Radio and Screen*, vii-xxiii. London: Faber and Faber, 2009.

Garrison, Alysia E. '"Faintly Struggling Things": Trauma, Testimony, and Inscrutable Life in Beckett's *The Unnamable*' in *Samuel Beckett: History, Memory, Archive*, ed. Seán Kennedy and Katherine Weiss, 90-110. London: Palgrave Macmillan, 2009.

Gascoigne, Bamber. 'How far can Beckett go?', *The Observer*, 12 April 1964.

Gontarski, S. E., ed. *A Companion to Samuel Beckett*. London: Blackwell, 2010.

Gordon, Lois. *The World of Samuel Beckett 1906-1946*. New Haven & London: Yale University Press, 1996.

Goulbourne, Russell. 'Introduction' to Jean-Jacques Rousseau, *Reveries of the Solitary Walker*, trans. Russell Goulbourne, ix-xxviii. Oxford: Oxford University Press, 2011.

Harmon, Maurice, ed. *No Author Better Served: The Correspondence of Samuel Beckett and Alan Schneider*. Cambridge: Harvard University Press, 1998.

Hartel, Gaby. 'Emerging Out of a Silent Void: Some Reverberations of Rudolf Arnheim's Radio Theory in Beckett's Radio Pieces', *Journal of Beckett Studies*, 19:2 (2010), 218-227.

Heppenstall, Rayner. 'Unnamed, At Last', *The Observer*, 10 April 1960.

Hill, Leslie. *Blanchot: Extreme Contemporary*. London and New York: Routledge, 1997.

Hill, Leslie. *Maurice Blanchot and Fragmentary Writing: A Change of Epoch*. London: Continuum, 2012.

Houston Jones, David. *Samuel Beckett and Testimony*. London: Palgrave, 2011.

Jakobson, Roman. 'Shifters and Verbal Categories' in *On Language*, ed. Linda R. Waugh and Monique Monville-Burston, 386-92. Cambridge, MA: Harvard UP, 1990.

Joyce, James. *A Portrait of the Artist as a Young Man*, edited by Seamus Deane. London: Penguin, 1992.

Juliet, Charles. *Conversations with Samuel Beckett and Bram van Velde*, trans. Tracy Cooke, Axel Nesme, Janey Tucker, Morgaine Reinl, and Aude Jackson. Châmpaign and London: Dalkey Archive, 2009.

Kalb, Jonathan. 'The mediated Quixote: the radio and television plays, and *Film*' in *The Cambridge Companion to Beckett*, ed. John Pilling, 124-44. Cambridge: Cambridge University Press, 1994.

Katz, Daniel. *Saying I No More: Subjectivity and Consciousness in the Prose of Samuel Beckett*. Evanston: Northwestern University Press, 1999.

Katz, Daniel. 'What Remains of Beckett: Evasion and History' in *Beckett and Phenomenology*, eds. Ulrika Maude and Matthew Feldman, 144-57. London: Continuum, 2009.

Kennedy, Seán. 'Edmund Spenser, famine memory and the discontents of humanism in *Endgame*', *Samuel Beckett Today/Aujourd'hui* 24 (2011), 105-120.

Kennedy, Seán. 'Introduction: Beckett in History, Memory, Archive' in *Samuel Beckett: History, Memory, Archive*, ed. Seán Kennedy and Katherine Weiss, 1-10. London: Palgrave Macmillan, 2009.

Kennedy, Seán. 'Preface' to Samuel Beckett, *Mercier and Camier*, ed. Seán Kennedy, vii-x. London: Faber and Faber, 2010.

Kennedy, Seán, and Katherine Weiss, eds. *Samuel Beckett: History, Memory, Archive*. London: Palgrave Macmillan, 2009.

Kittler, Friedrich A. *Gramophone, Film, Typewriter*, trans. Geoffrey Winthrop-Young and Michael Wutz. Stanford: Stanford University Press, 1999.

Knowlson, James. 'A Writer's Homes—A Writer's Life' in *A Companion to Samuel Beckett*, ed. S. E. Gontarski, 13-22. London: Blackwell, 2010.

Knowlson, James and Elizabeth Knowlson, eds. *Beckett Remembering Remembering Beckett: Uncollected Interviews with Samuel Beckett and Memories of Those Who Knew Him*. London: Bloomsbury, 2006.

Knowlson, James. *Damned to Fame: The Life of Samuel Beckett*. London: Bloomsbury, 1996.

Knowlson, James, and John Pilling. *Frescoes of the Skull: The Later Prose and Drama of Samuel Beckett*. London: John Calder, 1979.

LaCapra, Dominick. 'Trauma, Absence, Loss', *Critical Inquiry*, 25:4 (Summer, 1999), 696-727.

LaCapra, Dominick. *Writing History, Writing Trauma*. Baltimore and London: The Johns Hopkins University Press, 2001.

Lane, Richard, ed. *Beckett and Philosophy*. Basingstoke: Palgrave Macmillan, 2002.

Lanzmann, Claude. 'The Obscenity of Understanding: An Evening with Claude Lanzmann' in *Trauma: Explorations in Memory*, ed. with introductions, by Cathy Caruth, 200-20. Baltimore and London: Johns Hopkins University Press, 1995.

Laplanche, Jean. *Essays on Otherness*, trans. J. Fletcher. London: Routledge, 1999.

Laplanche, Jean. 'Notes on Afterwardsness' in *Essays on Otherness*, trans. J. Fletcher, 260-5. London: Routledge, 1999.

Leys, Ruth. *Trauma: A Genealogy*. Chicago and London: The University of Chicago Press, 2000.

Logue, Christopher. 'For those still standing', *New Statesman*, 14 September 1957.

Luckhurst, Roger. 'The Contemporary London Gothic and the Limits of the "Spectral Turn"', *Textual Practice*, 16:3 (2002), 527-546.

Luckhurst, Roger. *The Trauma Question.* London and New York: Routledge, 2008.

MacFarlane, Robert. *The Old Ways: A Journey on Foot.* London: Penguin, 2013.

McMullan, Anna. *Theatre on Trial: Samuel Beckett's Late Drama.* London and New York: Routledge, 1993.

Matthews, Steven. 'Beckett's Late Style', *Samuel Beckett and Death*, eds. Steven Barfield, Matthew Feldman, and Philip Tew, 188-205. London: Continuum, 2009.

Maude, Ulrika and Matthew Feldman, eds. *Beckett and Phenomenology.* London: Continuum, 2009.

Maude, Ulrika. *Beckett, Technology and the Body.* Cambridge: Cambridge University Press, 2009.

Mercier, Vivian. 'The Uneventful Event', *The Irish Times*, 18 February 1956.

Micale, M. and P. Lerner, eds. *Traumatic Pasts: History, Psychiatry and Trauma in the Modern Age 1870-1930.* Cambridge: Cambridge University Press, 2001.

Micale, M. and P. Lerner. 'Trauma, Psychiatry and History: A Conceptual Historiographical Introduction' in *Traumatic Pasts: History, Psychiatry and Trauma in the Modern Age 1870-1930*, eds. M. Micale and P. Lerner, 1-27. Cambridge: Cambridge University Press, 2001.

Moorjani, Angela. *The Aesthetics of Loss and Lessness.* London: Macmillan, 1992.

Moorjani, Angela. 'Beckett and Psychoanalysis' in *Palgrave Advances in Samuel Beckett Studies*, ed. Lois Oppenheim, 172-93. Basingstoke: Palgrave Macmillan, 2004.

Moorjani, Angela. 'Mourning, Schopenhauer, and Beckett's Art of Shadows', *Beckett On and On*, eds. Lois Oppenheim and Marius Buning (London: Associated University Presses, 1996), 83-101.

Mullen, Raymond. '"Stalking about London in a Green Suit": Beckett's *Murphy*, London and Flânerie', *Studies: An Irish Quarterly Review*, 95:379, 301-11.

Murray, Christopher, ed. *Samuel Beckett: 100 Years.* Dublin: RTÉ, 2006.

Nelson, Lycette. 'Introduction' to Maurice Blanchot, *The Step Not Beyond*, trans. Lycette Nelson, v-xxi. New York: State University of New York Press, 1992.

Nixon, Mark. 'Preface' to Samuel Beckett, *Texts for Nothing and Other Shorter Prose, 1950-1976*, edited by Mark Nixon, vii-xxiv. London: Faber and Faber, 2010.

Nixon, Mark. '"Writing Myself into the Ground": Textual Existence and Death in Beckett' in *Beckett and Death*, eds. Steven Barfield, Matthew Feldman, Philip Tew, 22-30. London: Continuum, 2009.

Oppenheim, Lois and Marius Buning, eds. *Beckett On and On*. London: Associated University Presses, 1996.

Oppenheim, Lois, ed. *Palgrave Advances in Samuel Beckett Studies*. Basingstoke: Palgrave Macmillan, 2004.

Oppenheim, Lois. 'Situating Samuel Beckett' in *The Cambridge Companion to the Modernist Novel*, ed. Morag Shiach, 224-237. Cambridge: Cambridge University Press, 2007.

O'Reilly, Édouard Magessa. 'Preface' to Samuel Beckett, *How It Is*, vii-xv. London: Faber and Faber, 2009.

Pattie, David. *The Complete Critical Guide to Samuel Beckett*. London and New York: Routledge, 2000.

Pilling, John, ed. *The Cambridge Companion to Beckett*. Cambridge: Cambridge University Press, 1994.

Pilling, John. *Samuel Beckett*. London: Routledge & Kegan Paul Limited, 1976.

Pountney, Rosemary. *Theatre of Shadows: Samuel Beckett's Drama 1956-76*. Gerrard's Cross: Colin Smythe, 1988.

Rabaté, Jean-Michel. 'Beckett and the Ghosts of Departed Quantities' in *The Ghosts of Modernity*, 148-70. Florida: University Press of Florida, 1996.

Rabaté, Jean-Michel. *The Ghosts of Modernity*. Gainesville: University Press of Florida, 1996.

Rabaté, Jean-Michel. 'Shades of the Color Gray' in *The Ghosts of Modernity*, 171-87. Florida: University Press of Florida, 1996.

Rank, Otto. *The Trauma of Birth.* London: Kegan Paul, 1929.

Richardson, Michael. *Gestures of Testimony: Torture, Trauma, and Affect in Literature.* London: Bloomsbury, 2016.

Ricks, Christopher. *Beckett's Dying Words.* Oxford: Oxford University Press, 1993.

Rothberg, Michael. *Traumatic Realism: The Demands of Holocaust Representation.* Minneapolis: University of Minnesota Press, 2000.

Rothberg, Michael. 'After Adorno: Culture in the Wake of Catastrophe', *New German Critique*, 72 (1997), 45-81.

Rousseau, Jean-Jacques. *Confessions*, trans. J.M. Cohen. London: Penguin, 1983.

Rousseau, Jean-Jacques. *Reveries of the Solitary Walker*, trans. Russell Goulbourne. Oxford: Oxford University Press, 2011.

Royle, Nicholas. *The Uncanny.* Manchester: Manchester University Press, 2003.

Rycroft, Charles, ed. *A Critical Dictionary of Psychoanalysis.* 2nd edition. London: Penguin, 1995.

Said, Edward. *On Late Style: Music and Literature Against the Grain.* London: Bloomsbury, 2007.

Said, Mariam C. 'Foreword' to Edward Said, *On Late Style: Music and Literature Against the Grain*, vii-ix. London: Bloomsbury, 2007.

Sconce, Jeffrey. *Haunted Media: Electronic Presence from Telegraphy to Television.* Durham & London: Duke University Press, 2000.

Sebald, W. G. *Austerlitz*, trans. Anthea Bell. London: Penguin Books, 2011.

Schiach, Morag, ed. *The Cambridge Companion to the Modernist Novel.* Cambridge: Cambridge University Press, 2007.

Smith, Russell. '*Endgame*'s Remainders' *Samuel Beckett's Endgame*, ed. Mark S. Byron, 99-120. Amsterdam and New York: Rodopi, 2007.

Solnit, Rebecca. *Wanderlust: A History of Walking.* 2nd edition. London & New York: Verso, 2001.

Szafraniec, Asja. *Beckett, Derrida, and the Event of Literature.* Stanford: Stanford University Press, 2007.

Tajiri, Yoshiki. 'Samuel Beckett et la Mécanisation d'Echo', *Samuel Beckett Today / Aujourd'hui: Présence de Samuel Beckett / Presence of Samuel Beckett: Colloque de Cerisy*, Vol. 17 (2006), 435-448.

Tanaka, Mariko Hori, Yoshiki Tajiri, and Michiko Tsushima, eds. *Samuel Beckett and Pain.* Amsterdam: Rodopi, 2012.

Thorpe, Vanessa. 'A new discovery for science and art: the cultural divide is all in the mind', *The Observer*, 24 November 2012.

Tiedemann, Rolf, ed. *Can One Live After Auschwitz?: A Philosophical Reader*, trans. Rodney Livingstone and others. Stanford: Stanford University Press, 2003.

Toynbee, Philip. 'Going Nowhere', *The Observer*, 18 December 1955.

Tynan, Kenneth. 'New Writing', *The Observer*, 7 August 1955.

Uhlmann, Anthony. *Beckett and Poststructuralism.* Cambridge: Cambridge University Press, 1999.

Vale, V., and Mike Ryan, eds., *J. G. Ballard: Quotes.* San Francisco: RE/Search Publications, 2004.

Van Hulle, Dirk. 'Adorno's Notes on *Endgame*', *Journal of Beckett Studies*, 19:2 (2010), 196-217.

Van Hulle, Dirk. 'Writing Relics: Mapping the Composition History of Beckett's *Endgame*', *Samuel Beckett: History, Memory, Archive*, ed. Seán Kennedy and Katherine Weiss, 169-182. London: Palgrave Macmillan, 2009.

Waugh, Linda R., and Monique Monville-Burston, eds. On *Language.* Cambridge, MA: Harvard University Press, 1990.

Weller, Shane. 'Preface' to Samuel Beckett, *Molloy*, vii-xx. London: Faber and Faber, 2009.

West, Sarah. *Say It: The Performative Voice in the Dramatic Works of Samuel Beckett.* Amsterdam and New York: Editions Rodopi B.V., 2010.

West, Sarah. 'Talking Ghosts', *Say It: The Performative Voice in the Dramatic Works of Samuel Beckett*, 64-87. Amsterdam and New York: Editions Rodopi B.V., 2010.

Whitehead, Anne. "'Ground that will remember you": trauma and landscape in Anne Michaels' *Fugitive Pieces*' in *Trauma Fiction* (Edinburgh: Edinburgh University Press, 2004), 48-78.

Whitelaw, Billie. *Billie Whitelaw… Who He?* London: Hodder and Stoughton, 1995.

Wood, David, ed. *Philosophers' Poets.* London and New York: Routledge, 1990.

Wood, Michael. 'Introduction' to Edward Said, *On Late Style: Music and Literature Against the Grain*, xi-xix. London: Bloomsbury, 2007.

Zilliacus, Clas. *Beckett and Broadcasting: A Study of the Works of Samuel Beckett for and in Radio and Television.* Abo, Finland: Abo Akademi, 1976.

Online Resources

Beckett Digital Manuscript Project, The. Accessed February 25, 2013. http://www.beckettarchive.org/introduction.jsp.

Birkbeck, University of London. 'Beckett and the Brain'. Accessed February 25, 2013. http://www.bbk.ac.uk/english/about-us/events-old/past-conferences/beckett-and-the-brain-24-june-2010.

Connor, Steven, 'Shifting Ground'. Accessed December 3, 2012. http://www.stevenconnor.com/beckettnauman.

Limit(e) Beckett 1 (2010). Accessed March 15, 2011. http://www.limitebeckett.paris-sorbonne.fr/one.html.

Oxford English Dictionary (OED). Accessed January 3, 2017. http://www.oed.com.

University of Warwick. *Beckett and the Brain.* Accessed February 25, 2013. http://www2.warwick.ac.uk/fac/arts/english/research/currentprojects/beckettandthebrain.

Van Hulle, Dirk, 'Beckett and Shakespeare on Nothing, or, Whatever Lurks Behind the Veil', *Limit(e) Beckett 1* (2010b), 123-136. Accessed March 15, 2011. http://www.limitebeckett.paris-sorbonne.fr/one/vanhulle.html.

Film

Shoah. Directed by Claude Lanzmann. New York, New Yorker Films, 1985.

Index

C

D

F

G

H

J

K

U

V

W

Z

ibidem-Verlag / *ibidem* Press
Melchiorstr. 15
70439 Stuttgart
Germany

ibidem@ibidem.eu
ibidem.eu